moving and knowing

LYDIA A. GERHARDT

moving
and
knowing

the young child
orients himself in space

PRENTICE-HALL, INC., Englewood Cliffs, N.J.

© *1973 by Lydia A. Gerhardt*

ISBN: P-0-13-604686-X

C-0-13-604694-O

Library of Congress Catalog Card Number: 77-37637

10   9   8   7   6   5   4   3   2   1

PRINTED IN THE UNITED STATES OF AMERICA

Prentice-Hall International, Inc., *London*
Prentice-Hall of Australia, Pty. Ltd., *Sydney*
Prentice-Hall of Canada, Ltd., *Toronto*
Prentice-Hall of India Private Limited, *New Delhi*
Prentice-Hall of Japan, Inc., *Tokyo*

To
FRANCES MINOR
in grateful appreciation
for her inspiration and encouragement
during the writing of this book

contents

2

orienting self in space   13

3

theory emerges from practice   35

4

designing curriculum   132

general bibliography   179

annotated bibliography   184

index   199

foreword

Right now, there is increasingly widespread interest in the education of young children. Researchers are seeking new understandings of cognitive growth. Body movement is being actively recognized as an underlying and essential component in the child's learning. These three areas of knowledge—knowledge of curriculum for young children, the process of knowing, and education through body movement—and their interrelationships are found in the forefront of thinking in early childhood education.

Head Start as a national endeavor made many more people recognize the importance of the early years of education. It also brought together people in various disciplines to think about and take action on the health, education, and welfare of children, particularly preschool poor children. Anthropologists, sociologists, pediatricians, educators, and others are collectively considering issues in the early years. The greatest upsurge is felt in nursery school education. Labor unions, women's liberation, and private enterprise are pressing for day care and home care for all children. Infancy education has been given a renewed thrust. There is also some rub-off in public education. The entire age span of early childhood education is rampant with divergent points of view and varying approaches. Experimentation continues to be paramount. The process of change, growth, and new knowledge in the field elicits positive conflicts.

Each child's acquisition of knowledge and his unique style of thinking is being reexamined. Piaget's research has come alive and attempts are being made to implement his theoretical framework in curriculum models.

Bloom, Bruner, Combs, Hunt, Gordon, Kohberg, and others are pursuing the understanding and interpretation of learning and young children. This knowledge forms the basis for continuous analysis of early childhood education.

Movement education is slowly seeping into early childhood education curriculum. This area has gained impetus from physical educators' re-viewing of body movement in human development and the human body's interaction with its environment.

The interdisciplinary rationale underlying this text brings fresh ideas to understanding the learning tasks of the young child. *Moving and Knowing* represents Lydia Gerhardt's extensive experience and deep knowledge of young children and their thinking. It also reveals her real involvement in the movement education field, both as a dancer and as an academic researcher.

A vital contribution of this book to the preprofessional student and the experienced teacher is the thorough analysis of selected observations of children's seeming development of concepts of space through their own body movement. Interwoven with this analysis of classroom observations is a sensitive synthesis of interdisciplinary literature which is critical to the reader's depth of understanding.

The recorded observations, anecdotal records, and structures for learning found in this book demonstrate insightful penetrations of the need to understand the human being in interaction (movement) with his environment as fundamental to learning. Dr. Gerhardt underlines the importance of the structure of the teacher's thinking, and her subsequent selection of opportunities that will facilitate each child's ability to orient himself in space. Implicit implications and resources for immediate learning encounters flow throughout the book.

With the concern for good education for all young children, the stream of new research in learning and this interdisciplinary view of the role of body movement in education, Lydia Gerhardt's *Moving and Knowing* will provoke a substantial theoretical and practical basis for change.

ELIZABETH ANN LIDDLE
Professor of Education
Director of Graduate Programs
Wheelock College
Boston, Massachusetts

preface

This book is concerned with the role of body movement in the child's conceptualization of space. Its intent is not to present a new body of knowledge but rather a re-viewing of what is known or sensed by authorities in many disciplines. Although anthropologists, biologists, genetic epistomologists, philosophers, neuro-physiologists, psychologists, artists, dancers and educators have long recognized a relationship between movement and conceptualization, no one has delineated the precise nature of the relationship. This textbook is built on an analysis and synthesis of this multidisciplinary literature. In addition to developing a conceptual framework, the textbook links this framework to teaching and learning through analyses of selected classroom observations of children's seeming development of spatial ideas through their body movement. Finally, it contains a chapter to help the classroom teacher design a curriculum that will facilitate the child's conceptualization of space through his body movement. It is hoped that the ideas explored will spark further thinking and experimentation on the part of both preprofessional and experienced teachers.

body movement, space, and the curriculum

Justification for the school curriculum lies in its ability to provide a sequence of opportunities that help each child build an understanding of, and ability to cope with, his world. One of the underlying assumptions of the curriculum is that the child is able to orient himself in space. The three-and four-year-old is expected to hang his coat *in* his "cubbie," run only when he goes *outside,* walk *around* the spilled juice, keep the paint *on* the paper, and find a *larger* block. The kindergarten child may be sent *down* to the cafeteria for the class's milk, asked to stand *behind* a line, or told to make a *circle* of chairs. The first grader is told to put his name *at the top of* his paper, place an *X near* the object that is *longest, begin* making the letter *e* in the *middle* of two lines. What does it take to perform any one of these tasks?

Later on, as the child learns to read and write he may be asked to find a sentence describing what happened to the boy in the story on his weekend trip. He must learn to differentiate *was* and *saw, car* and *far, b* and *d,* and *m* and *n.* He is expected to recognize the *beginning* and *end* of a book, a story, a page, and a sentence. He is given instructions, such as "*Begin* your *b* on the *top* line, draw a *straight* line *down,* stop on the next line, go *half* way *up* again and then make a *circle* to the *right*." What does it take to perform any one of these tasks?

As he begins to learn mathematics, the young child is asked to sort sets of objects. Notice what categories he uses. size? Shape? He comes to use number lines to solve problems of addition and multiplication, subtraction and division. (A number line is a sequence of numerals and shows that we use number names in an agreed order: 0, 1, 2, 3 . . .) What role does *directionality* play in the use of number lines? How many different number line shapes do you know?

Making a map or reading a map depends, among other things, upon ability to locate coordinate points in space. What else does it take to make a map?

Answers to these questions have to do with a point of reference, balance, size, shape, distance, area, volume, and other spatial ideas. It seems as if the child's conceptualization of his spatial world is fundamental to his ability to cope with reading, writing, mathematics, and mapping skills. With these skills in mind, this textbook is useful for professionals in early childhood education, special education, physical education, and child development and psychology.

early childhood education

Current trends in early childhood education focus on the need for teachers to articulate the uniqueness of each child's physical, intellectual, social, and emotional growth and development. The interrelationships among these factors develop his individuality. Movement and physical exercise have long been recognized as crucial to the development of physical well being. This approach, however, tends to minimize the importance of movement in the child's development of a body image and a sense of self. It also minimizes the role of body movement in the development of conceptual abilities. This textbook attempts to delineate the role of body movement in "knowing." Furthermore, it describes and illustrates particular classroom experiences that teachers have provided to facilitate the child's development. The last chapter is designed to help the teacher build a curriculum to develop the child's ability to orient himself in space. Without being prescriptive, it contains suggested opportunities that a teacher might provide to facilitate the child's development of concepts of space and spatial relationships.

special education

Increasingly, learning-disability specialists, teachers of retarded children, psychologists, and other special educators are recognizing the role of body movement in the education of the special child. These children often have poor gross and/or fine motor skills. Research reveals that such children's scores on intelligence and academic achievement tests have been significantly increased following "movement training" programs. Movement education has increasingly become an important part of the curriculum design for brain-damaged, emotionally-disturbed, and slow-learning children. This textbook provides a theoretical framework concerning body movement and learning as well as specific suggestions to the special educator for opportunities he or she might provide to develop the special child's conceptualization of his world through body movement.

physical education

Programs in physical education have moved from a game-oriented curriculum toward movement education. Through movement education, the child develops his own "movement vocabulary" that he can apply to a variety of movement activities. In an "activity-oriented" approach to physical education, the child is asked to skip in a particular way and, frequently, in a particular tempo and rhythm. The child who is developmentally unable to skip will probably "fail." In the child development (movement-education) approach to movement, on the other hand, the child may be given a task, such as, "Travel around the room using first one foot and then the other," and is free to solve the problem in his own way. This textbook provides a theoretical framework for a movement-education approach to physical activity for the young child. Body movement is the foundation of conceptualization and should be taught as an intellectual-physical skill. This book provides teachers with specific ideas for devising body movement experiences for the young child.

child development and psychology

The multidisciplinary rooting of the role of body movement in the child's conceptualization of space is of primary significance to educators of all disciplines. After all, body movement is central to life. The complexity of the child and his interaction with his spatial environment is a crucial theme developed throughout this book. To my knowledge there is no current text that describes the role of body movement in learning, although numerous books refer to its significance. Beyond this underlying theory, however, this book illustrates its theme with specific observations of three- to six-year-olds whose teachers seem to provide opportunities for the children to orient themselves in space. Moreover, this book attempts to weave theory with classroom practice to help teachers design a curriculum which will facilitate the child's orientation in space through body movement.

acknowledgments

Without my family, teachers, students, colleagues, and friends this book would never have been completed. It is impossible to give credit here to all who helped me in my work, but a few deserve special recognition.

I am deeply indebted to my mother and father who taught me most of what I know about teaching and learning; Kathleen Hinni who taught me to love "movement;" Frances Minor who gave so generously of her time and "knowing;" Irene Neurath and her teachers at the Corlears Community School who welcomed me, along with my tape recorder and camera, into their classrooms; Donna Harris who provided many photographs; Vera Maletic and Elizabeth Ann Liddle who made some constructive suggestions on the manuscript; Elizabeth Ann Liddle wrote the generous foreword to my book; and my students and colleagues who have willingly shared their "points of viewing."

Donna Harris, professional photographer at the Merrill-Palmer Institute, Detroit, Michigan, provided the following photographs: 3-1a, b, c, d, e; 3-2; 3-3a, b; 3-9; 3-11a, b; 3-14a,b; 3-15; 3-16a, b; 3-17; 3-19; 3-20; 3-21; 3-25a, b, c; 3-31; 3-32a, b; 3-33; 3-34a, b, c, d.

The dictionary definitions I have used throughout this text are from *Webster's Third New International Dictionary*, © 1966 by G. & C. Merriam Co., Publishers of the Merriam-Webster Dictionaries, and have been reprinted by permission of the Merriam Company.

moving and knowing

1

learning to move;
moving to learn

body movement in human development

Life begins with movement. The ultimate uniting of sperm and egg is dependent upon movement. During prenatal development, embryo and fetus are in constant motion as cell division and gradual differentiation prepare a new life for birth—movement into the world. This movement from a state of complete dependence to a state of relative independence requires rapid adjustments. The urge to survive forces the infant to move. He must breathe, eat, and excrete. He acts to maintain an equilibrium within his body and simultaneously responds to the external world. Hence, life reflects a creative interaction between the child and his environment. Initial impressions and responses are total and essentially undifferentiated, but gradually become more purposeful and selective. Through body movement the child discovers consistencies which, in turn, create patterns of response—knowledge in the making. He moves his head and mouth to find food. Movements that result in easing of hunger gradually become patterned to serve needs. The child learns that specific movements are required to satisfy his hunger, roll himself over, or find the limits of his crib. On the outside he merely seeks to cope; inwardly he is organizing his perceptions of his world. Movement is his means of expression and serves to help him gather impressions. It is his first communication with

1

the world—". . . his displacements, accommodations, assimilations, and adjustments to the world . . ." [1]—that tells him what the world is like. This adjustment to the world through movement begins preculturally. It is fundamental to life. Growth and development depend upon movement and man is designed to move. Muscles, joints, veins and arteries, body chemistry, lungs, and heart are all architecturally organized for movement. Thus, movement helps man to organize his world and man is organized to move.

As the living organism moves in order to cope with his world, his inner impressions undergo change. Processes group themselves according to function. The child moves—he reaches, touches, and grasps—and records relationships for later use. This "inner mapping" helps him to predict. An infant adjusts the shape of his hand to fit a familiar rattle or inspect a speck of food on his blanket.

> . . . every movement, however slight, causes modifications in the inner environment. For every movement made by the body a corresponding movement occurs in the central nervous system, which is thus being patterned and repatterned by every action. In this way, through a life of active response, the organism is building up within itself a model of the environment with which it is interacting; an inner map of events which enables it in course of time to anticipate external events and interpret phenomena by reference to its inner model. [2]

Movement is both cause and effect. It is constant. Even during sleep man moves. He is a constant mover. [3] The history of mankind is filled with evidence of man's movement. Man's ability to move has insured his survival. He has moved to obtain food, build a shelter, and make his clothing. He has moved to discover, to conquer, and to destroy. Body movement has always been a key to his cultural advancement.

> All that man has accomplished has been executed by bodily movement. The very fact that man is endowed with effective stepping movements and can go places has been and always will be influential in the cultural advancement of the human mind as well as assurance of man's survival. [4]

Movement has also been responsible for man's progress. Body movement stimulated early man to think.

---

[1] Eileen M. Churchill, *Counting and Measuring* (Toronto: University of Toronto Press, 1961), p. 48.

[2] Ibid., p. 47.

[3] Ray H. Barsch, *Achieving Perceptual-Motor Efficiency: A Space Oriented Approach to Learning* (Seattle, Wash.: Special Child Publications, 1967), p. 35.

[4] Margaret N. H'Doubler, *Dance, A Creative Art Experience* (Madison: University of Wisconsin Press, 1959), p. xvii.

Probably the first major impetus to thought was given when early men began to improve sticks and stones they picked up to use as tools and weapons. Chipping a blunt stone to the useful sharpness of other stones which had proved superior for cutting or scraping, coordinated eye and hand and brought a sense of achievement. Chipping flakes away generated thought models of connection and disconnection, whole and part.[5]

Movement directs man's achievements and thoughts, and thought in turn directs his movement. "It would seem to be the motor act under urge-to-live which has been the cradle of the mind. The motor act, mechanically integrating the individual, would seem to have started mind on its road to recognizability."[6]

Psychologists have used movement as a measure of thought. Bartlett has said, ". . . if we want to find out something definite about the nature and conditions of thinking processes, our best chance is to make use of clues that may be available from the study of simpler but related behavior."[7] In his study of thinking, he observed "adults in action." He was using body action as a reflection of thought.

Movement is apparently essential to one's ability to cope with the world. It stimulates man's thinking processes and it has played a vital role in the development of knowledge. Precisely how does body movement contribute to knowing? An examination of the relationship between body movement and sensory perception should begin to reveal the complexities inherent in the answer to this question.

the body movement and sensory perception relationship

Body movement serves man's perception and perception directs his body movement. The completion of nine months of prenatal growth and development, including a gradual differentiation of organs and systems, thrusts the infant into the world with complex survival mechanisms. Inner demands and outer reality simultaneously send messages to and from the brain. The infant's senses, responding simultaneously to changing environmental conditions and internal body needs, serve as an immediate source of information as well as a tool for response. The body acts and reacts in a continuing process of perception. Schachtel describes sensory perception as a "mode of relatedness" between the perceiver and the world around

[5] Gyorgy Kepes, ed., *The New Landscape in Art and Science* (Chicago: Paul Theobald, 1956), p. 41.

[6] C. Sherrington, *Man on His Nature* (Cambridge: Cambridge University Press, 1951), p. 169.

[7] Frederic Bartlett, *Thinking, An Experimental and Social Study* (New York: Basic Books, 1958), p. 11.

him.[8] As the body moves, sensory perception changes. Afferent systems carry impulses from sensory receptors to the brain which recodes them, sending new signals through an efferent system that forms the responses. "Perception includes the complex processes through which the individual receives, extracts, organizes, and interprets sensory information." [9] Sights, sounds, smells, tastes, and movements stimulate sensory mechanisms. The body itself responds to its responses, creating an interaction of modalities and systems. A dynamic process begins to emerge—action, reaction, and interaction.

Kephart describes the nervous system as a closed or continuous circuit allowing operation in either direction: input and output. In addition to sensory-motor responses, there can be motor-sensory responses. The output, or motor, phase can activate the input, or sensory, phase. Input can be developed by manipulating the output. Adequate motor responses can be obtained and developed by providing the proper sensory cues.[10] The human organism selects and processes cues from the environment. Working a puzzle, for instance, requires visual and tactile "output," the act of which affects sensory response—"input." Different puzzle shapes and color clues cause changing sensory responses (input) which alter subsequent action (output). The input is altered by the nature of the puzzle —size, shapes, and number of pieces, and picture—as well as by the child's puzzle memory, small motor skills, and feelings. The output is altered by internal physiological relationships, such as circulatory processes, neurological circuiting, and chemical balances. This internal network of interacting systems is both complex and invisible to the behavioral scientist. Characteristically, behavioral scientists interpret external response and infer the internal relationships. Similar external behavior within a group of individuals is the end product of a complexity of interactions which may be different and unique to each individual. Luria says,

> The most significant feature of a functional system is that, as a rule, it is based on a complex dynamic "constellation" of connections, situated at different levels of the nervous system, that, in the performance of the adaptive task, may be changed with the task itself remaining unchanged.[11]

[8] Ernest G. Schachtel, *Metamorphosis* (New York: Basic Books, 1959), p. 82.

[9] Judith L. Smith, "Kinesthesis: A Model for Movement Feedback," in *New Perspectives of Man in Action,* ed. Roscoe C. Brown and Bryant J. Cratty (Englewood Cliffs, N. J.: Prentice-Hall, 1969), p. 36.

[10] Newell C. Kephart, *The Slow Learner in the Classroom* (Columbus, Ohio: Charles E. Merrill, 1960), pp. 55–63.

[11] Aleksandr Romanovich Luria, *Higher Cortical Functions in Man* (New York: Basic Books, 1966), p. 24.

As the human organism moves through space, his sensory modalities respond to changing stimuli of light, sound, feel, smell, and taste. As environmental stimuli change, the ratio of sensory perception changes. In darkness, the organism depends on information he receives through his senses other than sight. While reading, information is received primarily through the eyes. Yet in darkness or while a person is reading the smell of smoke would stimulate a changed ratio of sensory response. "Sensation is always one hundred percent, and a color is always one hundred percent color. But the ratio among the components in the sensation or the color can differ infinitely." [12] The body seeks a balance and in this sense reacts predictably. If light is intensified, the sense of sound, touch, taste, and smell are affected at once. The media of the world—TV, telephone, print, even open fields and walls—each stimulate a variable ratio of sensory response. ". . . media as extensions of our senses institute new ratios, not only among our private senses, but among themselves, when they interact among themselves." [13] A complex interrelationship builds as sensory perceptions interact with environmental stimuli. An interdependence is sensed. Change in any part of the system affects the entire system.

The dynamic relationships between inner processes and outer experiences characteristic of perception only begin to reveal the complexities inherent in "knowing." What does the human organism do with perceived data? Sensory impulses travel to the association areas of the cortex where they are integrated and organized. Similarities and differences are juxtaposed to form patterns—images of sensed data. An examination of the role of imaging in the relationships among body movement, sensory perception and imaging should deepen the reader's grasp of "coming to know through body movement."

body movement, sensory perception, and imaging

Body movement causes changes in the inner organism. Sensed impressions derived from body movement travel through the central nervous system which is structured and restructured by every action. These structures are organized models—images. They are reflections of perceptions which mirror the past and serve to anticipate and interpret the future. Hence, when the body moves, sensory modalities react, and the human organism patterns his unique movements and perceptions in recorded images.

The formation of images derived from sensed impressions is characteristically human.

[12] Marshall McLuhan, *Understanding Media: The Extensions of Man* (New York: McGraw-Hill Book Company, 1965), p. 44.
[13] Ibid., p. 53.

Man explored his environment with his senses and learned about its form and textures; work and reflection revealed in nature, innate order and susceptibility to human organizing, bringing him a feeling of confidence and power. Out of the sensible richness of his environment, man built himself an image. . . . He sensed form-patterns in nature, the sun, the moon, a face, an ear of wheat, the shadow of a tree, and used them to break down his isolation within himself. Stored in memory, recreated in imagination, they built a feeling of being connected with the physical environment and with other human beings.[14]

That which connects builds a relationship. Relationships define patterns. Patterns become tools for understanding because they enable man to predict. They order, define, and structure experience. Similarities are juxtaposed with differences in a whole, a unit for subsequent comparison and prediction. "It is the capacity for organizing information into large and complex images which is the chief glory of our species." [15] Security derives from this sensed order preserved in images—controlled and understood.

Sensed forms, images and symbols are as essential to us as palpable reality in exploring nature for human ends. Distilled from our experience and made our permanent possessions, they provide a nexus between man and man and between man and nature. We make a map of our experience patterns, an inner model of the outer world, and we use this to organize our lives.[16]

Without organization we are disturbed; we cannot predict; we sense no patterns or relationships. The world lacks form and order. Kepes states:

Image-making was basic in enabling the human mind to grasp the nature of our surroundings. Isolating sensed forms was our first step in resolving a chaos of impressions into an articulated world. Visual images were formed of clearly defined entities—people and things—excised from the stream of sense experience. Men developed perceptual images according to the boundary lines which isolate objects visually from their surroundings.[17]

Images are, then, recorded experiences which reflect the past and help us understand the present and predict the future. If initial responses to the world are motor responses, then initial images must necessarily derive from motor experiences. "Feel" of one's own movement generates perception of self. As repetition of movement generates repetition of sen-

[14] Kepes, *The New Landscape in Art and Science,* p. 18.
[15] Kenneth E. Boulding, *The Image* (Ann Arbor, Mich.: Ann Arbor Paperback, 1961), p. 25.
[16] Kepes, *The New Landscape in Art and Science,* p. 18.
[17] Ibid., p. 29.

sation, patterns of sensation are recorded in images. "Images are a device for picking bits out of schemes, for increasing the change of variability in the reconstruction of past stimuli and situations, for surmounting the chronology of presentations." [18] Thus they are selective and personal, derived from interactions with the environment. Their personal nature is meaningful to the organizer who later learns to label them with words.

Images, then, serve as a bridge between sensed experiences and language. Impressions derived from movement in the world of concrete objects are preserved in an abstraction, removed from the concrete. Language does not replace images but is served by them and they, in turn, serve to restructure thinking by uniting the past with new data of the present. "The image method remains the method of brilliant discovery, whereby realms organized by interests usually kept apart are brought together." [19] Image-making may vary in mode or scope but ultimately unites a diversity of phenomena into a design of basic relationships.

A relationship implies structure. Structure is organization. Organization is meaning, a model of basic relationships. Its very nature connects individually unique pieces into a whole. "The image clearly does not reside in any one place or location. It is a pattern which pervades the whole." [20] Imaging is a form of structuring a whole in the mind. New experiences seep into the structure to find their place, altering the model to fit the needs of past and present. Thus, the relationships among the parts are dynamically altered by each new experience.

> Structure . . . is the created unity of the parts and joints of entities. It is a pattern of dynamic cohesion in which noun and verb, *form* and *to form,* are coexistent and interchangeable; of interacting forces perceived as a single spatio-temporal entity.[21]

New experiences are perceived either in or through formed patterns (images); or they serve to change formed patterns. When a new experience does not fit our established image, we build a new model— we extend the rules. Patterns, models, and images each suggest form. New experiences change this form. Meaning derives from interpretation of this interconnected whole. Man's survival depends upon his ability to shape his environment in accordance with his images. His ability to build a rapport with his world is reflected in the quality of his life.

Man structures the world while the world structures man. Out of

[18] Frederic C. Bartlett, *Remembering, A Study in Experimental and Social Psychology* (Cambridge: Cambridge University Press, 1964), p. 219.

[19] Ibid., p. 226.

[20] Boulding, *The Image,* p. 42.

[21] Gyorgy Kepes, ed., *Structure in Art and Science* (New York: George Braziller, 1965), p. ii.

the welter of interconnected, shifting, and changing impressions bombarding him through all his senses he finds order—a model of relationships.

> Man could not have ordered his world within the scale of his senses without breaking it up into separate things, freezing its movement and chopping up its continuity. . . . Measure became the means of separating; and separating by measuring appeared to be the key to interpreting nature. Today, however, interpretation has reached an impasse. . . . The more precise the measurement, the more difficult the act of isolation—because measure and measured interact. The act of measurement alters what is being measured.
>
> Although we have learned to express connection only in limited language, it has become obvious that not only what separates is important but what connects. The connections are not fixed. They are patterns and processes of nature's dynamics and as such, undergoing constant *transformation*. . . . The deeper connections are the dynamic organization of the successive patterns. They clarify relations of order, continuity and direction. . . .[22]

This body movement-sensory perception-imaging relationship serves as the seed of thought. Endowed with sensory perceptions, recorded in images, the human being acts further to identify, sort, evaluate, and interpret the unique contents of his own movement-perception images. He fills the gaps of his present perceptions with images derived from his unique interaction in the world.

body movement, sensory perception, imaging, thinking, and language

The beginning of this chapter stated that early man was stirred to thought from his own body movements. By manipulating the raw materials in his environment, man began to think about their potential for answering his particular needs. Clay could be molded and preserved, branches could be bent and lashed together, a stone could be sharpened, animal hides could be dried, cut, and sewn together. Man was thinking about materials and structures, whole and part, actual and potential. By being able to create a container, a shelter, a tool, and a weapon, man was mastering his world. He was able to create a new structure to suit a desired function. "Pottery-making gave man thought models of form and substance, permanence and change. The framework of thinking that grew from craft practices became an organizer of knowledge." [23] Seen in this way, focused body movement is the foundation and generator of thinking.

Yet, it was not movement alone. Man's complex of sensory mecha-

[22] Kepes, *The New Landscape in Art and Science,* p. 207.
[23] Ibid., p. 42.

nisms, which transmit sensations from movement for subsequent inner action, also react as basic transmitters of this primitive knowledge. Inner processing—sorting and ordering, to form patterns of sensed experiencing and preserve information—images are the next link in the chain which leads to thought.

> Thinking . . . is biologically subsequent to the image-forming process. It is possible only when a way has been found of breaking up the "massed" influence of past stimuli and situations, only when a device has already been discovered for conquering the sequential tyranny of past reactions. But though it is a later and a higher development, it does not supersede the method of images.[24]

Thinking, then, is a complex process catalyzed by present conditions but highly influenced by past experiences and memories—perceptual memories preserved in images. At the same time a thinker interprets his present perceptions, he manipulates them with previous perceptions (images).

Bartlett observed body movement skills in ball players, machinists, and surgeons and concluded that there was a continuing flow of signals from the environment of the performer which he interprets until the task is completed.[25] In addition to environmental signals, the performer picks up his own body signals which tell him about his movement as he is moving.

Bartlett further found a basic anticipatory function in sensory observation when items of evidence were presented in sequence. He noted that in daily life this anticipatory function is the result of grouping signal elements.[26] Thus, the individual is responding to a quantity of stimuli, many of which are not present in the "laboratory" setting.

> . . . the variety and *tempo* of natural events are often such that a simple anticipatory process resting upon inherent timing differences of single item stimulus-response behavior cannot satisfy the practical demand. The weight of emphasis is now shifted toward the structured character of grouped stimuli and events, and it is this structured character which can be used to project action towards a phase of behavior yet to come.[27]

It becomes apparent that observation of "concepts in formation" [28] must

---

[24] Bartlett, *Remembering: A Study in Experimental and Social Psychology*, p. 225.

[25] Bartlett, *Thinking, An Experimental and Social Study*, p. 14.

[26] Ibid., pp. 78–80.

[27] Ibid., pp. 79–80.

[28] Frances Minor, "Toward an Art-Science of Questioning: A Critical Inquiry into a Strategic Teaching Function" (Ed.D. dissertation, Teachers College, Columbia University, 1967), p. 182.

take place in the real world of daily activity. Here, and only here, will the complexities of stimuli which catalyze perceptions and order images leading to thought, be in operation.

Apparently, the thinker acts to structure present stimuli with images retained in memory. He groups items of evidence, outstanding because of their apparent regularity, symmetry, or numerical pattern, and weaves them into the structure of his images. Piaget describes this adaptive interaction between the organism and his environment as the relationship between two complementary processes—assimilation and accommodation.[29] As primitive symbols, images supplement direct sensory or perceptual response, increasing the range of "foreknowledge." Images also serve as a memory structure while present stimuli further direct behavior. "Skill, whether bodily or mental, has from the beginning the character of being in touch with demands which come from the outside world . . ."[30] or, more broadly, from objective evidence.

At this point the reader should be prepared for Bartlett's definition of thinking: "The extension of evidence in accord with that evidence so as to fill up gaps in the evidence: and this is done by *moving* [italics mine] through a succession of interconnected steps which may be stated at the time, or left till later to be stated."[31]

Our language describes thought in terms of movement: we focus on an idea, we seek order and we move toward a conclusion. Seen in this way, there is a harmonic relationship between body movement and thinking. Thought derives from action, thought determines action and there is movement in thought. Thinking emerges from a dynamic constellation of connections situated at different levels of the nervous system.[32] Action, perceptions, and images each have their function in thought. Words, too, serve thought; they also derive from movement.

> . . . at some time in man's human career, he began to create symbols for communicating with the world and the larger universe, with other human beings and with himself. . . . These early communications were probably nonverbal, using a variety of nonverbal messages such as . . . dances, change in gait or stance, postures, including bowing and kneeling and other forms of obeisance, gestures of arms and hands, facial expression and varied tones of voice (which apparently gave rise later to articulated language).[33]

[29] Jean Piaget, *The Origins of Intelligence in Children,* trans. by Margaret Cook (New York: W. W. Norton & Co., Inc., 1963), p. 7.

[30] Bartlett, *Thinking, An Experimental and Social Study,* p. 88.

[31] Ibid., p. 75.

[32] Luria, *Higher Cortical Functions in Man,* p. 24.

[33] Lawrence K. Frank, "The World as a Communication Network," in *Sign, Image, Symbol,* ed. Gyorgy Kepes (New York: George Braziller, 1966), p. 4.

Movement was probably man's first form of communication, accompanied initially by drums and chants. As sounds became associated with particular movements they grew to symbolize movement. Thus, words were born.

Words add further complexity to the complex process that creates and recreates images. Like images, words are representations of things that are not present. They also become symbols of personal experiences and tend, therefore, to have private meaning. In addition, words are used in social communications. Through a community of experiencing, words have not only private but universal meaning, and even then each listener and reader interprets words through personal experiences. Like images, words are abstractions, tools for structuring. They affect perception as perception affects their meaning. They are themselves concepts-in-formation. They represent only that to which they have been associated. They have no meaning in and of themselves; they must connect to both personal and social experience. Words can be said to be a distillation of the highly unique elements of personal experience.

> But once the individual uses the newly learned word, once a concrete situation is experienced through the agency of the word, the word contains the value of this symbolized situation. So the symbol . . . is a thing in process, containing and conveying the value which has become embodied in it, and communicating it in so far as there is community of experience between speaker and hearer.[34]

An analysis of language reveals that nouns differentiate objects while verbs define motion. Prepositions imply relationships, connections between things and movements. Thus, the genesis of language can be traced to movement. Vocabulary derives from movement, and language moves thought to higher levels. "The word was not the beginning—action was there first; it is the end of development, crowning the deed." [35] Language serves to refine thinking, it differentiates and abstracts experiences. It derives from perceptions, and in turn affects perceptions. Language reflects thought but is not itself thought. ". . . the structure of a person's thought processes is based on the complex structure of his language, which offers him certain categories and denies him certain others." [36]

The relationship between thought and language is a dynamic process. It is characterized by continuous movement from thought to word and

[34] Dorothy Lee, *Freedom and Culture* (Englewood Cliffs, N. J.: Prentice-Hall, 1959), p. 85.

[35] Lev Semenovich Vygotsky, *Thought and Language* (Cambridge, Mass.: M.I.T. Press, 1962), p. 153.

[36] Kepes, *Structure in Art and Science*, p. iii.

from word to thought. Thought establishes associations as it solves a problem, fulfills a function, grows and develops. Thought is not merely expressed in words but comes into existence through them. Since word meanings are dynamic rather than static formations, the complexity of this process becomes more evident. As the child develops and new demands are made on thought, the nature of word meanings changes and the relationship between thought and words changes. Words differentiate thought as they are united in a complete whole to express thought.

You may now begin to envision the development of an architectural form, a structure of interconnected elements uniting body movement with the development of sensory perception, imaging, thought, and language. Some relationships are apparent but the uniqueness of human experience in a spatial world should be examined in order to demonstrate its complexity.

summary

Body movement is the foundation of thought. It derives from, and contributes to, sensory perception, imagery, and thought. Each human being organizes his experiences into his own patterns. These patterns become his unique frame of reference in which, and through which, he assimilates new data. The systems of his body functioning interrelated with the systems of his environment build a complexity of dynamic relationships. As we move to examine the role of body movement in a very specific but fundamental task—the child's orientation in space—we will further explore this dynamic relationship.

2

orienting self
in space

One dictionary defines space in this way: "a limited extension in one, two, or three dimensions: a part marked off or bounded in some way: distance, area, volume." [1] Harvey Carr's definition describes the spatial attributes of objects: "their size, shape, stability, motility, and their distance and directional location in reference to each other and to the perceiving subject." [2] Objects help us define space, for their relationships can be measured, calculated, and changed. Without objects there can be no spatial measurement or relationships. In an empty room, for example, the walls define space by establishing measurable relationships. Objects further define that space by setting additional limits: they separate different parts within the whole space and establish new measurable relationships.

[1] Philip Babcock Gove, ed., *Webster's Third New International Dictionary of the English Language Unabridged* (Springfield, Mass.: G. and C. Merriam Company, 1968), p. 2180.
[2] Harvey A. Carr, *An Introduction to Space Perception* (New York: Longmans, Green and Co., 1935), p. 1.

definition of body movement

The definition of body movement is a human being's change of place, position, or posture.

differentiation: the genesis of spatial "knowing"

The newborn does not differentiate internal physiologic space and external space. His sense of space, a relatively undifferentiated and amorphous whole, is restricted to proprioceptive body experiences. Without movement he has only a tactual sense of weight against a supporting surface. Body movement links his physiologic space to the outside world of space. He moves and he is moved. He programs spatial information with his whole body as he stretches, kicks, rocks, and curls himself; as he is held, carried, cuddled, diapered, fed and put to bed. His body is formed by his movement as it is informed through his movement. Sensory perceptions are his tools; physical, social, and emotional needs, his motivations; and his body, the computer designed to program his world of space.

Early spatial perception is highly subjective, locked in degrees of comfort and discomfort. Sensations from body movement fall on a continuum between feeling satisfied and feeling strained or cramped. At this stage, the infant is primarily dependent upon his gustatory, tactual, olfactory, and kinesthetic modes of knowing. He exists in a space bounded by the length and reach of his body. It is a space which invites discovery. It can be reached, touched, felt, pushed, pulled, and changed by his body movement.

differentiating self from non-self

As his body makes contact, through movement, with objects in his spatial world, the human organism gradually separates self from non-self. Parts of his body come into contact with objects in the external world, and relationships begin to build. These first experiences of relating self to an object— the hand grasping the bottle, the foot kicking away the blanket, the mouth surrounding the nipple—are the foundations for subsequent spatial knowing. The child is himself the center of his spatial world, a personal *point of reference* through which spatial data are processed.

The body is a constant and thus a point of reference for perception of object constancies. Without a point of reference there can be no relationship—relationships exist as connections between two or more constancies or variables. The body, then, serves as the first point of reference for perception of space.

differentiating the parts of self

As the infant moves, he develops his sense of self. From gross and fine body movements, the human being accumulates bits of information that build his body schema. Through movement of both sides of the body against each other, against the force of gravity and in relation to stable objects, the child builds an awareness of the sides of his body, the top and bottom of his body, and the front and back of his body. Gravity is constant and gives stability to the infant's point of reference. The child exerts a counter-thrust to the force of gravity as he reorganizes his body parts to master pushing, pulling, stretching, rolling, crawling, creeping, walking, running, jumping, or skipping. Each new skill depends upon his ability to reorganize his body parts in movement. He spends most of his waking hours as a movement scientist—stretching and bending, twisting and turning, rocking and rolling, thrusting and counterthrusting—in a continuous search for a rhythm and dynamic balance to serve each movement skill. As he restructures the relationships among the parts of his body for each movement skill, he is increasingly able to differentiate his body parts—arms, legs, head, shoulders, hips, elbows, knees, feet, and hands. Each part plays a unique combination of roles in each moving skill. His development of a gradually more complex movement vocabulary helps him to differentiate the parts of self.

differentiating objective space

As the human being moves in a spatial surrounding, he gains awareness of the all-encompassing quality of that space. Sounds, smells, and sights exist in space relative to the front-back, top-bottom, and left-right of the body. The young child is at the center of his spatial universe, and perceives space in relation to himself. Self is still his point of reference. He perceives self relative to objects with multiple dimensions as well as relative to more than one object. Hence, he builds relationships based on self: self in relation to the dimensions inside of a car, to parts of a doorway, or to a table and chair. By observing his own body and the relationships among objects in space to parts of his body, he relates himself to the space outside of himself. Ultimately, the child shifts his point of reference from self to a point external to self. His point of reference becomes an object, part of an object, or a particular point in space. The child comes to use the steering wheel inside the car, the door itself, or the table as his point of reference. Eventually, the ground becomes his point of reference for judging the top and bottom of a building, as well as the top and bottom of self. The position of the driver's seat determines the front and back of a car; the magnetic poles are the point of reference for north, south, east and west; and the sun is the point of reference for the north and south magnetic poles.

The child's physical growth and his body development increase the complexity of his ability to differentiate objective space. Despite the dynamic changes in the relationships between self and the object world that growth and body movement create, there is constancy and predictability in both his body structure and the object world. The child must learn to differentiate between the stable and the variable. Looking at his highchair as he sits in it provides one point of view. When the child views that same highchair as he sits on the floor, or as he climbs into it, the relationships among the parts seem changed. Only through observing an object from many angles can the child come to perceive that there are stable relationships among its parts despite his body movement. By organizing his perceptions of stability and variability in objects, he discovers relationships and patterns. He can now predict and identify shapes.

> Things grow and disintegrate; they change their shapes, size, and position relative to themselves, to each other, and to us. These dynamics of the outside spatial world are amplified within us by our never-resting eyes, which are carried by our moving head and moving body. But in spite of all this mobility, the essential characteristic of the world as we perceive it is in fact, *constancy* and *stability*.
> The world as we perceive it is made up of things with persisting identity, existing in a frame of reference of stationary space.[3]

restructuring the parts

The child's discovery of patterns and relationships in the object world represents an ability to perceive a "new whole." In contrast to the amorphous whole to which he responded earlier, this new whole represents the child's restructuring of formerly differentiated parts. He now sees how the parts fit together. His sensed impressions are held through time, ordered in his mind's eye, and visualized as a whole. What he sensed to be located above, below, to the left, to the right, in front of and in back of him at each moment of his body movement now becomes part of his structured image. As he sees each object in its spatial relation to every other object, he is perceiving an interrelated whole. Gradually, the child learns to deal abstractly with spatial directions; that is, without his own overt motor activity. He comes to perceive the spatial relationships among objects. Kinesthetic, visual, auditory, and tactual sensing, stored in images, can be matched with present spatial perceptions to direct new spatial behavior and discoveries. The child projects the stability he perceives in the relationships among his body parts into the object world. Hence, it would

[3] Gyorgy Kepes, ed., *The Nature and Art of Motion* (New York: George Braziller, 1965), p. ii.

seem that the child's ability to stabilize the object world is a function of the stability of his body schema.

Body movement reflects the quality of the child's spatial images. As his repertory of recognized sequences of spatial perceptions increases, his ability to operate in a variety of spatial situations increases. To develop this operative spatial sense, the child must be able to focus his attention. Ontogenetically, focal attention develops with motor-sensory behavior, for movement activates sensory perceiving. Focal attention is activated when new demands are made on body movement skill and as body movement develops changes spatial perception. Later on, the child is able to focus his attention on the "idea" of an object or *relationships* among objects.

> Beginning with . . . first glimmering of the idea of object constancy, focal attention . . . becomes increasingly capable of being used in *thought,* instead of being tied completely to focal perception. The first step in this development is that the child not only becomes able to focus attention via the senses on an object seen, touched, and so on, but also becomes able to focus attention on the *idea of an object.* This focal attention to thoughts . . . together with the learning of speech—without which the capacity to have ideas of objects—could not go beyond an extremely primitive stage. Gradually not only objects but also their relationships, real or fancied, to the child and to each other become the objects of focal attention in thought.[4]

building dynamic body balance

establishing inner equilibrium

"The tendency to find equilibrium governs all natural order," [5] writes Kepes. Early survival in life depends upon an establishment of equilibrium between a person's physiological functions and his physical environment. Respiratory, digestive, neurological and circulatory systems establish a dynamic equilibrium with physical stimulation, food, air and temperature. Internal and external forces must be in balance if life is to be successfully sustained. With every movement, the human body's inner systems dynamically act, react, and interact to achieve balance. Physiological functioning in and through body movement becomes more complex as the human being grows and matures. Growth of limbs, which changes body proportions and the development of each new motor skill—crawling, walking, skipping, bicycle riding—affects body equilibrium. Throughout life, the intricate physiological interactions work toward the achievement of inner balance.

[4] Schachtel, *Metamorphosis,* pp. 257–58.
[5] Kepes, *The New Landscape in Art and Science,* p. 289.

structural axes of balance

The human body is built around three axes—a vertical, horizontal, and depth axis. The body rotates and revolves around these axes, the points of reference for all body movement. Rotation around the vertical axis (ex-

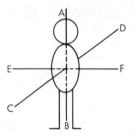

2-1. The three axes of body movement

tending through the body in line AB as shown in 2-1) can be illustrated by lying flat on the floor and rolling sideways from a face-up to a face-down position and back again. Rotation around the horizontal axis (extending through the body in line EF) occurs when the body performs a forward or backward roll. A cartwheel, or spin, performed while lying on the floor, illustrates rotation around the depth axis (extending through the body in line CD). (Interrelationships among the three axes will be discussed in the sections describing laterality and directionality.) Human movement, however, is more complex than these three rotations indicate. Bones, muscles, joints, tendons, ligaments, and cartilage are designed and organized to facilitate particular rotations, even as they inhibit others. Witness a child making "angels in the snow" (lying on his back and moving his arms and legs up and down along the floor), the longitudinal scribbling of the young child or any slow motion move of a "sport" skill.

body balance in and through movement

Dynamic body balance derives from a complexity of factors and is developed by the human organism in its own gravitational field. Gravity interacts as a constant with all body movement. As he moves, the child dynamically organizes his body parts in a continuous attempt to establish equilibrium against the force of gravity. Thus, the child builds dynamic body balance through his body movement. The interaction among his physiological systems contributes to his ability to balance his body in movement. The human body is endowed with components that facilitate balance: cerebellum, semicircular canals, proprioceptors, muscles, eyes, ears and skin. Since each body movement effects change in (1) physio-

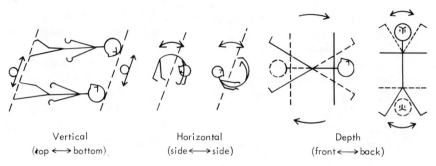

| Vertical | Horizontal | Depth |
| (top ←→ bottom) | (side ←→ side) | (front ←→ back) |

2-2. Axial rotations

logical systems, (2) the relationships among body parts, and (3) the messages received in the organs of balance, it would seem that an irregularity in any one of these factors would be reflected in dynamic body balance. Neurological impairment, learning of a new movement skill or nearsightedness each affect dynamic body balance. The ratio of significance of each factor is further altered by physical maturation and specific movement experiences, such as sudden rapid growth and learning a new body movement skill. Despite physical irregularities, maturation and the learning of new movement skills, the human body achieves balance, paying a price for it in degrees of body movement efficiency, which is unique to each individual.

The infant, with his immature physiological systems, body structure, and organs of balance moves against a strong gravitational field primarily around the vertical axis of his body. Gravity and his horizontal posture on the floor or bed are the primary factors in his body balance. Following the cephalo-caudal and proximo-distal progressions of development, body control proceeds from the head toward the toes and from the center of the body toward its extremities. The side to side movement of his head is the infant's first offensive force against gravity and achieving central balance of the head is a significant step in later body balance. He learns to elevate his head as he gains strength in his neck muscles; he lifts his upper torso as he gains strength in his arms. Preparing himself for independent locomotion, he initially pulls himself along, using the muscles of the top part of his body. As he gains strength in the lower part of his body, he is able to draw his legs under himself, thus preparing to creep. Creeping shifts the child's center of gravity which, in turn, effects changes in the relationships among the skeletal, muscular, and neurological systems already patterned by body movement. Bones and muscles work together to resist gravity and to facilitate movement around the vertical, horizontal, and depth axes of the body. The side-to-side motions necessary for creeping are primarily around the vertical axis while forward motion resists gravity primarily around the depth axis. When the child pulls himself upright to stand, he again changes the ways his bone structure, muscles, and nerves interact; he has to accommodate to a new center of gravity. His upright posture represents his dynamic resistance to gravity.

Initially, standing upright requires focused attention. Once upright, the body must use its movement skills to constantly maintain balance. As the child matures, his structural system becomes flexible enough to enable him to walk, run, jump, hop, skip, and ride a bicycle. His jointed body sets some limits of physical flexibility, but motor flexibility is almost limitless and, if exploited to its full extent, should signficantly expand his sense of balance and his "spatial knowing."

More specifically, the structure of the knee or elbow joint inhibits particular kinds of knee and elbow movement but each of these joints assumes a different combination of roles in running, jumping, and climbing. Each body movement involves balance and imbalance; hence, each movement structures and restructures the body parts in relation to (1) a chosen pathway in space, (2) a quantity of time, (3) degrees of muscular tension, and (4) the degree of movement control. A child receives different sensations from each movement skill whenever the emphasis on a particular aspect of motion shifts. Using the ideas above, sensation is different if one runs (1) in zig-zag floor patterns, (2) accelerating or decelerating speed, (3) by shifting body weight to "overbalance", or (4) expecting to have to stop at any moment. Dynamic body balance determines the quality of movement skill. The posture of the body while the body is in motion is a measure of dynamic body balance. Balance can be defined as stability produced by even distribution of weight on each side of the vertical axis. Sense of one's own weight—the pull of gravity on oneself—derives from muscle sensing in and through body movement and is necessary for achieving body balance.

Upright posture liberates the arms and hands for new explorations. Walking demands major adjustments from every part of the body—head, shoulders, torso, hips, legs, knees, and feet—in order that the body achieve balance. Gravity continues to impose a methodical processing on the early walker and is, in fact, a "major designing agent of physical structure." [6] Sustaining a stabilized and balanced course in his progressively complex world of space requires the walker to have homeostasis and homeokinesis of body functioning.

Since the three-dimensional organism is functioning in a three-dimensional world of coordinates, its achievement of balance must necessarily occur around three axes—vertical, horizontal, and depth. As the organism organizes groups of muscles for a multiplicity of movements, it is continually resisting gravity which exerts a constant force against

---

[6] Dudley J. Morton and Dudley Dean Fuller, *Human Locomotion and Form* (Baltimore: Williams and Wilkins, 1952), p. 277.

the body. Each movement changes the relationships among all the physiological systems in order to maintain the body's balance.

laterality [7]

Initially body movement is random, limited only by inherent structural relationships among skeleton, muscles, and joints. Through his own experimentation with movements the child gradually becomes aware of the difference between the two sides of his body. Later, as he matures, he is able to pull himself up on all fours. Movement from this position requires a shifting of balance from the center of gravity to a position that permits the releasing of an arm or knee. Alternate releasing of arms and knees around the gravitational center results in directional movement—falling to the side, falling back or front, but finally organized creeping. It is from this experimentation with locomotion that "sidedness of self" emerges. The child "senses" the sidedness of his movement as he seeks to balance. Movement on one side of his gravitational center necessitates a reciprocal movement from the other side to achieve balance or motor efficiency. Gradually, the child learns how to innervate one side against the other, how to sense which side has to move as well as how and when it has to move. As he senses his shifting body weight on each hand and knee, he simultaneously learns to center and decenter objects that lie in his line of vision. His structural bilaterality—two eyes, two ears, two arms, two legs—helps him coordinate his body in space.

2-3.   Center of balance

When the child finally pulls himself to an erect posture, he must realign the world in relation to this new verticality. His former sense of balance must be reorganized to serve his upright orientation: what was formerly parallel to his vertical axis is now perpendicular; what formerly was above his head is now directly in front of him.

Walking initially occupies the toddler's whole being as he seeks his center of balance. His muscles, skeleton, and neurological system are

[7] Kephart, *The Slow Learner in the Classroom*, pp. 42–46.

feeling out this new verticality. The toddler runs, tiptoes, climbs stairs and ladders, backs up and backs down, turns himself around, falls, reaches, reclines, and rolls. As he strives for more efficient movement he falls to the right, forward, to the left or backward. His feedback system records both motor errors and successes. Gradually, successes outnumber errors as the child senses the laterality of his body in movement.

This laterality is three-dimensional. These three dimensions can be illustrated by extending each of the three body axes into a plane. A plane of the vertical axis defines left and right; of the horizontal axis, front and back; and of the depth axis, top and bottom. Hence, the body has a left-top-front, a right-top-front, a left-bottom-front, a right-bottom-front, a

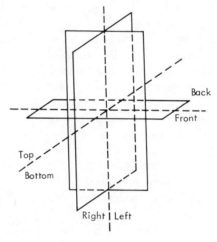

2-4.   Planes of the axes of body movement

left-top-back, and so on. When the body stands still, its relationships are constant, and objects in space exist relative to the front-back, top-bottom, and left-right of the body. Body movement, however, creates dynamic changes in the interrelationships. Furthermore, as the infant's point of reference changes from the horizontal (infant) to the vertical (toddler), the relationship of body parts to objects in space is also changed.

In addition to sensing laterality, the child learns to clearly differentiate the left side from the right side. His encounters with objects teach him that increased efficiency is achieved by leading with either left or right. He may find, for instance, that it is more comfortable to step up with the left foot first, or that the right eye is more informing than the left when peering into a small hole, or that the left hand is less likely to succeed than the right. Although psychologists still do not know how genetic and environmental factors influence sidedness, the establishment of a preferred side seems to be a factor of motor efficiency. The degree of sidedness also varies from person to person and from function to function.

directionality [8]

The young child uses stable objects to achieve his vertical posture. The bars of his crib, the sides of his playpen, the seats of chairs, and the legs of tables can be used for pulling himself upright. He is aligning his body against these objects; at the same time he is learning how it feels to be upright. He has, in fact, aligned himself with the stable objects in his world as he developed each previous movement skill. His movement efficiency is dependent upon his ability to align himself with external objects. In his performance, he matches his own sidedness with sidedness in his world. He learns that he has sides, and discovers that all objects have sides. Through experimenting with his body movement and aligning himself with objects, he learns that an object to his right may be reached by moving to the right. Initially, the relationship is that of self to object; later it becomes object to self. Much later, when the child shifts his point of reference from self to a point in space, he sees the placement of one object to the right of another object. Thus, directionality of objects is perceived through the laterality of self, as the child is able to relate specific body movement to objects in space. It is primarily through kinesthetic sensing and visual localizing of objects that directionality in the spatial world is perceived. Directionality is a projection of a sense of body sidedness (laterality) into objective space. Thus, as the child projects his body sidedness into space, he is constructing for himself the coordinates of left-right, up-down, and front-back. Kinesthetic coordinates within the body are matched with visual-tactual-auditory stimuli from the outside world of space. Thus, through body movement, the child builds directional orientation.

convergence

In addition to laterality and directionality, movement efficiency is dependent upon convergence. Convergence is a process of uniting separate skills to build functional efficiency. The bilateral human organism must learn to coordinate both sides of its body. Through movement of both hands it can simultaneously feel both sides of an object; by coordinating simultaneous impressions received in each ear it learns to locate and

[8] Kephart, *The Slow Learner in the Classroom,* pp. 46–49.

organize sound; through simultaneous fusion of both retinal images it comes to know the dimensions and locations of objects in space.

Convergence is built by the child through his body movement. The infant practices convergence as he explores an object held in both hands. Rolling, crawling, creeping, and walking also require sensory convergence as eyes, ears, arms, and legs seek rhythmic efficiency. Rhythmic efficiency in movement emerges from as it contributes to convergence. Hence, convergence is reflected in the rhythmic flow of body movement.

As convergence occurs in body sidedness, so it occurs in information processing. The human organism fuses the sidedness of his perceptions in a dynamic search for pattern and structure. As the architect of space centers, decenters, and recenters his attention on the dimensions of his experience, the dynamic structure of his thinking is built.

Man's brain fuses information received from bilateral sense organs. Without this fusion the information would be confusing, with a concomitant effect on efficiency.

As the human being moves, he perceives numerous dimensions of his spatial world and orders their relationships. His total spatial perceptions in any given situation include the relationships of objects and their parts to other objects as well as to himself. This becomes a structured image. The quality of a child's structured images is a function of the fusion of his vertical, horizontal and depth perceptions. He perceives objects bilaterally but his brain fuses this "sidedness" into a whole. His orientation in space derives from his fusion of "sidedness." This fusion of the vertical, horizontal and depth coordinates in conceptual space derives from his fusion of coordinates in percepto-motor space. Body movement is the foundation of conceptual architecture as perceptual and representational construction of space are predicated on body movement. At this point the reader may want to review Chapter 1.

> . . . both perceptual and representational construction are to some extent repetitive and possess a factor in common. This common factor is motor activity. Having already been the governing factor in representational images and, in all probability, the most elementary perceptions, motor activity now becomes the fountain-head of the operations themselves. The fact of its continuous existence through all the stages renders motor activity of enormous importance for the understanding of spatial thinking.[9]

"sensing" balance: a cognitive process

Psychological and cognitive feedback are basic to the learning of dynamic body balance. Only as the child learns the relationship of his body parts

---

[9] Jean Piaget and Barbel Inhelder, *The Child's Conception of Space,* trans. F. J. Langdon and J. L. Lunzer (London: Routledge and Kegan Paul, 1956), p. 13.

to his whole body in movement can he improve his efficiency. This is a physical, psychological, and cognitive task. As he moves his body in order to maintain balance, the child builds new programs into his space computer. With each movement is a counter-movement to achieve equilibrium. This is apparent when a person stumbles and instinctively corrects his loss of balance. The sensing of equilibrium requires a total body awareness, a sense of left-right, front-back, and top-bottom. Efficiency of body movement depends on a sensing of body location. Only as the child structures sensory feedback from his own movements is he able to improve his efficiency.

As the child learns to innervate one side against the other, front against back, top against bottom, he is learning body balance. His sense of balance or imbalance is a visual, auditory, and kinesthetic sensing of stability in his environment. As he organizes his own sensing of body balance, he finds relationships between his body parts and objects in his world. At any given moment, objects in his world exist relative to him and to one another—in front and in back of him, to the right and left of him, above and below him—despite his own body movement. He discovers consistency and regularity among spatial relationships. His moving body, head, and eyes facilitate his perceiving the constancy and stability in his world. The process of "seeing" the world of space is a complex five-step process, according to Harmon in Barsch: (1) light reflected on the retina must help the body come to a point of balance with that light and gravity; (2) the head, neck and body must cooperate to establish a point of reference in the visual space; (3) the organism must define its surroundings and the nature of its visual task; (4) the performer must define the details of the visual task—what exactly it will do; and finally, (5) vision must direct each step in the performance of the task. This dynamic sequence of "seeing" is repeated billions of times by a mobile organism whenever and wherever it looks.[10]

Since movement is continuous, the body is simultaneously performing all five steps in a continuing evaluation and reevaluation of the spatial perceptions in order to maintain its balance. The body uses muscles, nerves, bone structure for responding to perceptions of its shifting center of gravity to achieve perceptual-motor efficiency. The human organism will establish its own stability in perceptual space only as it feels stability in body balance. Interpretation as well as integration of sensory data affects the body's orientation in space. Sensory impairment or, more crucially, deficient processing of sensory data causes varying degrees of dis-

---

[10] Darell Boyd Harmon, "Body Restrained Performance as a Contributing Cause of Visual Problems," (paper submitted to Southwest Congress of Optometry, Fort Worth, Texas, 1965), as quoted in Barsch, *Achieving Perceptual-Motor Efficiency,* pp. 256–57.

orientation. For example, organic impairment, middle ear infection, or visual deficiency may distort perceptual organization.

With maturity, the organism depends more heavily on the eyes to carry the burden of the spatial perception task. Visual data feeds head and body movement directing the whole organism to assume a posture that can be maintained with a minimum of effort. The head is a crucial factor in location of the center of gravity. The eyes, transmitting to the brain a balanced or imbalanced image of space, depend upon the posture of the head. The posture of the head derives from the total body balance in the three axes of movement in a gravitational field. We now have come full circle in describing the interactions of body movement, body structure, body balance, and body posture in the child's orientation in space. The dynamic balance of self around the vertical, horizontal, and depth axes is a significant factor in spatial knowing. Each learner senses dynamic body balance both within his body and its relationship to the physical-motor demands of the world (his own movement) before he has a conscious awareness of balance. His "sense of balance" only later becomes a perceptual-cognitive process. As teachers we must come to know how the child organizes his perceptions. Body movement affects, as well as reflects, this unique organization and it is crucial that we recognize it.

> . . . spatial perceptions are by no means purely visual but are rather "visual-muscular labyrinthine" which concerns the attitude of the whole body in relation to gravity and the task.[11]

time of space; space of time

Orienting oneself in a given space necessitates ordering of a sequence of perceptual images. Locating one's position in an unfamiliar room, for example, necessitates perceiving the relationship of each wall to every other wall as well as the relationship of one's body to each wall. Such ordering requires a perception of body movement in space through time. Man has defined time in terms of movement. He developed his sense of time by observing movement patterns—rhythms—in his environment. He discovered a rhythm in the movement of the sun, a rhythm of day and night, a rhythm in the growth and development of plants and animals. He observed the waxing and waning of the moon, the ebb and flow of the tides, and relative change in the position of the stars. Rotation of the earth on its axis and its revolution around the sun—movement of an object through space—con-

[11] Charles Scott Sherrington, "Observations on the Sensual Role of the Proprioceptive Nerve Supply of the Extrinsic Ocular Muscles, Brain," 1915, as quoted in Barsch, *Achieving Perceptual-Motor Efficiency,* p. 267.

cretely define time. Complete spatial orientation is characterized by "spatial-temporal orientation which must proceed in terms of an inseparable and irreversible continuum of action." [12] Time is an inseparable factor of orientation.

internal time

The newborn is equipped with various physiological time systems. Each one—respiration, circulation, endocrine activity, or brain activity—maintains its own unique rhythm, but is also synchronized to operate within the organism as a whole. Organized in space, moving in time, the whole organic system can be considered as operating in "physiological time." As a machine with interlocking gears, the human being's rhythmical body functions become his temporal frame of reference for his movement in space. Change in any of these physiological rhythms affects the entire body and is reflected in body movement. Cerebral palsy, fever, asthma, and other disabilities affect change in physiological time as well as in "action time." The rhythmic systems of the body interact in space and through time to build a complex communication network in the central nervous system. "There is some temporal process in the central nervous system that limits and orders the perceptual events of the major sense modalities." [13] The composite tempo of internal body systems plays a vital role in the basic rhythm of daily living.

action time

The human being's physiological time is reflected in, and affected by, external body movement which builds a rhythm of action. Movements within the body are inextricably woven with movements of the body. Action time, or physical time, is a time of physical movement—the rhythmic flow of body movement. The rhythm and synchronization of his body movement reflects the child's sense of time. He builds a rhythmic flow into his walking, running, or crawling. This flow emerges from his internal time to join his syncopated and arhythmic perceptions in everyday living building a rhythm of transport. As the child's movement rhythm carries him through time it also moves him through space. Through body movement he comes to know a succession of points in space and a succession of points in time. He develops his own time of space (distance) and space

---

[12] Heinz Werner, *Comparative Psychology of Mental Development* (New York: International Universities Press, 1948), p. 180.

[13] C. T. White and P. G. Cheatham, "Temporal Numerosity: II. A Comparison of the Major Senses," *Journal of Experimental Psychology* 58 (December 1959), p. 444.

of time (duration). Estimating either distance or duration necessitates matching a sequence of objects in the environment with an established rhythmic body awareness. This is a crucial perceptual-motor task.[14] Hence, the child's perception of rhythm in his body movement serves as his point of reference for estimating both sequence and duration.

Sensing sequence and duration emerges from body movement and is a prerequisite to achieving movement skill. Some movement skills depend more on a particular sequence or succession of movements while others depend more on the simultaneous movement of many body parts. Success in building a tower of blocks, dressing and undressing, and manuscript printing depends more on a sequence of movements. Success in creeping, bicycle riding, or swimming is more dependent on the simultaneous movement of many body parts.

We tend to perceive distance in terms of duration. The distance between "here" and "there" is frequently calculated by "how long it takes to get there." Through many experiences, the child learns that the same span of space can be traveled quickly or slowly. He can control the rhythm and tempo of his movement. The child's movement rhythm reflects his sense of pattern in the time of space. The versatility of his body movement skills reflects the versatility of his rhythmic sensing and contributes to his spatial knowing. The extent to which the child acquires a sense of time in space is related to his movement efficiency. The tii. ng of movement, knowing when to move, and the ordering of spatial perceptions in time are critical factors in his orientation in space.

space thought in time; time-space in thought

For the infant, time "is embedded in a series of events—in a continuum in which space and time are not differentiated." [15] The young child, like early man, defines time through his discovery of rhythms in his environment. His sense of time emerges from his integration of the rhythms in his own physiological time, his action time, and the rhythms imposed by his environment. Initially, the rhythm of his basic physiological needs —hunger, fatigue, exercise—interacts with the rhythm imposed by the adults who provide for these needs. Gradually, he comes to know the rhythm of activities in his day—mealtime, bathtime, playtime, bedtime. Besides the rhythmic patterns of the day as his physiological needs are met, the child soon discovers a pattern in day and night, and a pattern in

[14] Jack D. Dunsing and Newell C. Kephart, "Motor Generalizations in Space and Time," in *Learning Disorders,* Vol. 1, ed. Jerome Hellmuth (Seattle, Wash.: Special Child Publications, 1965), p. 111.

[15] K. Lovell, *The Growth of Basic Mathematical and Scientific Concepts in Children* (London: University of London Press, 1961), p. 78.

his weekly activities. His sense of time soon expands into the past and future, from his own biological rhythms to the rhythms of sidereal time which are imposed by attending adults. The child's concepts of time derive from his body movement in regular routines of the day, weeks, months, seasons, and years. He learns sequence before he understands duration. He recognizes a particular succession of discrete events before he perceives the beginning to the end of an event.

The young child is able to orient himself in space only if he can carry out a succession of movements in a particular sequence. Initially, knowing how to go from "here" to "there" presupposes a particular sequence for him. A short cut disorients him. He wants to go to grandma's on the path he knows. He shrieks in protest when you take him to grandma's by a different route because he has identified a particular order of objects and events through his movement in time—a linear temporal-spatial translation of movement experience. This sequential "space-of-action" is an inflexible model for the very young child. He perceives a particular succession of movements through space. The child's memory also preserves a durational awareness of this succession of movement. He remembers the space of time and the time of space of his previous movement experiences. Memory elicits direction in thought. The thinker *moves* to fill the gaps between previous evidence and present perception. His thought connects points in time and space. "In every kind of skilled action from the simplest to the most complex, there is some kind of apprehension of the direction in which evidence is moving, or of the varied directions in which it might move." [16]

This suggests that the quality of thinking is inextricably interwoven with the structure built in the harmony of the time, space, and body movement of past experience.

> ". . . cortical activity, even when aroused by electrical stimulation, is revealed as a march of events with a definite temporal relation. The response obtained from any one point, at a particular moment, depends on what has happened before . . ." [17]

As movement in space is projected into the third dimension so is space thought. Initial experiences of rhythmic patterns of movement are photographed and stored in the mind. These images are continuously ordered and structured, their likenesses and differences are juxtaposed in rhythmic patterns.

[16] Bartlett, *Thinking, An Experimental and Social Study*, p. 78.
[17] Aleksandr Romanovich Luria, *Higher Cortical Functions in Man* (New York: Basic Books, 1966), p. 29.

> The essence of rhythm is the fusion of sameness and novelty; so that the whole never loses the essential unity of the pattern, while the parts exhibit the contrast arising from the novelty of their detail.[18]

Hence, the rhythm of movement pattern becomes the rhythm of pattern in idea. The flow of thought is an expression of cognitive rhythm. It serves to move man forward in his "space of time." It consists of elements from the past, perceptions of the present and planning for the future.

> Reaching, grasping, releasing—to reach again is the rhythm pattern for inquisitive man. The sequence is more meaningful when we express its rhythm as a reach-grasp-cognite-release (store) and reach again. This is inquiry. This is search. This is the melody of knowledge.[19]

Time permits thought to structure the dimensions of experience in space. Because the world is ordered, time and movement in space reveal this order—regularity and structure. Discovering patterns and relationships brings order to spatial knowing and awareness of sequences builds temporal order. An object in space is, in fact, different from each different viewpoint. By ordering each successive view in time, the viewer becomes able to anticipate a configuration sequence. "Knowing" an object that has been viewed from various angles is far more complex than knowing it from one particular angle. The ordering of a succession of views enables the viewer to perceive the three dimensions of space. With time being the fourth coordinate, orientation in space can be described only

> ". . . by stating the values of its four coordinates, three coordinates being required to fix its position, and one to fix its epoch. The epoch is the temporal coordinate that corresponds to the three spatial coordinates." [20]

Hence, body movement in time gives dimension to spatial knowing. The child, then, is the architect of dimension in his spatial knowing—he builds dimension in his knowing through his body movement. Content (space) and process (body movement) unite to form pattern and expectancy. Patterns of knowing emerge from body movement in space, and pattern serves as the point of reference for movement in thought. Using established patterns of knowing, the child moves to identify, classify and label the new. Knowing the essential characteristics of a sphere, for example, the child can move in his thinking to differentiate a ball, a penny, the earth, an orange, or a plate as "sphere" or "not a sphere." As old patterns leave gaps in interpretation of the new, thought is reorganized. Bits of old evi-

[18] Gyorgy Kepes, ed., *The New Landscape in Art and Science* (Chicago: Paul Theobold, 1956), p. 367.

[19] Barsch, *Achieving Perceptual-Motor Efficiency*, p. 310.

[20] G. M. Clemence, "Time Measurement for Scientific Use," in *The Voices of Time*, ed. J. T. Fraser (New York: George Braziller, 1966), p. 411.

dence are ordered in time to fit the new evidence. Time also permits practice of movement—development of increasingly complex movement skills resulting in expanded spatial knowing.

> Observations have shown that the relationships between the individual components of the higher mental functions do not remain the same during successive stages of development. In the early stages, relatively simple sensory processes, which are the foundation for the higher mental functions, play a decisive role; during subsequent stages, when the higher mental functions are being formed, this leading role passes to more complex systems of connections that develop on the basis of speech, and these systems begin to determine the whole structure of the higher mental processes.[21]

It is from actions that words flow; later, words flow into thoughts and thoughts direct actions. The child's speech is directly related to his dealings with the real world. The quality of his body movement and language experiences shapes his thinking. Words preserve actions through time. They label and thus generalize experience. As the human being moves through space and in time, he views his world from a multiplicity of angles. Learning to label each angle of viewing facilities his abstractions of essential similarities and differences, a key to conceptualization. Hence, time is a factor in conceptualization, for only in time and through time can the human being take in the many sides of his spatial world; time permits the ordering, structuring, and labeling of spatial relationships. Language and movement are the child's tools for expanding his spatial ideas in time. The complexity of his spatial knowing is dependent on the degree to which he differentiates his body movement. Thus, he expands his language of space through his body movement. The quality of his thinking is also a function of his integration in his speech-auditory systems. The child builds up a relationship between his motor experiences and the language he hears and learns to use. This internalization of the relationship between language and movement is the basis of his ability to verbally express himself and to receive verbal information.

To summarize: time is a significant ingredient of orientation in space. Physiological organization involves relationships among movement, space, and time. Body movement in space takes time and conceptualization of spatial ideas takes place in time.

conceptualization: a coming to know

Knowing begins with body movement. Body movement activates sensory analyzers which transmit perceptual information to create meaningful

[21] Luria, *Higher Cortical Functions in Man*, p. 37.

data. Initial knowing, as described by Piaget, is inextricably bound to motor activity—"sensory-motor" knowing. At this level, concepts are non-conscious " "spontaneous concepts." [22] The child focuses and acts on objects rather than focusing on the act of thought itself.

> The child becomes conscious of his spontaneous concepts relatively late; the ability to define them in words, to operate with them at will, appears long after he has acquired the concepts. He has the concept (i.e., knows the object to which the concept refers), but is not conscious of his own act of thought.[23]

As he reaches, touches, and grasps objects, and later crawls over, climbs up, walks around, and runs through objects, he senses shape, size, distance, direction, area, and volume. This sensory-motor practice feeds information to his central nervous system. As he interacts with his environment through body movement, he spontaneously assimilates schemes which he uses to explore new experiences. These schemes are ". . . behavioral forms or structures of the organism that correspond to the coordinating and organizing of external action." [24] The assimilation of these sensory-motor schemes forms the spontaneous concepts of early knowing.

> If every action implies assimilation and if assimilation is defined as incorporation of objects or of external links into schemes of actions, every action vis-a-vis an object transforms this object in its properties and in its relations. Thus every act of knowing includes a mixture of elements furnished by the object and by the action.[25]

"Scientific concepts" [26] emerge as the child learns to recreate his action in his imagination and associate words with his spontaneous knowing. Recreating action implies a focusing of attention on the elements of perception. As the human being focuses his attention, he simultaneously organizes his perceptions by separating and connecting the elements—a recognition of previous sensory knowing. This internalization of action is a generalization based on a particular sensory-motor act. Initially, the child considers each activity and object as a unique phenomenon. He is unaware of the regularities and patterns in his experience. Only as he perceives similarities among these discrete activities or objects is he able to generalize. He must discover the regularity and patterns in his experience. Cognition is an ongoing process which moves through various stages of structural

[22] Lev Semenovich Vygotsky, *Thought and Language* (Cambridge, Mass.: M.I.T. Press, 1962), p. 92.
[23] Ibid., p. 108.
[24] Hans G. Furth, *Piaget and Knowledge* (Englewood Cliffs, New Jersey: Prentice-Hall, Inc., 1969), p. 51.
[25] Ibid., p. 54.
[26] Vygotsky, *Thought and Language*, p. 82–93.

reorganization. Perception is restructured when the social world imposes words on experience.

> To become conscious of a mental operation means to transfer it from the place of action to that of language, i.e. to re-create it in the imagination so that it can be expressed in words.[27]

Developing with the mastery of language, scientific concepts reflect generalizations. Generalization requires more than ability to sense similarities. For instance, a figure with four straight sides and four right angles is a rectangle but it may also be a square. One can only differentiate a rectangle from a square when one recognizes that the adjacent sides of one of the two figures are different in length.

> The concepts of the manifold species and genera are supposed to arise for us by the gradual predominance of the similarities of things over their differences, i.e., the similarities alone, by virtue of their many appearances, imprint themselves upon the mind, while the individual differences, which change from case to case, fail to attain like fixity and permanence.[28]

The imperfect mind never retains the whole experience but rather a hazy impression which facilitates further generalization as a hierarchy of ideas develop. Conceptualization is then a gradual process of differentiation with a simultaneous process of structuring and restructuring of idea.

Symbols become links to connect motor activities, perception and conceptualization. Only through symbols can perceptions be classified, ordered, tabulated, discriminated, differentiated, and later retrieved. "Symbols . . . are signs that are produced or reproduced by the organism and directly follow from or lead to an internal action of knowing." [29] As such, they reflect the quality of operational intelligence. Symbols permit reorganization, restructuring and remembering—an "internal *action* of knowing." [30] "Not until we own the symbol do we feel that we hold a key to the immediate knowledge or understanding of the concept." [31] Language is a symbol system that transforms concrete experiences into conceptual knowledge. Words not only embody concepts but are themselves "concepts in formation." Words are generalizations which reflect images and connect "sensing" with thinking. Through language "human mental

[27] Ibid., p. 88.

[28] Ernst Cassirer, *Substance and Function and Einstein's Theory of Relativity* (New York: Dover Publications, 1923), pp. 14–15. Reprinted by permission.

[29] Furth, *Piaget and Knowledge,* p. 87.

[30] Ibid.

[31] Edward Sapir, "Language, an Introduction to the Study of Speech," in *Culture and Consciousness,* ed. Gloria B. Levitas (New York: George Braziller, 1967), p. 155.

processes are . . . elevated to a new level and are given new powers of organization, and man is enabled to direct his mental processes." [32]

summary

The main theme of this chapter is built through the juxtaposition of constancy and variability. Among the constancies in the human being's developing world of space is his body structure, a mobile and bilateral organization of muscles, joints, and systems designed for movement. Yet this structure varies among individuals. The human body further interacts with another constant—gravity—as the human organism moves through space seeking equilibrium. This search for balance is constant, universal, and fundamental to human survival, yet each individual builds his own dynamic body balance through his own body movement in his own environment. Body movement and space are universal constants; yet each individual's space and body movement vary at any one moment in time. Furthermore, the structure of body movement is variable and creates individually unique rhythms of movement.

The human organism's orientation in space is a unique and complex tasks. Each child structures his own world of space through his unique weaving of particular factors found in his unique body structure and the structure of his environment. What does this mean to each child? What does it mean for his teacher? What should the teacher look for in the child's environment? What should she look for in the child? To explore these questions, the following chapter examines body movement and spatial "knowing" using selected opportunities provided by classroom teachers of three- to six-year-olds.

[32] Luria, *Higher Cortial Functions,* p. 34.

3

theory emerges
from practice

This chapter looks at classroom practice through the ideas developed in the previous chapter. The material was collected in classrooms of children between three and six years of age whose teachers seemed to be providing opportunities for the children to develop concepts of space and spatial relationships through their body movement. The interactions among the children, teachers, and equipment are a mere sampling of opportunities that teachers are providing; here they are organized to illustrate children's seeming development of particular spatial ideas.

Analysis of these observations revealed that many factors of spatial relationships are inherent in each situation for each child. Each child's experience is uniquely his. The complexity of this analysis becomes more cumbersome when the situations themselves show increasingly complex interactions among the children, teachers, equipment, and ideas. I felt that the illustrations would more clearly mesh with the conceptual framework if they were organized to illustrate (A) what it takes to orient oneself in space and (B) some selected spatial ideas. To illustrate the inherent complexities, however, one observation—Lim climbing a ladder and a tree—is analyzed to isolate the complexity of spatial ideas relevant to this text as well as to a particular child's experience. The remaining observations have been classified and then analyzed to specifically illustrate particular factors of spatial knowing.

A. What It Takes to Orient Oneself in Space
  1. Children Move to Select Their Own Angle for Viewing Space
  2. Children Move to Find the Center of Balance in Space
  3. Children Move to Discover the Time of Space
B. Selected Spatial Ideas
  1. Children Move to Discover and Estimate Distance or Length in Space
  2. Children Move to Differentiate Shapes
  3. Children Move to Define Directions in Space
  4. Children Move to Connect the Dimensions of Space

LIM CLIMBS A LADDER AND A TREE

(a)

(b)

3-1. Lim climbing a ladder and tree

The teacher has provided a ladder with time and freedom for Lim to explore their climbing possibilities. Lim brings to the task climbing and hanging skills derived from previous experiences.

Climbing the ladder and hanging down from the tree limb requires a dynamic body "sensing" of distance, direction, shape, size, time, and body balance. As Lim takes each step up the ladder, he is estimating the distance he must lift each foot to reach the next rung, the direction in which it is to be lifted, and how long it will take to cover that distance. Simultaneously, he is estimating the distance he must lift each hand from where it is (point of reference) to the next place, the direction of lifting, how long it will take, and the shape and size of the object it will grasp. Each movement and new posture change Lim's center of balance, creat-

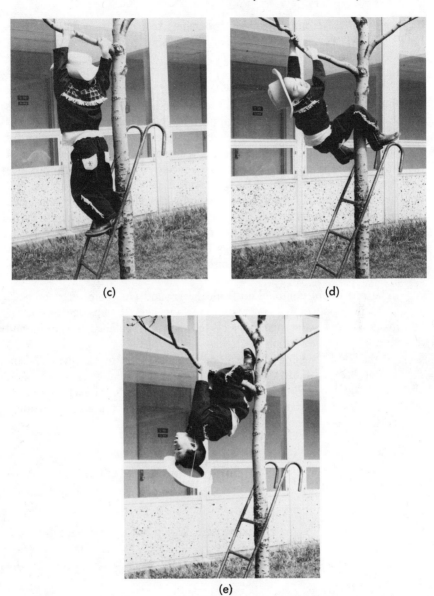

(c)

(d)

(e)

ing a need for a dynamic sensing of body balance. His body movement is evidence of a dynamic testing of the relationships among distance, direction, time, shape, size, and body balance from each point of reference.

Lim discovers that climbing the ladder to the third rung (3-la) enables him to reach up and grasp the tree limb with both hands—a spontaneous sensing of distance, direction, the time it takes to get there, and dynamic body balance. From the third rung, his new point of reference, he drops his feet from the ladder and hangs from the tree limb by both hands (3-1b). He is now spontaneously sensing body weight, the shape and size of the tree limb, and his new center of balance between his left and right sides.

Then, using the limb as his new point of reference, he reaches back (sensing the distance) to return his feet to the ladder. As Lim now climbs to the top rung (3-1c) he redistributes his body weight between hands and feet by placing his left hand on one side of the tree limb and his right hand on the other and pulling his feet up and around either side of the tree limb. His success is evidence of a dynamic "feel" of distance between the fourth rung of the ladder and a particular place on the tree limb which he grasps; the distance and direction in which he must pull his feet to wrap them around the tree limb; his center of balance as he pulls up his feet around the limb (3-1d).

Hanging by his hands and legs from the tree limb (3-1e) Lim now views the playground from a position upside down, his new point of reference.

The process of climbing up from the ground (his point of reference) provides an opportunity to explore "aboveness," "upside-downness," "downside-upness," the sidedness of self, gravity, balance, distance, and direction.

Total body "sensing" is the child's initial mode of "knowing." Sensory-motor "feel" of distance, direction, sidedness, balance, shape, size, "upness," "downness," is the essence of spontaneous concepts, formed by the self. Such spontaneous concepts form the foundation of later imaging and thinking—conceptualization.

children move to select their own angle for viewing space

using self as a point of reference for viewing space

JIM AND JOHN VIEW SPACE FROM THE TREE GYM

The teacher has provided a tree gym with time and freedom for Jim and John to climb up and view their playground (3-2). Each child comes to the task with climbing skills derived from previous climbing experiences. As each child climbs the tree gym, self serves as his point of reference for sensing up, down, left, right, between the rungs, over or under a rung, and through empty spaces. The point of reference for stepping to the next rung is the location of the foot before it takes a step; from this, the child estimates the distance to the next rung. Likewise,

3-2.   Jim and John viewing space from the tree gym

the point of reference for the hand is its location on one rung from which the child estimates the distance to the next location that will help to maintain body balance. Looking down from the top, self again becomes the new point of reference from which to note the top of objects, the distance down, the shape of objects from above, and their length, area, and volume. Although objects on the playground maintain a constant relationship to gravity; the child's angle of viewing changes as he moves.

LUCY VIEWS SPACE HANGING BY HER
HANDS AND KNEES

The teacher has provided an H-bar with time and freedom for Lucy to climb and hang down by her hands and knees (3-3). She comes to the task with previously-learned climbing skills. As she brings her feet and ankles over the bar (3-3a) and her upper body hangs down from the bar (3-3b), her body posture serves as her point of reference for viewing the new relationships of her body parts. She can observe that both hands and feet are "up," or that they are "higher than the rest of me," Hanging from the cross bar, she uses self as her point of reference as she views familiar playground objects upside down (3-3b). The objects in her playground world maintain a constant relationship to gravity and each other; Lucy's relationship to gravity is also constant but her body movement changes her point of reference.

(a)　　　　　　　　　　　　　　(b)

3-3.　Lucy viewing space hanging by her hands and knees

GEORGE BUILDS A TALL BLOCK BUILDING

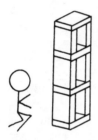

3-4.　George's block building

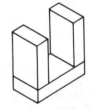

3-5.　George's block pattern

GEORGE:　It's getting so tall. Pretty soon I have to stand up to reach it. Mr. C., pretty soon I have to stand up to reach it (3-4).

The teacher has provided unit blocks with time and freedom so that five-year-old George may use them. He approaches the task with previous building skills and knowledge of unit blocks and other building materials. Initially the floor is his point of reference as he constructs the first pattern of three blocks (3-5).

He repeats this pattern vertically with each supporting block becoming the point of reference for the blocks placed on top of it. As he builds up the pattern to where he can no longer reach, George says, "Pretty soon I have to stand up to reach it." Self has become his point of reference for noting the height of his building. While he is sitting on the floor, his point of reference for estimating the height of his building is constant; as he repeats the block pattern and the height of the building increases, and is thus variable.

MICHAEL SEES TWO POSSIBILITIES
IN HIS WOOD WORK

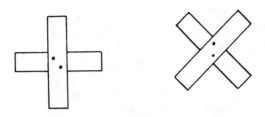

3-6. Michael's woodwork

MICHAEL: It's a plus sign. It could be a multiply sign. (*As he speaks he rotates his structure 45°.*)

The teacher has provided wood, nails, and a hammer with time and freedom for six-year-old Michael to work with them. He approaches the task with skills derived from previous experiences with woodworking. After he successfully hammers the two pieces of wood together (3-6) he says, "It's a plus sign." Self is his point of reference. Self continues to be his point of reference as he rotates his plus sign and declares, "It could be a multiply sign." Self as point of reference remains constant; movement of the wood is the variable.

Both George and Michael, in expressing their thinking about what they were doing, seem to provide evidence for Piaget's theory that knowledge derives from actions on materials.

using a point of reference external to self

JAMES'S POINT OF REFERENCE IS DIFFERENT
FROM HIS TEACHER'S

JAMES: These are gas stations on the bridge. (*He points to the four unit blocks on top of his bridge* [3-7].) I need more squares.
TEACHER: How many?
JAMES: Four . . . three . . .
TEACHER: How many? Four or three?
JAMES: Oh, you decide.
TEACHER: You tell me and I'll get what you want.
JAMES: (*Mumbles and nods head.*) Four and three.
TEACHER: Four *and* three?
JAMES: Yes!

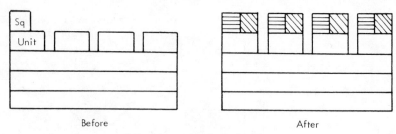

Before   After

3-7.   James's block building

The teacher has provided unit blocks for four-year-old James to build; she has also asked him questions to help him to clarify his thinking. He approaches the task with building, counting, and language skills derived from previous experiences with unit blocks and other building and "countable" objects. When James says, "I need more squares," the teacher asks, "How many?" James hesitates, "Four . . . three." The teacher's point of reference seems to be the single square block on the far left unit block. She thinks he needs three more but wants him to figure it out so she again asks, "How many? Four *or* three?" James replies, "Oh, you decide." She refuses, saying, "You tell me and I'll get what you want." Hesitating again, James states, "Four *and* three." His point of reference seems to be the "empty spaces" on top of each unit block. Hence, he needs seven blocks and to the teacher's question, "Four *and* three?" he replies, "Yes!" It would seem that the teacher's questions have focused his attention on precisely what he intends to do.

SAM CHANGES HIS POINT OF REFERENCE
AS HE VIEWS HIS CUISENAIRE RODS

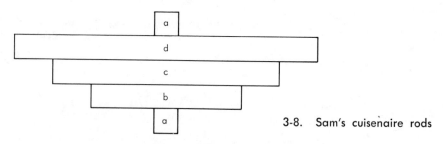

3-8.   Sam's cuisenaire rods

SAM: These are the short ends [a].
This is the littlest middle [b].
This is the high middle [c].
This is the top [d].

The teacher has provided cuisenaire rods and encouraged six-year-old Sam to arrange them and discover some spatial relationships. Sam approaches the task with manipulative and language skills derived from previous experiences with cuisenaire rods and similar materials. He has arranged the rods as shown in 3-8, and focuses his attention on the spatial relationships. Initially his point of reference seems to be the "short ends"—the *a* rods—which justify rod *b* as the "littlest middle." However, his point of reference seems to change to the longest rod (*d*) and the bottom rod, (*a*) when he says of rod *c*. "This is the high middle," and of rod *d*, "This is the top." Since Sam arranged the rods horizontally on the table and used the words, "top," and "high middle," it seems that he perceives these relationships horizontally using himself as a point of reference. Further, he has begun to generalize the meanings of "middle," "top," and "high middle," a key to conceptualization.

WHAT DOES IT TAKE TO SELECT AN ANGLE FOR VIEWING SPACE?

Self provides not only the first, but the most immediate and meaningful point of reference for viewing space. The human organism must learn to stabilize relationships relative to self despite body movement that changes spatial relationships. Through the use of outdoor apparatus, the teacher has provided opportunity for Jim and John on the tree gym, and for Lucy on the H-bar to discover the stability in spatial relationships despite varying points of viewing resulting from their own body movement. Through their actions on objects, George with unit blocks and Michael with woodwork have derived ideas about height and relative position of parts of a stable object when it is moved in space. James with blocks and Sam with cuisenaire rods, use points of reference external to self from which to perceive the relative position of particular blocks and some relationships within an arrangement of cuisenaire rods.

What then does it take to select a point for viewing space? "Point of view" is defined by *Webster's Third New International Dictionary* as a particular position in space or time development from which something is considered or evaluated. "Assuming a position" requires movement— either body movement or movement in thought; evaluation requires a focusing of attention on a task. As teachers we provide the materials; children then select and reveal their unique angle for viewing. Only to the degree that we pick up the clues the child provides can we help him move ahead in his thinking or help him shift his angle for viewing.

In what ways might a child reveal his angle of viewing? To what degree do the teachers in the illustrations above pick up the clues which each child provides? To what degree does each teacher help each child to focus his attention? To what degree do they help each child shift his angle for viewing when it is necessary?

children move to find the center of balance in space

3-9. Bobby balancing on the curb

The teacher has introduced a 4-inch-wide cement curb for three-year-old Bobby to walk along its edge. Bobby approaches the task with walking and balancing skills from previous experiences. He focuses his attention on his feet, suggesting that the curb is narrower than his usual walking stance. In order to balance himself while stepping forward on alternate feet, Bobby raises his arms and looks at each succeeding step. Each step changes the relationships among his body parts around his dynamic gravitational center. His success is evidence of his dynamic testing and "feel" of the sidedness (top-bottom, left-right, front-back) of his body—a spontaneous sensing of balance. His body structure is constant; body movement changes the relationships among the parts.

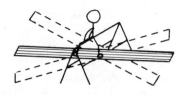

3-10. Balancing on the seesaw

The teacher has provided a sawhorse and plank for three-year-old Jane to explore. She approaches the task with standing and balancing skills from previous experiences. She focuses her attention on the placement of her feet on the plank—on either side of the saw horse, in this case; the placement of her hands on the top bar of the saw horse; and the arrangement of her body between her hands and feet. As she shifts her weight from side to side making the plank go up and down, the relationships among her body parts change around her dynamic gravitational center in relation to its position over the plank and sawhorse. Her success is evidence of her dynamic testing and subsequent "feel" of body balance—a spontaneous sensing and immediate responding to the sidedness of self in relation to the movement of the plank. Her body structure is constant; body movement changes the relationships among the parts.

DAVID AND PETER BALANCE ON A SEESAW

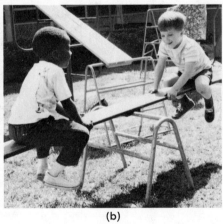

(b)

(a)

3-11. David and Peter balancing on a seesaw

The teacher has provided a sawhorse and plank (3-11a) for David and Peter to climb on. They each approach the task with climbing and balancing skills from previous experiences. Each child's attention seems focused on the relationship between his own movement-posture and the movement-posture of the other child. Each child's body movement will alter the relationships among his own body parts as well as those of the other child's movement-posture. Their success (3-11b) is evidence of their dynamic testing and subsequent "feel" of balance—a spontaneous sensing of the relationships among their own movement-posture, the movement posture of the other child and the location of the board on the sawhorse.

Each child's body weight and the position of the board on the sawhorse is constant; body movement, however, changes the relationships among the board, the sawhorse and each child's body parts.

KIM BUILDS WITH UNIT BLOCKS

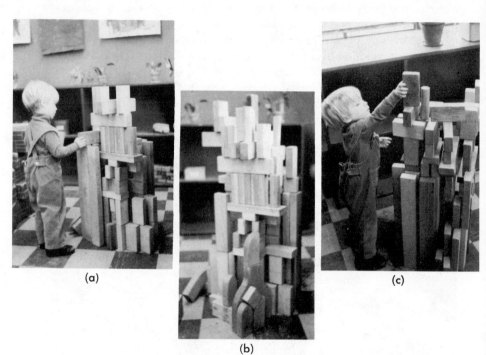

(a)

(b)

(c)

3-12. Kim building with unit blocks

KIM: Hey! It's so steady. Look! Anoder bridge! I have a tunnel that you can't see. It's so dark in there. Hey, I did it over a bridge. (*Balanced a block*) Here's the window! Look what I did!

The teacher has provided unit blocks with time and freedom for three-year-old Kim to build. He approaches the task with skills and knowledge from previous building experiences. He focuses his attention on balancing each block. As he "tries out" each block to see if it will balance, it seems he is feeling the dynamic relationship between his action on the blocks and the other supporting blocks. His success is evidence of a spontaneous sensing of the center of balance. His comments suggest a conscious knowing of balance: "Hey! It's so steady! Look! Anoder bridge! I have a tunnel that you can't see; it's so dark in there. Hey, I did it over a bridge." The blocks themselves are constant in size and weight; Kim's action on them changes their center of balance.

SALLY BALANCES HER BOX SCULPTURE

3-13. Sally balancing her box sculpture

(b)

(a)

SALLY: I'm going to put this cup here. I hope it will balance. [3-13d, e, f]

The teacher has provided boxes, scotch tape, glue, and a cardboard base with time and freedom for three-year-old Sally to build a box sculpture. Sally approaches the task with some knowledge and skills in pasting and sculpture from previous experiences in similar tasks. In 3-13b, Sally tries to balance the weight of the long paper-cup box by placing a paper cup on the LaRosa box. She says, "I'm going to put this here. I hope it will balance." She struggled for at least five minutes, seeming to sense the weight of the overbalanced paper-cup box. Finally, she selected the salt box (3-13c) and inserted it under the end of the paper-cup box. This unbalanced the original right-hand portion of her construction, so she placed a paper cup between the paper-cup box (3-13d) and the My-T-Fine pudding box. "Now it's balanced" she said. Initially, the imbalance was related to the weight of the paper-cup box and counterweight of the boxes to which she had it glued (3-13b). Ultimately, she achieved balance by leveling the paper-cup box on the salt box and the original base boxes and paper cup (3-13d, e, f). Finally, she glued another paper cup on top of the paper-cup box (1-13g). Her success would seem to be evidence of a spontaneous "feel" of both kinesthetic and visual balance, as well as a conscious use of the word, "balance."

(c)

(d)

(e)

(f)

(g)

WHAT DOES IT TAKE TO FIND THE CENTER
OF BALANCE IN SPACE?

"Balance" can be defined as stability produced by even distribution of weight on each side of the vertical axis. From this definition, it would seem that balance can only be achieved through movement that distributes weight equally on each side of a vertical axis. Since weight is the force of gravity on a body, a sense of balance requires a sensing of weight distribution during movement around a vertical axis. The vertical axis thus becomes the point of reference, or the fulcrum, of balance. In Chapter 2 (see pp. 17–26), we discussed how the child programs a dynamic sense of body balance as he develops body movement skills. It would seem that Bobby on the curb, Jane, David, and Peter on the seesaws have each focused their attention on redistributing their body weight and are sensing dynamic body balance. Sally manipulating boxes and Kim building with blocks are each "acting on" materials and seem to consciously perceive balance and imbalance. Movement is a key to finding a center of balance in space.

In what ways might a child reveal his sense of dynamic body balance? To what degree does the teacher pick up the clues which each child provides? To what degree does she help him move ahead in his "spontaneous sensing" or "conscious conceptualization" of balance in space?

children move to discover the
time of space

DAVID THROWS AND CATCHES A BALL

The teacher has provided a large rubber ball with time and freedom for David to throw and catch. David comes to the task with ball-throwing and catching skills derived from previous experiences. While he focuses his attention on the ball, reaches up, and stands balanced on his toes, he is also estimating the direction in which the ball is traveling and the speed at which it is falling. His success further depends on his posture and position relative to the path of the ball, the distance and direction of his movement, his timing, and anticipation of his grasp on the ball when it comes down. Crucial to his success is the interrelationship of the time and the rhythm of his body movement, and his estimation of the time of the movement of the ball. Conceptualization of movement through space includes a "sensing" of the time-space of body movement.

(a)

(b)

3-14. David throwing and catching a ball

BETSY JUMPS ROPE

3-15. Betsy jumping rope

The teacher has provided a rope with time and freedom for Betsy to practice jumping. Betsy approaches the task with jump-rope skills derived from previous experiences. She grasps one end of the rope with her left hand and the other end with her right, rotates her arms in a circular motion—back-up-forward-down—on either side of her body causing the rope to form an arc and move in a circular path. She bends her knees and springs off both feet simultaneously as the rope approaches and goes under her body. Crucial to her success is her coordination of the rhythm in her arm-rotation and the rhythm of her jump—a dynamic time-of-thought and time-of-action relationship. Thought, "sensing," and action become integrated into a spontaneous knowing.

BETSY JUMPS ROPE WHILE THE TEACHERS
TURN IT

3-16.   Betsy jumping rope while the teachers turn it

The teachers help Betsy practice jumping. She stands between the teachers, swings her arms to the right, bends her knees and leans to her left and toward the rope in preparation to jump (3-16a). Simultaneously, she focuses her attention on the movement of the rope and springs off both feet as the rope approaches and goes under her body (3-16b). Crucial to her success is her coordination of the rhythm of her jump with her estimation of the rhythm of the movement of the rope. This indicates a dynamic relationship between a time of thought and a time of action. Again, her thought, "sensing," and action become integrated in a simultaneous spontaneous knowing.

RUNNING IN SPACE-TIME

3-17. Cindy, Lisa, Ann, and Dorothy running

A runner propels himself forward with a force equal to the force of his push against the ground. This force determines the speed of movement which, in turn, affects posture, balance, and the speed and angle of arm and leg rotation. Coordinating the arm and leg swing is itself a rhythm that affects the length and direction of the stride and the tempo of movement. Interaction among force, friction, rotation, balance, posture, angle of knee bend, moving center of gravity, and arm swing in running is a space-time coordination involving rhythmic interaction and time judgments. Running involves a dynamic relationship among body parts in motion through space in time. It requires total body involvement.

WHAT DOES IT TAKE TO DISCOVER THE
TIME OF SPACE?

Being aware of the duration of an action would require experience with body movement. Since time can be thought of as a space interval, and space as a time interval, body movement links space with time. Movement in space is a relationship between distance and duration. Distance between "here" and "there" is constant, while the duration of movement varies.

Spontaneous sensing of space-time is evident in David's movement to catch the ball, Betsy's jumping rope, and the running of the four girls. In the activities analyzed above, each child selects his movement, and through it reveals his grasp of particular space-time relationships.

In what ways might a child reveal his space-time knowing? To what degree does each teacher in the illlustrations selected pick up the clues that each child provides? To what degree does she move each child ahead in his "spontaneous sensing" or "conscious conceptualization" of space-time?

children move to discover and estimate distance or length in space

SANDY ESTIMATES AND DISCOVERS THE
LENGTH OF A PLANK

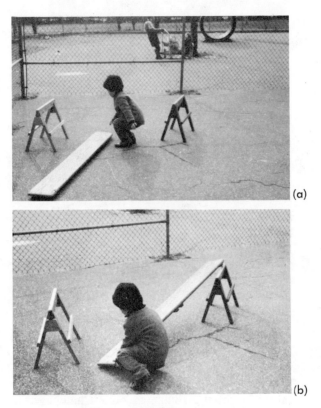

(a)

(b)

3-18.   Sandy estimating and discovering the length of a plank

The teacher has provided time and space for Sandy to work with a plank and two sawhorses. Four-year-old Sandy brings to this task previous experience with moving and building. He focuses his attention on one end of the plank, which he picks up and balances on one sawhorse (3-18a). This end of the plank now serves as a point of reference as he picks up the other end of the plank to place it on the other sawhorse (3-18b). Ultimately, Sandy moved the sawhorses in line with each other and close enough to allow the plank to bridge them. Sandy's success is evidence of his spontaneous estimation of the length of the plank, the height of the sawhorses, and the distance between the two sawhorses necessary to simultaneously hold up each plank.

ROGER ESTIMATES AND DISCOVERS THE
HEIGHT OF THE TILE WALL

3-19.   Roger estimating and discovering the height of the tile wall

The teacher has provided the hollow blocks and a tile wall with time
and freedom for Roger to stack the blocks and look over the wall. Roger
comes to the task with skills learned from previous building and climbing
tasks. He makes a stack of four blocks against the tile wall and uses another
block as a step. Climbing up on the stack of blocks and looking over the
wall (3-19) would seem to provide a spontaneous sensing of both the height
of the wall and the height of the hollow blocks. Climbing requires the child
to "feel" how far to lift a leg, reach an arm, or place a foot.

TORI AND WIN DISCOVER THE HEIGHT OF
THE PLAY PLATFORM

The teacher has provided a play platform and ladder with time and freedom for Tori and Win to climb. Both children come to the task with skills
from previous experience with climbing tasks. Climbing a ladder
requires a kinesthetic sensing of the distance one must lift a leg to
reach each rung. Climbing from the ground to the platform further provides a "feel" of the total distance traveled. Win, who has climbed part-
way up the ladder "feels" the distance between each step, as well as the
distance from the ground to his present height. As he looks down (3-20)
his kinesthetic sensing of the distance is visually reinforced.

3-20. Tori and Win discovering the height of the play platform

The teacher has provided a tree gym with time and freedom for Randy to climb. Randy approaches the task with climbing skills derived from previous climbing experiences. He hooks his right knee on an upper cross rung and his right hand grips the same rung near his knee. With his upper body resting horizontally on a lower rung and his left leg and hand reaching down to a still lower rung, Randy seems to be arranged to spontaneously "feel" multiple distances: the distance between (1) the rung under the right knee and the rung behind the left ankle; (2) the right knee and the left hand; (3) the rung that the upper body is resting on and

3-21. Randy discovering the distance between the rungs

the rung that the left hand and left ankle touches; and (4) the bar supporting the right knee and right hand and the rung against which the left ankle and the left hand are resting. Climbing up the tree gym and getting into this position further provides opportunities for spontaneous sensing of the distance from the ground to this height and the distances between the rungs.

BILLY, ADAM, SHERRI, AND YARA ESTIMATE
AND DISCOVER DISTANCE

BILLY: I want to make it higher. (*He begins to lift one end of the board.*)

SHERRI: I can't jump that high! (*Cries.*)

TEACHER: Let's try it and if we can't do it we'll put it back.

SHERRI: (*Continues to cry, saying she can't do it.*)

TEACHER: Mrs. A. will make a high one over there and we'll have a low one here. (*For some reason she leaves the latter one high, too.*)

ADAM: (*Jumping and half crying.*) I want it lower!

BILLY: (*Slapping his hands on the board.*) I don't want it higher.

TEACHER: (*Lowers board and children continue to bounce and jump off.*)

ADAM: (*Pushes two large hollow blocks into the jumping space.*)

YARA: (*Crying.*) I want to jump. I want to jump very far.

TEACHER: (*To Adam.*) Yara said she wants to jump very far. What will happen if the blocks are here?

ADAM: (*Hangs head and slumps on blocks.*)

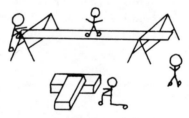

3-22.   Estimating and discovering distance

The teacher has provided two sawhorses, a plank, and two large hollow blocks for Billy, Adam, Sherri, and Yara (all three years old) to climb, jump, and verbalize their understanding of the distances inherent in their play. The children come to the task with climbing, jumping, and language skills derived from previous experiences.

Billy. Lifting the plank and saying, "I want to make it higher" suggests that Billy has a conscious knowing of "higher." Later he slaps his hand on the plank and says, "I don't want it higher," seeming to confirm his grasp of this word and his thinking about height.

Sherri. Crying "I can't jump that high" suggests that Sherri is using herself as a point of reference and, from past jumping experience, thinks that the height of the board is beyond her jumping ability—a conscious knowing of height in relation to jumping skill.

Adam. Adam's crying "I want it lower!" suggests that he has a conscious kinesthetic-visual sense of the height he is able to jump from. Later, when the teacher says, "Yara said she wants to jump very far. What will happen if the blocks are here?" Adam's slumping down suggests that he knows that the blocks are in Yara's way. He is aware of the distance Yara thinks she can jump.

Yara. Looking at the blocks Adam has pushed in front of the jumping board, Yara says, "I want to jump very far." She, too, seems to have a kinesthetic-visual knowing of her ability to jump a given distance in space and has abstracted her knowing through language.

BARBARA STRUGGLES TO GRASP A COMPLEX
DISTANCE-TIME RELATIONSHIP

Excerpt from a discussion in the kindergarten about a trip to River Park on the previous day.

TEACHER: OK. Let's get around to someone else now who hasn't had a turn. Barbara?

BARBARA: We saw the boats what was gonna pull the other boat—we were talking to the man—under a bridge, 'cause the bridge was too high and when the water got lower, then he could go under it. And he was going to help pull the boat under the bridge because it was too low for the sailboat to go in there—under the bridge.

TEACHER: Right! Remember that boat. Barbara's telling us about that boat with the big high point. What's that called?

BARBARA: A sailboat.

TEACHER: It was a sailboat and what's that part called? The mast? The mast was so high that it couldn't go . . .

BARBARA: Under the bridge.

TEACHER: So what was he waiting for, Barbara? You were saying something about the water.

BARBARA: The water had to get lower.

TEACHER: The water had to get lower. Uhuh! That was a very exciting thing that happened on our trip yesterday. I'm glad you brought that up, but there were lots of other things, too. Judy?

JUDY: The bridge was the Brooklyn Bridge.

TEACHER: That was the one that was *too low*. We'll have to check that the next time we're down there to see if the Brooklyn Bridge is really the lowest bridge. (*There are three bridges visible from the River Park.*) Sal, what did you want to say?

The teacher has taken the children on a walk to the River Park where the tugboat captain told them that the mast of a particular sailboat was too tall to fit under the Brooklyn Bridge at high tide, and when the tide went out, the tugboat would pull the sailboat under the bridge. The teacher has also provided an opportunity for Barbara and the other children to discuss their trip to the River Park. Barbara is trying to grasp the relationship between the essentially stable heights of the bridge, boat and mast, and the changing water level due to the changing tide. Because the teacher focuses her attention on the word "mast," and does not further question Barbara's thinking, it is not clear whether Barbara understands how the water gets lower and why it will be lower at another point in time. She says ". . . when the water got lower, then he could go under it," which shows she is thinking about a future point in time when the water will be lower and the mast will then fit under the bridge.

MITCHELL ESTIMATES AND MEASURES THE
TIE-STRING FOR HIS CROWN

(a)   (b)

3-23. Mitchell estimating and measuring the tie-string for his crown

MITCHELL: Mrs. G., I need some string for my crown.
TEACHER: Well, I have some of this. How would this be?
MITCHELL: How much do I need?
TEACHER: Well, Mitchell, what do you think?
MITCHELL: I don't know.

TEACHER: How will we figure it out?

MITCHELL: Cut it here! (*He indicates a length which turns out to be too short.*) It's not big enough!

TEACHER: Well, maybe we need another way of measuring. How could we do it?

MITCHELL: I need this much. (*Stretches his arms out.*)

TEACHER: Will that be enough, do you think?

MITCHELL: I don't know. Yes, I think so!

TEACHER: Show me where I should cut it.

MITCHELL: (*Indicates another place that is too short.*) It's still too little! (*Exasperated!*)

TEACHER: Maybe we need another way of measuring it.

MITCHELL: (*Pulls string from spool and holds it under his chin* [3-23a].) Is that big enough? (*3-23b.*)

TEACHER: Let's see. (*Helps him to measure it accurately, cut it and secure it to his crown. Mitchell leaves to join the other crown wearers.*)

The teacher has provided Mitchell with collage materials including paper, string, and glue. She has also raised questions to help Mitchell think through how to measure the string for his crown. Mitchell would like the teacher to make the decisions for him and initially does not sense how to estimate or measure a realistic quantity of string for tying his crown. He asks, "How much do I need?" The teacher turns the question back to him: "What do you think?" She continues to let him make his own decisions even when he twice cuts a piece that is too short. When she finally suggests "Maybe we need another way of measuring it," he pulls a long piece of string from the spool and holds it under his chin in his first attempt to estimate realistically how much he needs. The teacher's statement, "Maybe we need another way of measuring it" seems to help Mitchell focus his attention on the specific nature of his task—measuring string for tying his crown. He picks up the clue and moves ahead in his thinking.

KIM MEASURES HIMSELF AND HIS FRIENDS

KIM: (*Pushing Nancy against chart.*) Let's see how bigger you are. (*3-24a*). (*Walks around behind Sandra.*) I'm almost bigger (*3-24b*). (*Reaching toward top of chart.*) Pretty soon I'll be that bigger (*3-24c*).

The teacher has provided a height chart on which each child's height and name is marked on a line. A tape measure is affixed to the wall next to the chart. Kim notices the chart as he stands near it with his friends. All the children are three years old. (The teacher reported that he knows and is most concerned with the fact that he is the shortest child in the group. She has thoughtfully included the measurements of two younger siblings as well as a ten-year-old on her chart.) Kim moves to stand be-

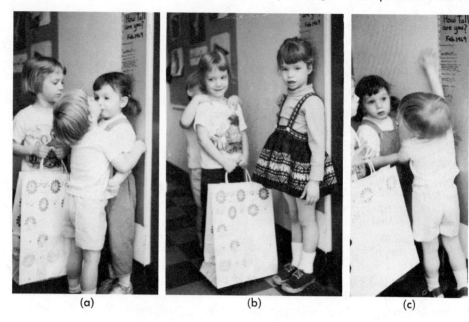

(a)   (b)   (c)

3-24. Kim measuring himself and his friends

hind Sandra to compare his height to hers. When he states, "I'm almost bigger" it is not clear what his point of reference is, but he seems to sense his own height in relation to Sandra or something else he is thinking about. Pushing Nancy against the chart saying, "Let's see how bigger you are," again shows he has no clear point of reference, although it would seem to be either the chart or his own height. He seems to be equating "bigger" with vertical height in both instances. When he finally reaches up on the chart and says, "Pretty soon I'll be that bigger" he seems to be comparing his present height against the chart as well as his height in the future. He seems to grasp the idea that he will grow taller in time.

WHAT DOES IT TAKE TO DISCOVER AND ESTIMATE
DISTANCE OR LENGTH IN SPACE?

"Distance" may be defined as the amount of separation between two points, lines, surfaces, or objects in space or time. "Length" may be defined as distance or extent in space, often expressed in units of linear measure. Piaget considers length as "filled in space," and distance as "empty space."[1] With these definitions in mind, we may conclude that estimating distance or length in space necessitates movement through time between any two points in space, one of which is the reference point for

[1] K. Lovell, *The Growth of Basic Mathematical and Scientific Concepts in Children* (London: University of London Press, 1961), p. 108.

the other. In the previous observations of children, movement has in-cluded climbing and jumping, as well as manipulating objects, such as building blocks, planks, and string. Kim compares his height with that of his friends and against the chart, while Barbara struggles to image the downward movement of the water at low tide so that the sailboat may pass under the bridge.

In what ways might a child reveal his grasp of distance and length in space? To what degree does the teacher pick up the clues each child is providing? To what degree does she help each child move ahead in his spontaneous sensing or conscious conceptualization of distance and length?

children move to differentiate shapes

SCOTT CLIMBS A TRUCK TIRE

(a)	(b)	(c)

3-25.   Scott climbing a truck tire

The teacher has provided time and freedom for Scott to explore a truck tire cemented into the ground. In 3-25a, Scott has gripped the top of the tire with both hands while he leans on his lower arms, a spon-taneous response to roundness of this truck tire and an estimation of its height and depth. He balances his body by placing his right foot on the ground at the side of the tire in order to lift his left leg across the width of the tire while he leans his upper body against the top of the rounded surface. His posture is primarily vertical but he leans slightly left and for-ward over the top of the tire. His body is surrounding part of the tire.

In 3-25b, Scott has redistributed his weight to pull his upper body further over the top of the tire; he lifts his right foot from the ground, moving his left leg toward the center of the tire, leaning his head and shoulders over the opposite side. His upper body leans forward and toward the horizontal, while the lower part hangs vertically—he has moved up and around the tire.

In 3-25c, he finally stands upright, balanced between both feet, swinging his arms forward as he prepares to jump. The sequence of these movements has brought him success in climbing on top of the tire.

KINDERGARTEN CHILDREN DIFFERENTIATE A
CIRCLE, A SQUARE, A RECTANGLE,
AND A TRIANGLE

Four observations in one kindergarten found a teacher providing opportunities for children to differentiate various shapes, including a circle, square, rectangle, and triangle.

1. The teacher asked the children to sit along the sides of a six-foot square which she outlined on the floor with masking tape. Through her questions she focused the children's attention on the differences between this square and their usual "juice circle."
2. Several weeks later the teacher placed a six-by-three-foot rectangle next to the square and directed the children to sit along the sides of this new figure. She then focused their attention on the differences between this whole new rectangle and the former square.
3. Several weeks later, the teacher asked her children to first trace their own square among the 24-inch square floor tiles, move in a number of different ways (tip-toe, step, jump) among the floor-tile squares and finally imitate these geometric shapes with their bodies.
4. Some weeks later, the teacher provided sticks for three children to construct a square, rectangle, and triangle. She then focused the attention of the entire group on the similarities and differences among these geometric shapes.

Through these four observations, the uniqueness of individual thinking and language skill emerges. Steven notes some essential differences but struggles to find the appropriate vocabulary. In contrast, Amanita seems to grow in her ability to verbalize her thinking about relative differences among the three shapes. Hal's comments reflect his noticing a range of differences, but he is unable to verbally organize his comparisons. Peter limits himself to one point of view and clings to it despite the teacher's questions and the discussion among the other children. Brooke is the master at perceiving significant relationships and verbalizing the organization of her thinking.

Discussion: Sitting Along the Sides of a Six-Foot Square

TEACHER: What is different about juice today? (*The children usually sit in a circle.*)

JENNY: Today it's a square. Before we had a circle.

TEACHER: What are the differences?

MATTHEW: A square has sides and a circle doesn't have any sides.

PETER: A square has straight sides and a circle has bendy sides.

ERICA: Circles don't have any points but squares do have points.

HAL: It has points just like the cots do.

STEVEN: A square has lines but a circle doesn't have lines.

ERICA: A square has straight lines but a circle has lines that are all bended.

TEACHER: (*To Matthew.*): Would you agree to that?

MATTHEW: No! A circle has bended lines.

TEACHER: Supposing we made a triangle on the floor to have juice on. Would there be any differences then?

GEOFFREY: It would have just three corners.

PETER: It has a point at the top.

ERICA: If you had lots of different triangles you would have a lot of private places for everyone.

JENNY H.: It would be a different shape.

AMANITA: Why don't you make lots of little shapes around the room— triangles and squares?

ROBERT: A triangle has three points and the points are just points.

MATTHEW: A triangle has three sides.

TEACHER: Is that different from a square?

MATTHEW: Yes, because a square has four sides.

HAL: A triangle doesn't have a side on top.

GEOFFREY: A square is like this (*draws square with his finger*) and a triangle is like this (*draws triangle with his finger*).

TEACHER: Everyone do what Geoffrey did. A square is like this (*children make motions*) and a triangle is like this (*more motions*).

PETER: Sometimes people say triangles have three points.

STEVEN: A triangle has three points and a square has only four.

TEACHER: There are lots of differences aren't there? So maybe we should make a triangle some day and sit on it.

Discussion: Sitting Along the Sides of a Six-by-Nine-Foot Rectangle

TEACHER: Remember the last time we had juice in the block corner?

SHAWN: We didn't have chairs and the juice circle was littler.

TEACHER: Anyone else notice what Shawn is talking about?

PETER: Now we connected an oblong to the square.

STEVEN: The reason we connected an oblong to the square is . . .

3-26. New rectangle made by adding a small rectangle to the original square

(*points to* c) that's the line we had before. Now the square is bigger by connecting an oblong.

TEACHER: Can you say anything different about it?

JENNY: We never sit in a square.

PETER: The square got bigger 'cause you connected an oblong.

TEACHER: What's the difference between an oblong and a square?

PETER: The first square was bigger. (*Peter is sitting at point* x *and seems to be consistently comparing the small added rectangle to the former square. He does not seem to notice the new whole rectangle* [afeg].)

TEACHER: How exactly did I do it?

HAL: An oblong is bigger than a square.

TEACHER: How do you know?

HAL: This line (*points to* f) is bigger than that line (*points to* e). That one's higher (*points to* f *again*).

TEACHER: Go point to it.

HAL: An oblong is like this (*walks around the new rectangle*). See how fat the square is (*points to former square*).

AMANITA: A oblong is skinnier than a square.

TEACHER: How come?

JEFF: A square they made with littler wood.

WENDY: When you have a square they're the same on each side. When you have an oblong it's not.

HAL: When you have a rectangle this line (*points again to* f) is longer than this line (*points to* e).

TEACHER: Say that again.

HAL: When you have a rectangle this line (*points to* f) is bigger than this line (*points to* e).

TEACHER: What about other lines?

SHAWN: The square is not as good as before. It doesn't look good as before (*it is slightly rubbed away*). Oblong is skinnier. Square is fatter.

STEVEN: Oblong is bigger but it's skinnier.

BROOKE: This whole thing (*circles arms to indicate the whole new rectangle*) is an oblong because this line (*points to* e) is littler than this line (*points to* g), when you attach it together.

TEACHER: There're two ways to see it. Which one did you look at first?

BROOKE: (*Points to* f.)

TEACHER: Then you were looking at which?

BROOKE: (*Points to* e.)

ERICA: This line (*points to* f) is bigger than this line (*points to* e) because a rectangle is bigger than a square.

TEACHER: What makes it bigger?

HAL: Oblong is longer and skinnier.

TEACHER: What makes it skinnier?

HAL: The sides.

TEACHER: Show us!

AMANITA: If they're connected.

TEACHER: Are the sides the same in an oblong?

ERICA: Some sides are shorter. Some are longer.

PETER: You had to connect an oblong to make space for all the children.

HAL: The sides are different. They're not the same.

SARAH: This line (b) is bigger than that line (*points to* a).

STEVEN: Because this line was littler (*points to* a.)

SHAWN: (*Puts his foot on square floor tile—8″ × 8″.*)

TEACHER: What's different about the sides of a rectangle? (*Children are looking at a mobile that was made by them and consists of their own uneven rectangular pieces of construction paper.*)

BROOKE: There are no squares up there because that line is bigger than that line. This one is shorter than this one. (*She's right!*)

HAL: That one over there (*pointing vaguely to mobile*) has longer sides like this one (*points to* a).

Body Movement Using Floor Tiles

3-27. Tile floor pattern

TEACHER: Find a square that's not touching anyone else's square. That means that it is this big (*encircles a set of 9 tiles, a 3-tile square*). No part—not even a corner of your square—should be touching another person's square. Draw a line around your square with your finger (*3-28*a, b). Now get up and walk around your square (*3-28*c, d). Hop around your square. Change your feet so you don't get too tired out on one foot. . . . On your square, Shawn. Watch those lines. . . . Now stand on one corner of your square (*3-28*e). Now take a giant step and reach to another corner of your square (*3-28*f). Now bring your feet together. . . . Now take big steps and walk from one corner to another corner but not a diagonal corner. Now that's a tricky word. Jeff?

JEFF: What's a diagonal corner?

(a)

(b)

(c)

3-28. Moving around on the floor tile patterns

TEACHER: What's a diagonal? If I stand here and I go to this corner of my square, I'm making a diagonal. But let's walk around in big giant steps all *around* the square. Francesca, you're out of your square. Where's your square? I want to see you walk from corner to corner. Good, Amanita! Very good! Let me see you walk around and then I have something even trickier. . . . All right! Now let's go—keep walking back and forth in a diagonal. Make a diagonal. That's it, Jeff. Back! Now try the other diagonal, Jeff. This is a little tricky to figure out—diagonals. It's hard enough to figure out what they are. Now, everybody stand inside the little square inside your big square. Put both feet inside the little square inside your big square. Let's stand there for a minute. Now look around and you'll see there's a little brown square here and then there's a light one here and a brown one here (*she points to the center square of each set of nine squares*). I want you to walk from one *little* square to another (*3-28*g). Jeff, be careful that your heels and everything gets inside that square. Walk—the whole way around—the whole big space. Walk from little square to little square. Now jump from little square to little square (*3-28*h, i, j, k). Good! Good! Good! Good! Hey, that was great! Francesca, you took a diagonal jump! Little square to little square. Watch out! Watch where you're going. You have to look up as well as down. Good, Kerry! Jump! Keep jumping. Jeff almost did a double one, there, didn't you Jeff? See if you can make it—can you make it almost to here, Jeff? (*He is jumping over one center brown square to the second center square—double!*) How long can you jump? Hey, that was a nice leap you took, Kerry! OK, jump back to your square. Jump back to your own square. Sit down on your square. Sit down on your square. Now, let's see if you can use one line of your square and both legs to make a triangle. Can you use one line of your square and your both legs to make a triangle? Look what Shawn has here! (*3-28*l). Here's a leg and a leg and one line here. Can you do it another way? One line of the square and two legs to make . . . now his triangle is standing up! He has a standing up triangle! Hey, that's a bit of a different shape. Yes! Jeffrey, where's your line of your square, Jeff? Here's the line of this square he's using and then this comes up and down. And Kerry, is this your triangle? Where's your bottom line? On the floor? Yours goes across like this . . . and up and down. (*Teacher is tracing the sides of each child's triangle as she moves around the room.*) Hey, isn't that great? Now you've got one going like this. Is that right, Shawn?

SHAWN: A bent one!

TEACHER: A bent one? Where are your three lines, Shawn? (*3-28*l).

SHAWN: Dum, dum dum!

TEACHER: I see, sort of one leg. Now let's see you, Erica. You've got a standing-up one here. And what is this part? . . . Now, make your own square using your body and the floor—maybe one line of your square—your own square! Make your square. You be part of the square as well as part of the square on the floor.

JENNY: I made an oblong (*3-28*m).

TEACHER: Yup! You did! Now, where's yours, Matthew?

MATTHEW: Here and here and here and here! (*3-28*n).

TEACHER: Here and here and here and here. Uhuh!

BROOKE: Mrs. G., look!

(d)

(e)

(f)

(g)

(h)

(i)

(j)

(k)

(l)

(m)

(n)

TEACHER: Let's see. Oh, you used your whole body. Across here and here and here and here. Let's see who can make a circle now, inside your square. Use your body to make a circle *inside* your square. How would be a good way to do that?

BROOKE: I made my whole body!

TEACHER: A circle in a square. All right! This is her circle and she's sitting inside her square. Let's see. Where's your circle? Let me see the rest of your circles! Well, it kind of has points doesn't it, Matthew?

JENNY: I tried to make a circle.

Discussion and Action on Sticks

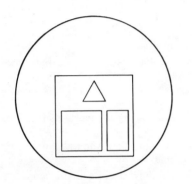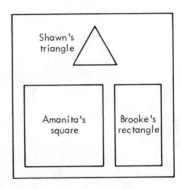

3-29. Children's construction of three geometric shapes

The teacher has spread a 36-by-36-inch blanket on the floor in the middle of the "juice circle." On the blanket she placed six 8-inch green sticks and six 4-inch red sticks from the tinker toy set.

TEACHER: Today I brought some sticks to the juice circle. You know, we've been talking a lot about shapes. You've been making shapes in different ways. I thought today we would make different shapes from these sticks right here in juice. . . . Does anybody think, using these sticks—think about this for a minute—that you could make a square?

MARGIT: I could make a . . . one shape out of these.

TEACHER: What shape do you think you could make?

MARGIT: I could make two shapes.

TEACHER: You could make two shapes. Do you know the name of your shapes? . . . Do you think you could make a square, Margit? All right, come over and do it. (*Margit shakes her head, "No." Amanita interrupts.*)

TEACHER: All right, Amanita, do you want to try? You keep your idea in your head, OK Erica? (*Erica has tried to enter.*)

AMANITA: (*Standing and trying to put corners together in the air, vertically.*) I just can't play with them all.

TEACHER: Well, get down and you can use one at a time and I'll hold them if you want me to. (*Amanita kneels, still holding the sticks verti-*

cally.) No, you can put it flat down here, Amanita. . . . (*Amanita succeeds in making a square using four green sticks* [*3-29*].) OK. Amanita says that this is her square. What do you think about that? Does anyone think . . . Yes, Robert?

ROBERT: I can make . . .

TEACHER: First of all, let's find out what people think about this shape. (*Brooke raises her hand.*) Brooke, what do you think about that?

BROOKE: That is not a rectangle. It's a square.

TEACHER: Brooke, how do you know it's not a rectangle?

BROOKE: Because I looked at the table (*She points to the table that is called the "rectangle table" by the teacher and children.*) and I looked at the rectangle and the rectangle is short and longer but these (*points to Amanita's square*) are the same.

TEACHER: But all of these (*points to side of square*) are the same here. Brooke, could you take some of these sticks and make a rectangle? Since you brought this up, let's see. (*Brooke makes a right angle with a red stick and a green stick.*) All right, she did that first . . . and that (*third side*) . . . and that. Let me just get these corners together. Now, Brooke says that this is a rectangle (*points*) and this is a square (*points to square*).

AMANITA: (*Pointing to rectangle.*) That could be a square also, in one way.

TEACHER: Amanita says, this (*rectangle*) could be a square in one way, also. How could it be a square, also in one way?

AMANITA: Some windows are like that and they're still called a square.

TEACHER: I wonder why they call them a square. (*Steven raises his hand.*) Steven, what do you think about this?

STEVEN: Because, if that was a square (*points to square*) and that was a rectangle (*points to rectangle*) what do ya think? A square would be larger than a rectangle.

TEACHER: If this was a square (*points to square*) and that was a rectangle (*points to rectangle*), then the square would be larger than the rectangle. How is that?

STEVEN: Because a square . . . because a rectangle has longer lines than a square.

TEACHER: A rectangle has longer legs than a square?

STEVEN: Lines! (*Points to longer sides.*)

TEACHER: And it has longer lines right here? (*Points to long sides of rectangle.*) OK. What's the difference between this rectangle and this square? What makes this a rectangle? (*Hal raises his hand.*) Hal?

HAL: (*Pointing to rectangle.*) That one doesn't look quite like a rectangle. That one (*square*) looks more like a rectangle.

TEACHER: Why does this one (*square*) look more like a rectangle?

HAL: Because it's more longer.

TEACHER: You mean if something is longer, no matter what, it's a rectangle, Hal?

HAL: (*Mumbles.*) It is . . .

TEACHER: It *is* a rectangle. Well, then, what is this? (*Pointing to square.*)

HAL: (*Pointing to square.*) A square!

TEACHER: This is a square. Margit, you disagree. Why? (*She mumbles.*)
Are you going to tell us why?

AMANITA: I'll tell you why.

TEACHER: Let's let Margit. You don't want to tell us? All right. Maybe
you'll think of a reason later. Amanita, you tell me why you disagree.

AMANITA: (*Points consistently to the correct shape.*) Because, this is not
as long as that and a rectangle is supposed to be long, not fat. And a
square is supposed to be fat, not long.

TEACHER: A rectangle is long—not fat. And a square is fat and not long.

AMANITA: Right! And this is fat (*points to square*) not long. This is long
(*points to rectangle*) not fat!

TEACHER: What do you think about that? Somebody else. (*Brooke raises
her hand.*) What do you think about that, Brooke?

BROOKE: Well, because this one . . .

TEACHER: This rectangle (*points to rectangle*) . . .

BROOKE: The part over here (*points to one short side*) is shorter than
here (*points to a long side*).

TEACHER: Now, Brooke says . . .

BROOKE: Now these (*circling her arm over square*) are all the same.
That's why it makes this (*points to rectangle*) a rectangle and yours a
square (*points to square*).

TEACHER: Margit, did you listen to that? Listen! Do you know what
Brooke said? You listen and see if you have something to say about it.
And Margit, see if you agree with this. Brooke says that the reason that
this is a rectangle is because this (*pointing to the long side of the rectangle*) is longer than this (*pointing to the short side of the rectangle*).
Right, Brooke? This side of the rectangle is longer than this side and on
a square every side is the same. Is that right, Brooke? That's why this
(*pointing to rectangle*) has to be a rectangle and this (*pointing to
square*) has to be a square. That's what Brooke said. Now . . . Amanita
agrees. Steven, you had your hand up.

STEVEN: I agree.

TEACHER: You agree with Brooke? Mark?

MARK: I agree with Brooke.

SHAWN: I do, too.

ROBERT: I agree with Hal.

TEACHER: Hal, what do you want to say? Maybe you have another idea.
(*Hal mumbles.*) I think Hal has something interesting he's thinking
about . . .

SHAWN: I want to make a triangle.

TEACHER: All right, Shawn, you come make a triangle. And then . . .
here, I'll put that back together, Shawn, and you make a rectangle.

SHAWN: A triangle!

TEACHER: A triangle! Excuse me! Now, Shawn is going to make a triangle. Oops! Just put the two ends together, Shawn. (*He has upset the
rectangle by scuffing the blanket with his foot.*) OK. Now, we have
three different shapes. The new one is called a triangle. What do you
have to say about that? How is that different from these other shapes?
Somebody who hasn't spoken very much. Robert?

ROBERT: A triangle is just about like . . . it's just about . . . long and it's not fat like a square.

TEACHER: OK. He says it's long and not fat like a square. Amanita?

AMANITA: Well, the triangle is like a teepee.

TEACHER: Like a teepee. And how is it different from the square or the rectangle?

AMANITA: Because, these two (*points to square and rectangle*) are not like teepees and this (*points to triangle*) is.

TEACHER: I see.

AMANITA: And this is one with (*pointing to square*) . . . And this (*pointing to rectangle*) is sort of the same as that (*pointing to square*) because all these are the same amount of side . . . all these sticks.

TEACHER: Hey, Amanita noticed something that was *the same*. That the sides . . . this has three . . . all the sides are the same on this triangle and all the sides are the same on this square. The same size. Right?

AMANITA: Right!

TEACHER: The same. You just counted them. Did I see you just count them? These are the same number?

AMANITA: No! This (*square*) is four and this (*triangle*) is three.

TEACHER: Oh, so that's a different thing. OK. (*Brooke raises her hand.*) Brooke?

BROOKE: Well, I can see it two ways because if you stand like this and this . . . (*She walks around the triangle pausing at each of the three triangle bases.*)

TEACHER: (*Laughs*) It depends on where you're sitting, the way you see it. Is that right, Brooke? And if you're sitting there, Brooke, which . . .

BROOKE: I can see it this way.

TEACHER: And which part seems to be the bottom line? . . . when you're right there?

BROOKE: This line (*she points correctly*).

TEACHER: And when you're right there . . . (*She moves to each base in turn.*)

BROOKE: Then it's this one.

TEACHER: And when you're right here, it's this one . . . I was wondering is there any other difference between a triangle and a square? . . . of the rectangle and the triangle? What about the corners? Is there any difference between the corners of all of these shapes? Steven?

STEVEN: 'Cause these (*points to square and rectangle*) have four corners and this (*triangle*) has only three corners.

TEACHER: Uh, huh. What about the rectangle?

STEVEN: That has four corners, also.

TEACHER: Hey. The rectangle . . .

STEVEN: Those two (*square and rectangle*) have four corners. That (*triangle*) has only three corners.

TEACHER: OK. Somebody else, now, who hasn't said too much. Sarah?

SARAH: The triangle has only three sticks.

TEACHER: And the other shapes . . . ?

SARAH: . . . have four.

TEACHER: Francesca, you wanted to say something?

FRANCESCA: I can make another shape.

TEACHER: OK. I'm going to leave these sticks out in a box. Let's see how many other shapes you can make. You can work on it by yourself because I think there are a whole lot of other shapes we could make, too. Hal, you wanted to try a funny kind of circle. Jonathan, you wanted to try something, too . . . Well, I'm going to put these sticks together someplace and see what other kinds of shapes we can make.

A CLOSER LOOK AT STEVEN, AMANITA, HAL,
PETER, AND BROOKE

Steven. Steven's difficulty in finding vocabulary to express his thinking is revealed in the first discussion about the square. He seems to be using "lines" as his word to describe "straight lines," when he differentiates a square and a circle saying, "A square has lines but a circle doesn't have lines." Later, in this same discussion, he distinguishes a triangle from a square by the number of "points": "A triangle has three points and a square has only four."

In the second discussion Steven focuses on size as he differentiates the former square and the new rectangle. He says, "Now the square is bigger by connecting an oblong." Later on in the discussion, after several children have used the word, "skinnier," Steven says, "Oblong is bigger but it's skinnier." The original square seems to be his point of reference, as he compares it first to the new whole rectangle and then to the added rectangle ▯ . He still focuses on size but also notes the relative length of the sides of an oblong. Later in the discussion he refers to the short side (a) of the oblong a▯ as "littler"— "Because this line is littler." Side a now seems to be his point of reference because it's "littler" than either f or $g,$ the long sides of the new whole rectangle $\begin{smallmatrix}f\\g\end{smallmatrix}$▯ . Because the teacher does not question his point of reference or use of words, his thinking is not made clear.

In the body movement experience with the floor tiles, Steven accurately traces his square with his finger (3-28b), tiptoeing around the edge of his square (3-28d) and jumping from "little square to little square" (3-28j).

In the discussion about the three geometric shapes, Steven again differentiates the square and rectangle according to relative size, saying, "A square would be larger than a rectangle." Here the teacher questions his thinking and Steven focuses on one difference: ". . . because a rectangle has longer lines [note use of vocabulary] than a square." Later, the teacher's question "Is there any difference between the corners of all these shapes?" focuses Steven's attention on the number of "corners."

Steven states that the square and rectangle have four corners and the triangle has only three. When the teacher asks, "What about the rectangle?" Steven replies, "That has four corners, also." Then Steven synthesizes his thinking about the number of corners: "Those two (square and triangle) have four corners. That (triangle) has only three corners."

Amanita.   Amanita ,eems to grow in her ability to verbalize her thinking with each of the three discussions.

In the first discussion when the teacher tries to direct the children's attention to the differences among a square, a circle, and a triangle, Amanita focuses on Erica's comment about "lots of different triangles" and "private places." She says, "Why don't you (teacher) make lots of little shapes around the room—triangles and squares?"

In the second discussion, Amanita reveals her ability to distinguish the length of the sides of an oblong from a square when she says, "An oblong is skinnier than a square." Using the square as a point of reference, she seems to be focused on the added rectangle. She also seems to recognize that a "whole" oblong consists of connections (corners): she answers, "If they're (sides) connected" to the teacher's question "What makes it (oblong) skinnier?"

In the floor tile experience, Amanita distinguishes a square by walking around it. In the final discussion, Amanita constructs the square herself by connecting the ends of four sticks of equal length. As she struggles to verbalize her thoughts, she focuses on the similarities in the square and rectangle (four sides and/or four right angles). Pointing to the rectangle, she says, "That could be a square also, in one way. Some windows are like that and they're still called a square." Furthermore, in comparing a rectangle with a window she indicates that she has an image of the four-sidedness, or the four right angles, of a window. Ultimately, however, she synthesizes her thinking about length and width by stating the essential differences between a square and a rectangle: "Because, this is not as long as that and a rectangle is supposed to be long, not fat. And a square is supposed to be fat, not long." Here she seems to use one shape as a point of reference for the other. This also suggests that she is simultaneously conserving the length and width of a square and a rectangle.

Later on in the same discussion, Amanita makes an analogy between a triangle and a teepee, suggesting she has an image of their three-sidedness. She further distinguishes between the triangle and the square and rectangle: "These two (square and rectangle) are not like teepees and this (triangle) is." Then she goes on to count the number of sides on the rectangle and square: "And this (rectangle) is sort of the same as that (square) because all these are the same amount of side . . . all these sticks." The teacher seems to focus on the length of sides, ". . . all the sides are the same on this triangle and the sides are the same on this square. The same size. Right?" But Amanita is focused on the number of sides: "This (square) is four and this (triangle) is three."

Hal. Hal's comments seem to reflect his focus on numerous single differences but he seems unable to verbally organize them into a whole idea.

In the first discussion, he seems to image right angles: "It (square) has points just like the cots do." Later, he distinguishes between a square and triangle by pointing out, "A triangle doesn't have a side on top." What opportunities should the teacher provide to help Hal clarify his thinking?

In the second discussion, Hal begins to grasp the essential differences between a square and a rectangle but again he never accurately verbalizes what he seems to grasp. Is it because he keeps selecting a new point of reference? "An oblong is bigger than a square," he says, focusing on size. When the teacher asks, "How do you know" he adds, "This line is bigger (long side of new whole rectangle) than that line (long side of small added rectangle)." When the teacher says to point to it, Hal shows his comment "That one's higher." now is referring to the added rectangle ☐ not the whole new rectangle ☐☐ . Later, he again says, "When you have a rectangle this line (long side) is longer than this line (short side)." When he says, "Oblong is longer and skinnier," he reveals that he is focusing on two dimensions. After that, he says, "The sides are different. They're not the same." Is he referring to a rectangle? What does he mean by "different"? The teacher doesn't ask. Finally, pointing out one of the rectangles hanging from a mobile, he says, "That one over there has longer sides like this one," revealing he is able to identify a rectangle vertically as well as horizontally.

Peter. Peter seems to focus on a single factor in each discussion despite the teacher's questions and the verbal interaction of the other children.

In the first discussion, he says of the triangle, "It has a point on top." In the second discussion it is clear that he focuses on the small added rectangle and does not seem to perceive a whole new rectangle based on the former square. "Now we connected an oblong to the square," he says. (He was sitting on the short side of the added rectangle.) Later, he states, "The first square was bigger." Than the new rectangle?—the teacher doesn't ask. Peter seems to be distinguishing between the areas of the square and the added rectangle. His final remark still concerns the added rectangle. When the teacher asks, "Are the sides the same in an oblong?" and Erica replies that some sides are shorter, some are longer, Peter says, "You had to connect an oblong to make space for all the children." Neither the teacher's question nor Erica's contribution changes his thinking. He seems to be fixated on the oblong connected to square. Are his words affecting his perceptions?

Brooke.   Brooke is adept at perceiving significant relationships and verbalizing her thinking. Her first statement in the second discussion distinguishes the different lengths of adjacent sides of a rectangle: "This whole thing is an oblong because this line is littler than this line, when you attach it together." Although the teacher doesn't ask "Attach what together?" Brooke later confirms her ability to distinguish squares from rectangles by pointing out rectangles on a mobile. She says: "There are no squares up there because that line is bigger than that line. This one is shorter than this one." By pointing out a vertically-hanging rectangle, she confirms her ability to abstract the essential differences between the relative length of the sides in a square and a rectangle.

In the final discussion, Brooke again demonstrates her ability to differentiate the relative length of the sides of a rectangle. When the teacher asks, "Brooke, how do you know that it's not a rectangle?" Brooke replies, "Because I looked at the table (rectangular) and I looked at the rectangle and the rectangle is short and longer but these (sides of square) are the same." At the teacher's request, Brooke then constructs a rectangle using the tinker toy sticks. Later, when comparing the square with the rectangle, she focuses on the length of their sides. Of the rectangle she says, "The part over here is shorter than here"; of the square, "Now these (sides) are all the same. That's why it makes this a rectangle and yours a square."

After the triangle has been constructed, Brooke seems to recognize from her chair at the side of the circle (a single point of reference) that "a triangle is a triangle is a triangle" no matter which line is viewed as its base. She then stands at each base and confirms her discovery. She has a perceptual flexibility which is a prerequisite for abstraction.

FOUR-YEAR-OLDS DISCUSS THE SHAPES

OF FAMILIAR OBJECTS

The following discussion again clearly reveals the uniqueness of individual perception and conceptualization when children's attention is focused on shapes of familiar objects. Sarah and Susan reveal differences in style of perception: Sarah focuses on the whole, Susan on parts. Paul, Chantel, and Mathew abstract essential similarities from familiar objects, a crucial step in conceptualization.

> TEACHER: Karen, what was different about the way we put our chairs for juice, yesterday?
>
> KAREN: It was like a *A*.
>
> BRIAN: Like a square.
>
> TEACHER: Brian says that it was like a square. Would someone like to show me, not with words, but in some other way what kind of a shape it was yesterday? Now that's hard to do. Who thinks they can do it? (*Chantel raises her hand.*) Chantel?

CHANTEL: (*She traces the four edges of a floor tile.*) Like that!

TEACHER: She pointed to something that is on the floor. This is what Chantel did (*traces the same square*). She said, "Like that!" Can someone else think of another way to show me? (*Brian raises his hand.*) Brian?

BRIAN: (*Brian traces two adjacent squares—a rectangle!*)

TEACHER: Now Brian did something a little bit different. Are you watching his finger? Brian did this (*She repeats what Brian did.*) all the way around . . . what?

SARAH: The whole brown block.

3-30.   Tile floor pattern

TEACHER: The whole brown block, Sarah says.

BRIAN: And then I went down there (*He retraces the long side.*)

TEACHER: And then you went down there. And what was that?

SARAH: There were two pieces—parts!

TEACHER: So it can be what?

SARAH: Broken so we can have two.

TEACHER: Broken so we have two. Two what?

SARAH: Two squares.

TEACHER: Yes. In other words, he showed us two squares, didn't he? Can you think of any other way to show me? (*Susan raises her hand.*) Susan? Let's watch Susan's fingers.

SUSAN: (*Susan traces a + between four tiles.*)

TEACHER: Hmm. She did something very interesting. Would you go around those shapes one more time and let us watch that? Wait! Can you keep your finger down? Do it one more time and keep your finger down and don't lift it up so that we can really follow it as you go.

SUSAN: (*Repeats the +*) It can be broken in four pieces.

TEACHER: It can be broken in four pieces. Did you see what Susan was doing? This is what Susan did. She did her finger down like this and she did her finger across like that. And she said that made four pieces. Can you think of another word you might use.

MATHEW: Four squares!

TEACHER: Four squares, Mathew says. Very good! Right! Well, today Mr. A. put the chairs up for our juice time. Did he make a square?

PAUL: An eggie.

JOHN: A egg.

TEACHER: He made an egg?

SEVERAL CHILDREN: Yeah!

TEACHER: Does this look like an egg?

SALLY: No, a circle.

PAUL: An eggie!

TEACHER: Well, what's the difference between a circle and an egg shape?

PAUL: This is the shell (*children on chairs*) and that's the yolk (*points to center of circle*).

TEACHER: Oh, here's the shell on the outside. So we're the what?

PAUL: The shell and that's the yolk.

TEACHER: That's the yolk inside. That's very funny, Paul . . . I see something we've just been using that looks a little bit like the shape of an egg—the shape the way the chairs are. It's right near me and I wonder if anyone can see it. What do you see that's kind of that shape? It's not on me.

CHANTEL: This! (*The juice tray is an oval shape.*)

TEACHER: Let's take it up and hold it where everybody can see it. Does this look like an egg shape?

CHILDREN: Yeah!

TEACHER: Well, since you have such sharp eyes, maybe you can find something else that's a shape like . . .

JENNY: (*Picks up cracker basket which is an oval shape.*)

TEACHER: Oh, Jenny. Boy are you quick!

PAUL: I can find another egg shape.

TEACHER: Can you Paul?

PAUL: (*Picks up identical basket.*)

TEACHER: Oh, yes, here's the red basket. Sit down a minute. I want to ask you something. What's the difference between an egg shape and something round? What's the difference? They look kind of alike to me. Maybe you can tell me what's different.

MATHEW: A round ball.

TEACHER: What's a round ball? What about a round ball, Mathew?

MATHEW: (*Makes a circle with the thumb and forefinger of his right hand.*)

TEACHER: Mathew did it with his finger. Can you do it with your fingers, Paul? Show me a round shape with your fingers. Jenny did it this way (*using both thumbs and both forefingers*). Mathew did it this way. See if you can do it with your arms. (*Experimentation!*) The only thing that no one has explained to me that I'm still thinking about is, what's the difference between an egg shape and a circle? Can you find a circle anywhere up on this chair?

CHANTEL: Yes! This (*runs to pick up paper cup*).

(*Mathew comes to pick up the top of the juice container.*)

TEACHER: Yes! And the top of this. Look!

MAYA: The bottom, too.

TEACHER: Maya says the bottom, too. Let's look at the bottom of the cup. What's the difference between the round shape and the egg shape. (*She holds up paper cup and tray.*)

CHILDREN: I don't know.

TEACHER: I don't think you're thinking very much.

PAUL: We are but we just don't know.

TEACHER: You are but you just can't think how to say it? We'll have to think about that another day. We'll get some more egg shapes and some more circles and see if we can figure it out. I guess it's a little bit hard, that question.

A CLOSER LOOK AT SARAH, SUSAN, MATHEW,
CHANTEL, AND PAUL

Sarah. Sarah initially labels the two adjacent brown squares as "the whole brown block." She then differentiates the "two pieces—parts." When the teacher asks, "Two what?" she replies, "Two squares." The teacher's question seems to have helped her to change the focus of her attention as well as verbalize her perception.

Susan. While looking at the same floor tile pattern, Susan's attention is focused on the center lines of a block of four floor tiles—a +. Because the teacher does not question the specific nature of Susan's perception, it is not clear how Susan views what she has traced, but her perceptual style differs from that of Sarah.

Mathew. Mathew is able to correctly label "four squares" when Susan traces the + between four adjacent floor tiles. Later when the teacher asks, "Can you find a circle anywhere up on this chair?" Mathew, without words, picks up the top of the juice container, a conscious abstraction of "roundness."

Chantel. Chantel's ability to differentiate whole geometric shape is revealed when she traces around the four sides of a square floor tile distinguished for her on three sides by the color of adjacent tiles. Later she accurately perceives the oval shape of the juice tray and the circle shape on the top and bottom of a paper cup. Like Mathew, she abstracts the essential similarity without the use of words.

Paul. Paul distinguishes the juice tray's oval shape from the square floor tiles. He answers the teacher's question, "Did he make a square?" by saying, "An eggie." His point of viewing does not change even when Sally calls the shape a circle. He further explains his own analogy saying, "This is the shell (children on chairs) and that's the yolk (points to center of oval)." His ability to abstract "ovalness" from "egg shape," in the arrangement of chairs and the cracker basket suggests a perceptual grasp of ovalness or egg-shaped. When the teacher asks, "What's the difference between the round shape and the egg shape?" and says the children are not thinking very much, Paul replies, "We are, but we just don't know." This suggests that his attention is focused on the question but he is as yet unable to verbalize what he can visually differentiate. The two-dimensional circle and the three-dimensional egg shape may be a confusing analogy for him.

WHAT DOES IT TAKE TO DIFFERENTIATE SHAPE?

Shape may be defined as a fixed contour or spatial form; *form* as a visible and measurable unit defined by contour: a bounded surface or volume or a system of visible elements. A shape has dimension and a boundary. It would seem that differentiation of shape is dependent upon ability to differentiate the whole contour of a form. To differentiate two-dimensional geometric forms would therefore require ability to distinguish the top and bottom, left and right of a shape and to distinguish the relationships among the sides. What is the relative length of each side? How many sides does a particular shape have? At what angle is each pair of sides juxtaposed?

Finding differences among two-dimensional geometric shapes requires an ability to differentiate at least one relative difference (number of sides, length of sides— ☐ △ or ☐ ▭). Finding similarities among two-dimensional geometric shapes (triangles) requires ability to differentiate both relative differences (length of sides) and relative similarities (number of sides) △ ◁▭ ◁ .

THE ROLE OF BODY MOVEMENT IN THE DIFFERENTIATION OF SHAPE

Scott, having climbed up on the truck tire, has used his whole body to explore roundness. The kindergarten children were asked to explore a square for themselves, and each drew a line around a square, walked and hopped around a square, stood on one corner of a square, and giant-stepped to reach another corner of a square. The four-year-olds have traced shapes as they differentiated them on the floor tiles. Moving the whole body or part of the body was inherent in each task. There are multiple factors interacting in a dynamic ratio for each child as he performs each movement. Included among these factors are each child's ability to—

1. differentiate all sides of a shape. (How many sides does it have? What is the relative length of each side? Which sides are curved and which are straight?)
2. locate a point of reference from which to move.

3. sequentially organize all sides of a shape so that he perceives the whole shape.
4. balance his body with reference to his movement.

The dynamic ratio among these factors serves as each child's point of reference in his execution of each subsequent movement and/or the clarification of his thinking.

In what ways might a child reveal his ability to differentiate shape? To what degree does the teacher in the observations cited pick up the clues each child is providing? To what degree does she help each child move ahead in his "spontaneous sensing" or "conscious conceptualization" of shape?

children move to define directions in space

JENNY, ANNE, AND BRYAN CLIMB ON THE TREE GYM

3-31. Jenny, Anne, and Bryan climbing on the tree gym

The teacher has provided time for Jenny, Anne, and Bryan to climb a plank and tree gym. They come to this experience with climbing skills and confidence derived from previous climbing experiences. Jenny crawls forward on the board; Anne steps down; Bryan leans forward and to his right over the top bar—each child moves from his or her particular point of reference. Jenny seems to focus her attention on the forward end of the plank, as she grips either side of the board and crawls forward. Anne seems to focus her attention on the placement of her left foot which is stepping down while she grips a vertical and horizontal bar and supports herself with her right foot. Bryan seems to focus his attention on his hands as he grips the supporting bar beneath him. In all these body movements, the children seem to focus their attention on the relationship between the location of supporting body parts and the particular body parts that will be moved. They are finding and maintaining a dynamic center of body balance among the body parts used as supports. Climbing up, down, forward, or over seems to require a spontaneous "feel" of the direction of movement of the whole body as well as of particular parts.

LINCOLN CLIMBS UP THE LADDER AND
OVER THE RAILING

(a)   (b)

3-32. Lincoln climbing up the ladder and over the railing

The teacher has provided a climbing bridge and ladder with time for Lincoln to climb. He comes to this experience with climbing skills and confidence derived from previous climbing tasks. As Lincoln reaches the top of the ladder, he grips the railing on the climbing bridge with both hands, supports himself on his right foot and focuses his attention on his left foot which he lifts to place on the bridge siding (3-32a). Then, supporting himself again on the right foot, he swings his left leg over the railing (3-32b). Directing his body up and over the railing takes finding and maintaining a dynamic center of body balance among supporting body parts during movement. Lincoln's climbing up the ladder and over the railing requires a kinesthetic, visual, and tactual "feel" of dynamic body balance during his up-and-over movement, from his selected point of reference at the bottom of the ladder.

HENRY CRAWLS UP THE SLIDE

3-33. Henry crawling up the slide

The teacher has provided a slide, with time for Henry to climb it. Henry comes to this experience with climbing skills and confidence derived from previous climbing experiences. He seems to focus his attention on the top of the slide as he grips each side and pulls himself forward and up toward the top. It would seem that his body movement forward and up on the slide would take finding and maintaining a dynamic center of body balance among supporting body parts during movement. Henry's climbing the slide on his hands and knees would then provide a kinesthetic, visual, and tactual "feel" of this forward-and-up body movement.

TEDDY, MARK, KEN, AND MARGARET
JUMP OFF A PIPE

The teacher has provided a large cement pipe and ladder with time for Teddy, Mark, Ken, and Margaret to climb up and jump off. They each come to this experience with previous climbing and jumping experiences. Teddy seems to focus his attention on the ground (3-34a). As he jumps, he tilts his body slightly left, lowering his left arm and tilting his head to the left. As Mark jumps (3-34b) he also raises his arms, but bends them at the elbow, and he holds his left foot slightly ahead of the

3-34. Teddy, Mark, Ken, and Margaret jumping off a pipe

right. He, too, focuses his attention on the ground. Ken's arms are held straight and slightly raised over his head as he, too, focuses on the ground (3-34d). Margaret (3-34d) jumps up, throwing her arms back and pulling her knees up. Jumping from the pipe seems to require a focusing of attention on the dynamic relationship among body parts in takeoff, we well as in flight, in order to maintain balance. Jumping from the pipe (point of reference) requires a kinesthetic and visual "feel" of forward and down as each child acts to control his movement.

DIRECTED BODY MOVEMENT CLARIFIES "UP" AND
"DOWN" FOR A GROUP OF THREE-YEAR-OLDS

TEACHER: (*The teacher has cleared a space on the floor and gathers the children around her.*) Would anyone like to tell us, what does *up* mean?

ROBIN: Up means up into the sky.

TEACHER: Up into the sky.

ROBIN: This is up (*raises arm*) and that's down (*lowers arm*).

YOLANDA: No, up means when you go down (*brings arm down*), up (*raises it*), down, up.

ROBIN: This is down. This is up (*moves both arms down and up, once*). This is east and this is west. (*Moves both arms front left to right.*)

TEACHER: I see. Adam R., what did you want to say?

ADAM: Up means up and down means down.

TEACHER: Up means up and down means down. Does anybody else have ideas about up and down?

ABIGAIL: Up and down! Up and down! (*She lifts right arm up and down as she speaks.*)
(*Several children stand and begin to jump.*)

YOLANDA: No! That's not how you do it. Jack-in-the-box, Jack-*in*-the-box. Jack-*out*-of-the-box.

CHILDREN: (*Children begin to jump up and down.*) Jack-in-the-box. Jack-out-of-the-box.

TEACHER: Everybody show me with your whole bodies, where's down! Down! Down! (*3-35*a)

YOLANDA: Down means down!

TEACHER: Down means down. All the way down.

ROBIN: Up means up.

TEACHER: Now show me *up* with your whole body. Up! How high up? How high up can you go? (*3-35*b)

ADAM: Look! I can even go high when I jump!

TEACHER: Evan, how high can you go *up*?

CHILDREN: (*Jumping.*)

TEACHER: Can you jump up to the ceiling?

EVAN: I'll show you how high I can go! Look at how high I can . . . (*Bumping and confusion.*)

TEACHER: Easy, easy, easy. We do have to be careful not to bump somebody else.

ADAM: Look, Mrs. R.!

TEACHER: Everybody down. Everybody down. All the way down. All the way down. All the way down.

TEACHER: Can you move one leg up? (*3-35*c) Good! And move it down again. Now . . .

YOLANDA: I've got a way to do it!

TEACHER: Now, can you move . . . can you move one arm . . . one arm up and one leg up? One arm and one leg. (*3-35*d) Good! Now move the other arm up and the other leg up.

LISA: I can do this!

TEACHER: Lisa has two arms up and two legs up. Can anybody else do that? Good! Good! Good! All right. Can you make your whole body go down? Can you make your whole body go down? Your whole body go down . . . down, down—your whole body. Make your whole body go down. I see Abigail's whole body down. I see Yolanda's whole body down.

CHILDREN: Look at me! Look at me!

TEACHER: OK. Now. Can you make your whole body all the way down? O.K. Can you make one leg go up—one leg go up? And one leg down. And another leg up? Good! Let's see Yolanda! One leg up. Good!

CHILDREN: Look how I can do it. Teacher he bumped me.

TEACHER: Yolanda moved one leg up.

YOLANDA: Look how I can do it!

DANNY: Look how I can do it!

TEACHER: OK. Danny, come over here. That's it. All right! Now! Can you lie down again and put both legs up in the air . . . all the way up in the air. Good! Good! (*3-35*e)

DANNY: I can, too.

YOLANDA: Look at me!

TEACHER: Up! Way up! And now put your legs down again. Good! OK.

(a)

(b)

3-35.   Children exploring "up" and "down"

(c)

(d)

(e)

The teacher has focused her children's (they are three-year-olds) attention on the meaning of "up" and "down" first through her questions: "What does 'up' mean?" "Does anybody else have ideas about up and down?" She has further directed the children to move their whole bodies "down" and "up." Finally, she directs them to move parts of their bodies either "up" or "down."

Yolanda, Abigail, and Robin each define "up" and "down" through body movement: they move one arm or both arms up and down as they say, "This is up and that's down." Several children pick up on this movement and begin jumping up and down.

Then the teacher directs their activity by focusing their attention on their "whole bodies." She says, "Everybody show me with your whole bodies, where's down!" Later she directs, "Now show me 'up' with your whole body."

Figure 3-35a shows a number of children lying flat on their backs in response to the teacher's direction to show her "down"; 3-35b shows a number of children stretching "up" as the teacher directs, "Now show me 'up' with your whole body." Each child who moves up and/or down is feeling "up" and "down" through the muscles of his body. The teacher continually reinforces her direction saying, "Up! How high up? How high up can you go?" as the children are moving "up." The teacher's words are connected to the children's actions, providing them with auditory as well as visual, tactual, and kinesthetic associations with "up" and "down." The teacher increases the complexity of the task by directing the children to move one arm up, then one arm and one leg up. Later she says, "Lisa has two arms up and two legs up. Can anybody else do that?" Now the children focus their attention on the movement of parts of their bodies in different directions. This requires their thinking about the movement of particular body parts in particular directions. At no time, however, does the teacher help each child to discover what points of reference he is using. Can one define "up" or "down" without designating a point of reference? Under what conditions?

TRYING OUT BODY MOVEMENT IN
PARTICULAR POSTURES

*(Children, age four, are sitting with the assistant teacher at the edge
of a large empty space in their classroom.)*

TEACHER: Will everyone—sitting down, not standing up—slide yourself to a spot that's not close to anybody. That's your own private little spot. Gee, you slid yourself into kind of a circle. Here's a big empty space, Micky, for you. OK, I want to see everyone get as *little* as they can. Make yourself so little that you are just a *wee* spot on the floor. Let's see if you can get so *tiny* that I can hardly see you. (*3-36a*). Oh, you can squeeze up smaller than that, Martin. Let me see you squeeze up, Bret. Good! Now, see how *tall* you can get with your knees still on the ground. (*3-36b*). Oh, you can still stretch your bodies more than that. Can you

(a)	(b)

3-36. Body movement in particular postures

get a little *higher?* Now, keep stretching but put one foot on the ground
—with one knee. Can you turn in that position? See if you can hold
your balance and lift that one foot off the floor! Now, put one hand and
one knee on the floor and see what you can do! Now with both arms in
the air, stand up. Now I want to see you walk around the room—wait
'til I'm finished so you know what to do—with your arms and hands as
high as you can reach them. Now with your head still *high,* try walking
with your hands as *low* as they will go. Keeping that way, walk to *one
side.* Now to the other side. Stop!

  Now we are going to make believe that everybody here just stepped
in some sticky chewing gum and they can't pick their feet *up.* Make believe that those feet are stuck and you just can't get them *up* but you
want very much to move and get off that spot. Stick your feet *down,*
Micky, and don't let them move. Can you move your bodies in all kinds
of ways without those feet moving? How many ways can you do it?
Let's see. Look Micky is going *around* this way. Is that the only way you
can do it? Is there another way? How about an *up* and *down* way? That's
one way with bending the knees. That's a good way.

BRIAN: I have another way.

TEACHER: That's another way. Brian turned around so far that he could
see *behind* him.

PEPPY: Watch! I got a way!

TEACHER: Peppy thought of another way—back and forth this way.

The teacher in this experience has used directed body movement
to focus the children's attention on a series of spatial ideas including size
and direction. Initially, the teacher directs the children to "get so tiny
that I can hardly see you." Then (3-36a) she says, "Now, see how tall

you can get with your knees still on the ground (point of reference)." In order to become "tall" while kneeling, the children have to move upward from their "tiny" shape. This experience provides them with an auditory, visual, and kinesthetic "feel" of upward movement. Then the teacher directs: "Put one foot on the ground—with one knee. Can you turn in that position? See if you can hold your balance and lift that one foot off the floor! Now put one hand and one knee on the floor and see what you can do!" Following these directions requires the children to focus their attention on the relationships of body parts (one knee and one foot on the ground) and to consciously move in a particular direction (turning or traveling in that position). This provides, simultaneously, an auditory, visual, and kinesthetic "feel" of the relationships of body parts in a particular position as well as during movement in that position. This would also be provided by the execution of the teacher's subsequent directions: "Now, I want you to walk around the room, with your hands as high as you can reach them. Now with your head still high, try walking with your hands as low as they will go. Keeping that way, walk to one side. Now to the other side. Stop!"

The teacher asks the children to make believe their feet are stuck. She again focuses their attention on directional movement as she says, "Can you move your bodies in all kinds of ways without those feet moving? How many ways can you do it? Let's see!" She encourages their discovery of different ways of moving: "Look, Mickey is going around this way. Is that the only way you can do it? Is there an up and down way?" Trying out different directions of moving with a single limitation provides children with a conscious "feel" of movement of parts of the body from a particular point of reference; they are also encouraged to think about further possibilities.

FINDING THE WAY BACK TO YOUR
OWN CLASSROOM

Returning from the outdoor playground, a group of three-year-olds and their teacher come through another classroom on their way to their own room. (See 3-37.)

JON: (*While the children stand at point* A.) Let's go and see if we can find our school.

TEACHER: Yes, Jon, we'll come back again when Mrs. A's group is outside. Which way do you think we should go to get to our part of the school?

JON: This way. (*Points toward point* B.)

TEACHER: Let's try it. (*As they approach point* B.) Now which way should we go?

JON: This way. (*As the group heads toward point* C.) Here it is!

SEVERAL CHILDREN: Here it is!

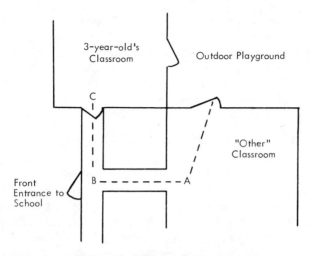

3-37. Floor Plan of Classrooms

The teacher has taken her children through another classroom on their way back to their own classroom. When Jon expresses concern about finding "his school" the teacher focuses his attention on possible directions asking, "Which way do you think we should go to get to our part of the school?" He hesitates, but points down the hall. The group follows. Then the teacher again asks, "Now which way should we go?" Other children are already walking in the correct direction when Jon answers, "This way." The teacher's questions seem to have helped him to focus his attention on the possibilities. In the first instance the possibilities are somewhat limited, for the children have just come from one door and there is only one other door in the room. In the second instance there are three possibilities, but the other children seem to recognize the right way and may have influenced Jon's thinking. Jon expresses concern and uncertainty. "Let's go and see if we can find our school," he says, apparently equating it with "room", and he hesitates in responding to the teacher's questions. However, the teacher's questions seem to have helped him to focus his attention, and the attention of the whole group, on available possibilities, encouraging independent thinking.

DIFFERENTIATING THE DIRECTIONS OF TRAVEL
OF A ROCKET AND AN AIRPLANE

Excerpt from a discussion in a kindergarten in 1967 (American astronauts circled the moon in December 1968).

MICHAEL: You need a rocket to go to the moon. I have a rocket at home. It is silver and red. Kendell and I play rockets if his brother is not home.
KENDELL: You can take an airplane (*to go to the moon*).

TEACHER: To go to the moon?
KENDELL: Uhuh.
TEACHER: Do you really think you can take an airplane?
RICHARD: No, because airplanes go sideways. (*Indicates horizontal direction with his lower arm.*) Rockets go up. (*Indicates vertical direction.*)
TEACHER: Don't airplanes go up?
RICHARD: Yes, but then like this. (*Again indicates horizontal direction.*)

The teacher has provided a discussion time during which two children begin to talk about rockets and airplanes. She also raises significant questions to help them clarify their thinking. Richard differentiates up from sideways by moving his arm and hand up (perpendicular to the earth—his point of reference) and sideways (parallel to the earth) while he says, "Airplanes go sideways. Rockets go up." The teacher's question, "Don't airplanes go up?" elicits, "Yes, but then like this (parallel to the earth)" from Richard. Richard seems to sense "sideways" as horizontal and relative to the surface of the earth; and "up" as against gravity and thus vertical to the earth. The teacher's questions have focused his attention and helped him to verbalize his perceptions.

WHERE DID YOU GO?

Excerpt from a discussion with a three-year-old:

TEACHER: Where did you go with Miss G.?
TIM: To the mailbox.
TEACHER: How did you go? I didn't see you after you left here.
TIM: (*With each statement he changes the position of his hand on the table 180°, thus including left, straight ahead, and right.*) We went that way. Then we turned that way. Then we turned on the sidewalk. Then we went that way. Then we turned onto the grass. And then we turned and came back another way.
TEACHER: You made a lot of turns didn't you?

The teacher questions Tim concerning the way the children walked to the mailbox that morning: "How did you go? I didn't see you after you left here." Tim uses his limited vocabulary and the movement of his hand to differentiate left, right, and forward. It seems clear that Tim has a sense of the changes in direction made on the walk and that the teacher's question has helped him to image them.

WHAT DOES IT TAKE TO DEFINE
DIRECTIONS IN SPACE?

Direction may be defined as the line or course on which something is moving or along which something is pointing or facing; or a channel or direct course of thought or action. *Line* may be defined as the course or direction of something in motion or treated as if in motion. *Route* is a straight line oriented in terms of at least temporarily stable points of reference. It would seem that defining direction in space requires movement on a line through time from a point of reference. In the observations selected, children are climbing forward, down, over, or up; jumping down; moving their whole body, or parts of their body, up, or down; walking back to their classroom; and indicating direction by gesturing. Each child has moved on a line through time from a point of reference.

In what ways might a child reveal his ability to define direction in space? To what degree does the teacher in each observation cited pick up the clues that each child provides? To what degree does she provide opportunities to help each child move ahead in his "spontaneous sensing" or "conscious conceptualization" of direction in space?

children move to connect the dimensions of space

CAROLENORE AND AMEE DESCRIBE THEIR
BOX SCULPTURES

CAROLENORE: This is the library and this is the door (*single egg carton section affixed to cardboard base and small box*).

VISITOR: Could you tell me how you made it, Carolenore?

CAROLENORE: First I put this thing (*cardboard base*) on the bottom and then I glued it together with these boxes. And I put the door (*egg carton*

(a)   (b)   (c)

3-38. Carolenore and Amee describing their box sculptures

section) in and I taped it because it wouldn't stay. And after I put all these boxes together, I put this piece on top. That's the roof! And then I painted all this and then I made this around here (*points to painting on base*).

VISITOR: Did you paint it first?

CAROLENORE: No! After it dried we painted them. And then we painted them. This is where the people are going in (*egg carton section*). And then they go up the stairs and they go right in there (*points to slits in fruit box*). Then they look at all the books and then they go upstairs. And if they don't like those books, then they go up here (*grasps square box [3-38a]*) and these are the children's books. And then way up here they look at all the grownup's books (*cylinder*).

VISITOR: Where are the grownup's books?

CAROLENORE: Up here! (*cylinder*)

VISITOR: And where are the children's books?

CAROLENORE: Down here! (*lowest box, beneath fruit box*) And these are the father's and mother's books (*fruit box*) and these are the uncle's and aunt's (*box above fruit box*). And these are the children's books, again (*box she is grasping [3-38a]*).

VISITOR: That means that there are children's books in two places.

CAROLENORE: And grownup's books in two places, too.

VISITOR: Do you know a library that's made like that?

CAROLENORE: Yup! It's by my house. You just have to walk four or ten blocks and you go inside the library.

VISITOR: How do you get up on the top floor of the library?

CAROLENORE: You go up on different elevators.

AMEE: I made a dinosaur.

VISITOR: Tell me how you made your dinosaur.

AMEE: I put this on the bottom (*cardboard base*) and I took a milk bottle and I put it here and I glued it here.

VISITOR: And how did you do this part? (*Top piece*)

AMEE: I cut it off the milk bottle, and I put it on his—up from here, on the top of his head.

CAROLENORE: And this is an egg carton. Right Amee?

VISITOR: How did you know how to make a dinosaur like that?

AMEE: I don't know.

CAROLENORE: She looked in the Museum of Natural History. Right, Amee? She looked at all the dinosaurs.

The teacher has provided cardboard bases, boxes, glue and paint with time and freedom for the children to construct a box sculpture. Several days after the construction experience a visiting teacher asks the children about their structures. In describing hers, Carolenore (age four) begins, "First I put this thing (cardboard base) on the bottom. . . . And after I put all these boxes together, I put this piece on top." Subsequently, she states, "This is where the people go in. And then they go up the stairs and they go right in there." Later she says, "Down here!" in answer to the teacher's question about the location of the children's books. She also holds to her sequence of which books are on each floor. Beginning at the bottom; children's, mother's and father's, uncle's and aunt's, children's, grownup's. She confirms this arrangement by agreeing with the visitor's conclusion, "That means that there are children's books in two places, too." The visiting teacher doesn't question her further so the fact that she actually has three "floors" of adult books is not clarified. Her accurate use of "up," "bottom," "top," "in," "inside," and "down," suggests that she has a verbal, visual, kinesthetic, and tactual sense of these relationships both from acting on the materials and from being in a similar library in her neighborhood.

In describing her sculpture, Amee reflects, "I put this on the bottom . . ." And later she says, "I cut it off the milk bottle, and I put it on his head—up from here, on the top of his head." Her grasp of "bottom," "on," "up," and "top," also seems to be a verbal, visual, kinesthetic, and tactile sensing of these relationships derived, in part, from her action on the materials.

STEVEN AND ERICA EACH MAKE A SCULPTURE

(a)   (b)

3-39. Steven and Erica making a sculpture

The teacher has provided each child with two pieces of wood, a dowel, a one-foot square piece of styrofoam, glue, and a knife (for cutting the styrofoam) for building a sculpture. Each child comes to the ex-

(c)   (d)   (e)

perience with skills and confidence derived from previous construction tasks. In 3-39a, Steven points to the top of his sculpture as he explains it to Mark. He has already glued a piece of wood and the dowel to his base. Having cut the styrofoam into a triangle, he has glued it to the top of the vertical piece of wood. In 3-39b and c he seems to be trying out another piece of styrofoam, first balancing it between the dowel and the upright piece of wood and then centering it only on the dowel.

Using the same materials, Erica also stands up her dowel but she tries to balance a long thin piece of wood on top of it (3-39d). Subsequently, she glues it flat on the base board and lays a square piece of styrofoam next to it. (3-39e).

It seems that both Steven and Erica by acting on their materials, are tactually and kinesthetically feeling balance, top, front, back, left, right, square, triangle, and cylinder.

PETER, ROBERT, AND STEVEN BUILD
A BUS STATION

The teacher has provided the children with blocks, a bus, and two trucks. The children have all had previous experience with unit blocks and some ideas about bus stations. During a three-day period they have worked and reworked a model of a bus station, parking lot, and ramp. This model of a bus station seems to be evidence their kinesthetic, visual, and tactual sensing of the three dimensions of a building. The bus station has an upper-level parking lot and two ramps that connect the parking lot with

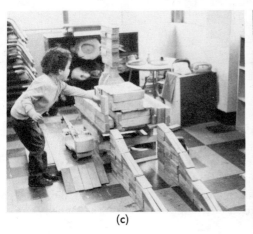

3-40. Peter, Robert, and Steven building a bus station

the ground level. A close look at the photographs will reveal that many size and shape relationships are inherent in this construction. Three different kinds of ramps blocks were used (see 3-41).

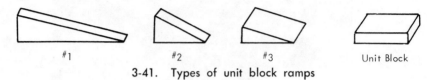

#1   #2   #3   Unit Block

3-41.   Types of unit block ramps

These ramp blocks are set up to make a continuous ramp from the top to bottom level of the bus station. The ramp was built on a supporting structure of unit, and double-unit, blocks. To construct the ramp seems to require perception of the relationships of the shape and size of each ramp block. Block 1 is a double-unit long, a half-unit wide, and a double-unit high; block 2 is one unit-block long, a half-unit wide, and a double-unit block high; and block 3 is one unit-block long, a unit-block wide, and a unit-block high. Blocks 1 and 2 are always used in pairs (two are equal to a one-unit width), and are placed against two units in height; block 3 is used singly and is placed against only one unit width. Thus, each block requires a different point of reference and a different spatial relationship to adjacent blocks. The trying-out of each block would provide a kinesthetic, tactual, and visual "feel" of the relationships involved—a perception of height, width and depth.

3-42.   Ramp construction using unit blocks

The stack of blocks on the top of the building (clearly visible in 3-40b and d) illustrates the children's perception of the length and width of the blocks used. Two unit blocks are separated by a double unit "roof" board, suggesting that the builder had a "feel" of the length and width of "roof" boards, and the length and width of two unit blocks placed end to end. It would seem that action on these unit blocks to build the ramp and bus station reflects the children's dynamic testing of the dimensions of space.

3-43.   "Roof" boards and blocks stacked up

The teacher has provided three-year-old Susan with crayons and paper. Susan has had previous experiences with drawing materials. Using herself as a point of reference, she first locates, "where *I* live," then "my grandmother's house, (my) school." She draws lines to connect the three places (See 3-44). Her drawing seems to express her kinesthetic, visual, and tactual sensing of the separation in space of her home, her school, and her grandmother's house.

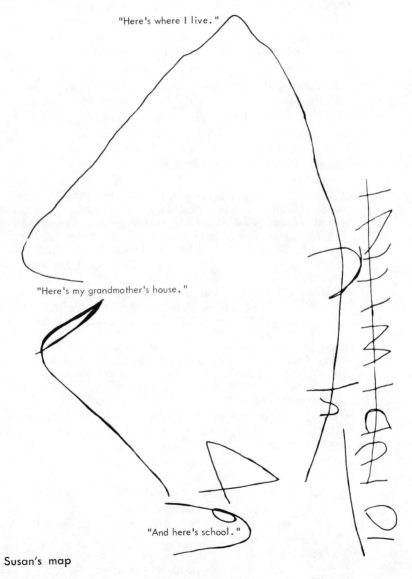

"Here's where I live."

"Here's my grandmother's house."

"And here's school."

3-44. Susan's map

FIVE-YEAR-OLDS CONSTRUCT A 3-D MAP
OF THEIR CLASSROOM

The teacher has provided a large piece of tagboard, a felt marking pen, and unit blocks of various sizes and shapes. In addition, she raises significant questions to focus the children's attention on what a map is, and to help them clarify their thinking about the map. As the discussion progresses, each child demonstrates the uniqueness of his thinking. Margit seems to grasp essential relationships but is inarticulate with her ideas except those concerning size. Kerry seems to focus on parts of the discussion without verbally relating the three objects she mentions to the rest of the room or the map. Peter seems to have a single point of viewing and resists changing it. Hal is able to perceive and talk about significant spatial relationships. Brooke, too, grasps spatial ideas, but in one instance, becomes disoriented. It seems significant, too, that the group is concerned first with objects which are regularly "acted on," such as the sink, blocks, book cases, tables and cots, while the very large and obvious posts, which are used primarily for picture hanging and as separators within the room, are among the last items to be included. In what way is body movement contributing to the children's thinking here?

TEACHER: We have something on the floor here. I don't know if everyone's noticed that Miss G. just went and brought in some blocks from another room. Now! We have a piece of paper and some blocks. I have an idea. Let me sort of just tell you a little bit about it, and as you listen you get your ideas and see what you think of it. Yes, Brooke?

BROOKE: And also you have some footprints, too. (*There are footprints on the tagboard.*)

TEACHER: That's right! I think we can use those, too. They'll be very helpful for what I'm going to do. You know, we've been talking about Manhattan—Manhattan Island, New York City, all kinds of things. We've had a little trouble figuring out exactly what all these things are, and a number of people—I think Matthew was one and Jenny G. was one—were thinking that what we ought to do was to get a map of these places and just find out. We have a lot of questions. Right, Jenny? We ought to figure them out. Well, a map . . . a map. Can anybody tell me a little bit about a map? Margit?

MARGIT: The part that we were talking about was really part of the world.

TEACHER: Part of the world. Uhuh. What about a map? Who has their hand up? Mark?

MARK: If you want to go somewhere, a map tells you what it is.

CHILDREN: Where!

TEACHER: Where it is. Where it is. All right! How about that? Geoffrey?

GEOFFREY: A globe tells you where *everything* is.

TEACHER: A globe helps you to see where everything is. Is that a kind of map, Geoffrey?

GEOFFREY: Uhuh!

TEACHER: I see. Steven, what do you think about maps?

STEVEN: Well, it tells you when you cross the road—it tells you which road to go.

TEACHER: It tells you on which road to go?

CHILDREN: Yeah!

TEACHER: I see. That's true. Any more ideas about maps? Jonathan?

JONATHAN: We need almost a bigger piece of paper.

TEACHER: For what?

JONATHAN: To make a map. We need some crayons to draw one. We need some crayons to draw a map.

TEACHER: Why would we need a bigger piece of paper?

JONATHAN: So you could put more stuff on it.

TEACHER: More stuff on it. Well, that's an idea. But supposing Mark, supposing we wanted to make a map of our room. Supposing there was somebody that we knew that had never seen our room before and we wanted to make a map to show them exactly where everything was in our room. Matthew?

MATTHEW: We'd have to make dots and tell people where people would be. We'd have to make dots and lines coming from one dot to another and then figure out which person lives on what dot.

TEACHER: Is this a map of the room you're talking about, Matthew, or another kind of a map?

MATTHEW: A room!

TEACHER: A room map. Well, that's an idea. Anyone else have an idea about how we could make a map of the room? How could we make a map of the room? Brooke, do you have any ideas?

BROOKE: No!

TEACHER: You don't sound very interested.

BROOKE: No I don't!

TEACHER: Well. Maybe . . . Let's see. We could try . . . Yes, Brooke?

BROOKE: I know what we could do. We could make the East River going into the ocean.

TEACHER: We could make a map of that. Right! Hey, that's a great idea. Maybe, we could do that sometime. Would you like to make a map of that, Brooke?

CHILDREN: (*Yes's and no's*)

TEACHER: OK. Steven, you had your hand up. What did you want to say, Steven?

STEVEN: You know, we could make the East River going into the . . . river!

TEACHER: Right! Now, I think before we make that map, let's very quickly—and you look around the room and tell me how I can start to make a map of this room and what we'll need.

CHILDREN: (*Noise and confusion.*)

TEACHER: Wait! Wait, wait, wait! I'm going to put something in. Look, first. I'm going to tell you one thing that I'm going to put in first. Brooke, and all of you over there are sitting in front of the cubbies. Right? Right! Now, I'm going to pretend—we'll pretend. We have to do a lot of pretending. And I'm going to pretend that this is some cubbies and this is some more cubbies (*two double unit blocks*). And these are the cubbies.

Now everybody look. These are the cubbies that are in back of you. Matthew and Francesca and Sean and Jenny and all of you right there. (*3-45*a) Yes, Brooke?

BROOKE: You have to put a little square one right there 'cause then it makes a turn.

TEACHER: All right. Brooke says that the next thing I should do is a square one. Unfortunately, . . . Can I use this size, Brooke?

BROOKE: Yes!

TEACHER: I don't have a square one right here. (*To assistant*) You might go over and bring some squares.

BROOKE: I mean a rectangle!

TEACHER: Oh, you meant a rectangle. Why a rectangle? Do you think a rectangle would be better than a square?

CHILDREN: Yes . . . !

TEACHER: Why?

PETER: It wouldn't be long enough. Neither would a square.

TEACHER: What Peter? It wouldn't be long enough? Neither would a square? Margit?

(a)

(b)

3-45. Making a 3-D map

MARGIT: It looks longer to me!

TEACHER: Which looks longer?

MARGIT: (*Runs to corner of cubbies*) This!

TEACHER: Do you want to take a look? Right there, Margit. See how those cubbies come together! Just Margit come over. If we wanted to make it look just like this, Margit, (*points to the corner where two sections of cubbies come together*) look at the corner, here. Can you see how that corner comes together? Right there!

How do you think would be the best way to do it, here? (*Points to the unit block at right angles to two double units.*)

MATTHEW: The way you did it, Mrs. G.

TEACHER: Matthew, would you say . . . is that all right now?

CHILDREN: Yeah!

TEACHER: All right. So now we have Amanita's and Jonathan's and Margit's and Sean's cubbies. Now, what comes after that? Put your hands up. Robert?

ROBERT: The outside.

TEACHER: The outside? How do you mean the outside?

ROBERT: Well, the outside has little holes.

TEACHER: A hole there . . . (*He seems to be talking about the backing of the cubbies which is made of perforated pasteboard.*) Yes, Amanita?

AMANITA: Well, we needed this space.

TEACHER: We needed this space?

AMANITA: Because that's how we get into the room! (*She is referring to the space between the unit block that represents the four cubbies and the edge of the paper—3-45b*)

TEACHER: That's how we get into the room. So should I leave this here?

CHILDREN: Yes!

TEACHER: Now, what am I going to put—if we leave this space—then what comes next over here? If you can't see it from where you are, try to remember. (*She's referring to the shelves behind the cubbies and therefore behind the children.*) Geoffrey?

GEOFFREY: The wall.

TEACHER: The wall. Let's see . . . I'll leave that space and I'll put the wall right . . . (*Unit block in lower center of 3-45b.*) OK. Now, where should I go from there. Brooke?

BROOKE: A sink. A sink right here.

TEACHER: A sink right here. I'm going to have to use this (*square block standing in right hand corner*). Can you pretend? We're going to have to pretend that this is the sink. Now where should it go? No, wait a minute. Let's ask Brooke. This is her idea.

BROOKE: Right here (*far right corner of map—3-45b*).

TEACHER: Right there.

BROOKE: And then we'll need the paper towels at the sink.

TEACHER: Well, I'm going to need more little things, Brooke. Can we go on and get the big things in and then we're going to put in those little things. Now. . . . now. Yes, Sean?

SEAN: The bench.

TEACHER: We need the bench to be where, Sean? (*He points.*) Right on that side of the cubbies. (*To assistant teacher.*) Could I have a long one of those squares—you know they're on that side, there? All right, if we have this part here, Sean, where am I going to go from here? What am I going to put in next? Someone who hasn't said anything. Matthew?

MATTHEW: You know what? The bench should be right next to where— right against the cubbies.

TEACHER: Sean said about here (*small block behind cubbies block [3-45b]*).

MATTHEW: No, Matthew!

TEACHER: Well, Sean pointed earlier when you weren't listening, Matthew. OK? Would you agree?

MATTHEW: Yes.

TEACHER: OK. Let's get on around. You know, we have only one part of our room. Sarah, what shall we put in next?

SARAH: We can put, um . . . the juice circle around.

TEACHER: The juice circle right in and around the chairs or around . . . All right. I'm going to need a magic marker. Steven?

STEVEN: We need more cubbies. (*There are additional cubbies for another group along the wall next to the sink.*)

CHILDREN: Yes!

TEACHER: We need more cubbies. Well, Steven . . .

STEVEN: We need twenty cubbies.

TEACHER: We need twenty cubbies. All right. Well, supposing I were to do this. Do we have any more space to do more?

CHILDREN: Nooo!

TEACHER: No, we don't!

STEVEN: We could move that over.

TEACHER: Move what over?

CHILDREN: The cubbies!

STEVEN: The cubbies. What else?

TEACHER: Move all of this over? (*Points to two double units and single unit representing cubbies.*)

MATTHEW: And put it over there on that side.

STEVEN: And then we could put more blocks . . .

CHILDREN: Yeah!

TEACHER: Well, now wait a minute, Steven. Wait, Amanita. If I move everything over, what am I going to do about all of the rest of the room? How am I going to get all of this (*points to part of the room the children are facing*) in? If I start moving everything over . . .

MATTHEW: You could move it over just to here (*edge of paper*).

TEACHER: Just to there? And would that give me enough room?

CHILDREN: (*Yes's and no's.*)

TEACHER: Yes . . . no? Margit, what do you think?

MARGIT: We should put the portfolios right there (*points to corner by door*).

TEACHER: All right. Now, just hold on a minute. I'm going to write "portfolios" here. Port . . . folio. All right. Now, Margit, what did you say? If the block corner is right here, where would the block shelves be? Margit? Margit says, let's put the block shelves right here.

MARGIT: How are we going to make the blocks in the shelves?

TEACHER: Well, that will be tricky. Well, let's pretend that some of these blocks are block shelves (*double units*). Do you want to pick out . . . how many you will need? How many block shelves are there along there?

STEVEN: Two!

TEACHER: All right. Two large ones. OK. What are you going to use to put in the block shelves? This . . . where . . . Matthew, could you please put your signal up? I know you know how to use it. Put one, where? (*Steven placed two double units along upper edge.*) All right. And the next one, where? Right, here. OK. Now! Wow. We're getting there, aren't we? Now.

MATTHEW: We'll put the book corner over here.

TEACHER: You think the book corner should be over here?

STEVEN: There!

TEACHER: Where? Amanita, yes?

AMANITA: Well, if we're going to make the block corner over there, then we'll have to make the toy shelves.

TEACHER: Hey! How about that? Where? Would you (Amanita) pick out . . . How many of those shelves do we have there?

CHILDREN: Two!

TEACHER: All right! Would you place those please? You want two of those. All right. (*Amanita places two units—3-45b*) OK. All right! OK! We're getting somewhere. I'm going to look around. Would somebody please tell me . . . where I should . . . someone who hasn't done . . . Hal, what would you like to . . .

HAL: We could put one there for the book shelves on that side . . .

TEACHER: Would you come and do it? Come and do it. Take your blocks and do it and say what you're doing as you do it.

HAL: There's one book shelf and there's the other (*3-45c*) . . . (*mumbles*).

TEACHER: And what is this one here?

HAL: Part of the book shelf.

TEACHER: This is part of the book shelf? Hal, would you take another look in there and see how many shelves we have!

BROOKE: Three!

SEVERAL CHILDREN: Three!

CHILD: Three because the toy one.

TEACHER: Now, wait a minute. Hal, did you put in the toy one, too? Or are you just putting in the book shelf?

HAL: The toy one, too.

TEACHER: The toy one, too. This is where you would like it to be? Right next to the book shelf?

HAL: Yes!

CHILDREN: (*Yes's and no's.*)

TEACHER: Robert, would you like to come and put it where you think it ought to be? (*Robert separates Hal's two unit blocks.* [*3-45e*].) OK. Thank you, Robert. Now, what else do we have over there? We have now our book corner, our toy shelf. . . . What else is over there that we need to put in? Let me have Mark. You haven't come to do it. What do you want to put in?

MARK: There used to be a table . . .

TEACHER: Right, but it's been moved hasn't it?

MARK: Now it's next to the door.

TEACHER: All right. Do you want to put that where you think it should be? Kerry, if you sit down, then I can call on you. What do you want to use for it? What sort of a shape? (*Directed to Mark.*) All right. He's going to use this square block. Now, here's the toy shelves. Now, take a look, Mark. Where do you think the table should be? Or about where is the door? Show me where I should mark "door."

MARK: Right next to here (*points appropriately*).

TEACHER: Right here? Here. Here? OK. I'll just put it . . . I'll just make little marks 'cause we'll want to fill this in later. I don't have the right color. That's the door. Where are you going to put the table, now? Right there. Now! Thank you, Mark. (*Square block in front left center is table—3-45e.*) What next? What shall we fill in with here? Someone who hasn't come . . . Matthew, have you come?

MATTHEW: The oblong table is right along here.

TEACHER: In front of the door?

MATTHEW: No!

CHILDREN: Nooo!

TEACHER: Here! Matthew is going to use this (*double unit*) . . . oblong table. (*3-45d*) How about that? All right. Now, what is missing?

CHILDREN: The circle table. The circle table.

TEACHER: Everybody now, Sean, needs to look carefully around the room. We are missing things. Look around. Think where you want to put it. Peter, now what do you want to say?

PETER: The oblong table should be on that side.

TEACHER: Which side?

PETER: This side. (*He is pointing to the "wrong side" of the "red door".*) And the door should be on this side. (*The door is accurately placed— standing unit block in left front center of 3-45e.*)

BROOKE: No! We mean the red door!

CHILDREN: Yeah . . .

MATTHEW: Yes. We mean the red door.

BROOKE: We mean the red door.

TEACHER: (*to Peter*) Which door?

SEVERAL CHILDREN: The red door. The oblong door.

PETER: (*mumbles*) I guess they do mean that's the red door.

TEACHER: Peter, we do mean that this (*two short marks on map—between Matthew's hands—3-45d*) is the red door, there (*points to side red door*).

(c)

(d)

(e)

CHILDREN: Yeah . . . !

TEACHER: Does that help, Peter? Is that what you meant?

PETER: Umhum . . . Unless that wasn't . . . but if that was the place we go out there . . . then it would be on the other side. (*The "red door" is an outside door. The only other door in the room is an inside door. It is located on the short wall between the unit block representing the short group of four cubbies and the unit block representing the wall on the right side of the map.*)

TEACHER: Oh, on the other side . . . I see. Good. That was good thinking. What else do we need? Jenny G., you haven't been up yet.

JENNY: You could use one of those short blocks to put the table over there in front of the red door.

TEACHER: Short blocks? You mean these? To use for this table, Jenny?

JENNY: For the door!

TEACHER: Oh, for the door. Would you put it in—how you think it ought to be . . . (*stands a unit block upright on long wall where the teacher has marked the door*). All right. Very good. Next. What else do we need? Sarah?

SEVERAL CHILDREN: The round table.

SARAH: What else are we missing? That's the problem.

TEACHER: Right. What else are we missing?

CHILDREN: The round . . .

TEACHER: Wait. Wait. Let's let Sarah . . .

SARAH: The lights and . . . the table near the door.

TEACHER: The table near the door? I think we have that table. Mark, did you put that table in?

MARK: Yes!

TEACHER: Would you show her? (*He does.*) It's that! The lights . . . and how are we going to put in the lights? Do you think we should have lights on our map?

CHILDREN: Nooo!

HAL: We don't need them.

TEACHER: Hal says we don't need them. Why not, Hal?

PETER: 'Cause it's already lit.

TEACHER: Wait. Let's let Hal say what he thinks. What do you think, Hal?

HAL: I don't know . . . maps are for the bottoms of things not for the tops of things.

TEACHER: Hey! My goodness, do you know what Hal said? Now, nobody mentioned this. We ought to talk about this.

BROOKE: What?

TEACHER: He says that maps are not really for the tops of things. They're just for the . . .

CHILDREN: Bottoms!

TEACHER: Is that what you mean, Hal?

HAL: Yeah . . .

TEACHER: I see. Well . . .

SARAH: Not always.

TEACHER: Not always. Sarah says, not always. OK.

ROBERT: Once I had a map that was for the bottom and the top.

TEACHER: I see. Wait a minute, Robert. OK?

SARAH: We didn't do the little rectangle table.

TEACHER: We didn't do the little rectangle table. Let's have Sarah put in the little rectangle table. This is going to be tricky.

SARAH: Not so tricky!

TEACHER: Not so tricky? OK. Good! Let's see if . . . (*Sarah places a unit block appropriately in the upper left hand corner on the long wall— 3-45e.*) And that little rectangle . . . that's the smaller one than these big ones. Hey, that kind of works out doesn't it? Sarah, can we let someone else have a chance? Thank you. Now, Jonathan, you haven't had a chance to put anything down. What do you think we should put in now?

JONATHAN: A juice circle.

TEACHER: A juice circle. Let's wait to do that a little later. OK? Let's put the furniture in first.

SARAH: Mrs. G., I already said that!

TEACHER: You already said it. Right! OK, I'm going to start around with Kerry.

KERRY: The mice! The mice,

TEACHER: But before we put in all those wonderful little things, we have to get the rest of the furniture in.

KERRY: The mice are in a cage.

TEACHER: Right! We'll do that maybe another time. Let's see. Peter? Wait, you've had . . . Let's start here again with Margit. You haven't been out here for awhile.

MARGIT: You should put this thing, there (*points to post and a spot on the map*).

TEACHER: Would you do it, please? And what kind of a block are you going to use for that? All right! And where do you want to put it? Right about there. This is the post. (*3-45f*) OK. You think this is the best place for it? It's a little tricky to figure out where it goes. Robert? Think! Think and then tell us. Mark, what did you have in mind?

MARK: The cots!

TEACHER: The cots. Would you please put the cots in. What size do you think? Very long? Very long!

MARK: (*Holding double unit*) Too big.

STEVEN: Much too big.

OTHERS: Much too big.

TEACHER: Too big! Well, what do you think, Mark? Peter, you said . . . this. (*Peter wants to use a unit block.*)

STEVEN: Nooo!

OTHERS: Nooo!

TEACHER: Well, what do you think? Mark says he really feels that this (*double unit*) is a better shape. Why do you think that that is a better shape? Are the cots then, as big as the oblong table, Mark?

MARK: No.

CHILDREN: Nooo!

TEACHER: Well, what do you think? We'll use this for the cots but we'll pretend they're smaller. But could we use a smaller block?

SEVERAL CHILDREN: Yes . . .

MARK: You have to make it a little teenier.

TEACHER: This (*double unit*) has to be a little teenier?

MARK: I changed my mind.

TEACHER: OK, you changed your mind. OK. Now what would you like to use? Here, am I holding something? You say right there. (*Mark places unit block in the approximate center of the far "long side"—3-45g*) All right! How does that seem? Now, are the cots as little . . . All right! Maybe now . . . Jeffrey, is there anything else?

PETER: The circle table.

TEACHER: Let's let Jeffrey say it.

MATTHEW: We made that.

MARK: Where?

TEACHER: Jeffrey?

JEFFREY: Everything's done.

(f)

(g)

TEACHER: Everything's done. Some people disagree. Peter, the circle table? Would you want to use this? (*Plaster of paris disc.*) Where are you going to put it? Where should the circle table be? Oh, you have a different shape you want to use.

PETER: The circle table's a little fatter. It's not square, either.

TEACHER: It's a little fatter . . . Well, Peter, let's pretend again 'cause we're having trouble finding exactly what we need. We're doing the best we can. Now, where should that be?

CHILDREN: No, not there. (*Peter has placed it accurately.*)

TEACHER: The circle table, then, is right in front of the post? Is it right in front of the post?

CHILDREN: (*No's and yes's.*)

PETER: I can't see the circle table (*from where he's sitting*).

TEACHER: Should it be over there?

BROOKE: But it should be on the other side, because we're facing it—this way from the cubbies.

TEACHER: Show me what you mean, Brooke.

BROOKE: If we're going to be on the cubby side and the cubbies are over here and we're facing the post thataway, then the circle table should be over here (*indicates a place between the cubbies and the post—actually where they are building the map; she's wrong*).

PETER: No, it should be on the other side.

TEACHER: Well, now wait, Peter. Let's sort of think about this. Who else has an idea? No wait, I'm going to pick it up and hold it until we work this thing out. This is the post that Margit put in and those are the cubbies over there. Now, which side of this post, Brooke, or anyone, is . . . Hal, what do you think?

HAL: That one.

TEACHER: Which side is the circle table on?

CHILDREN: This one. That one . . .

TEACHER: (*To Hal.*) You would say here. Robert, what would you say?

ROBERT: I would say this side. (*He's correct.*)

TEACHER: Right on this side.

BROOKE: Me, too!

TEACHER: You changed your mind. Why did you change your mind, Brooke? What made you change your mind? Did you see something that you hadn't seen? (*No response from Brooke.*) Oh, all right. Now, Steven.

STEVEN: We need the other post.

TEACHER: We need the other post.

KERRY: We need the record player.

PETER: There's only one post. (*He can see only one from where he's sitting.*)

KERRY: The record player.

STEVEN: No, what about that post?

TEACHER: What about this post? All right. Now Steven says, this post should be right about here. (*Steven places a unit block to represent the second post. Margit had used a double unit to represent the first post.*)

MARGIT: But that one's bigger than that one's supposed to be.

TEACHER: This post (*new block*) is bigger than . . .

MARGIT: . . . than that one. But it's not supposed to be because it really isn't bigger than the ceiling.

CHILDREN: (*Laughter*)

TEACHER: Margit, is this post (*second*) higher than this post (*first*)?

CHILDREN: Nooo!

MARGIT: This one is fatter (*second*) than this one. (*She's right.*)

TEACHER: This one is fatter than this one.

MARGIT: And this is higher. (*She is referring to the double unit used to represent the first post.*)

TEACHER: This one is higher than this one?

MARGIT: Look! It can't be because we changed. See!

STEVEN: They're both the same size.

AMANITA: No they're not.

STEVEN: Yes they are.

HAL: They have to be.

TEACHER: Hal says they have to be. Why do they have to be?

HAL: 'Cause the ceiling doesn't get higher on one side.

TEACHER: Hal says the ceiling isn't higher on one part than another part. Margit, you said this should be changed. Do you want to change it since you're the one who put it here? (*The unit block is replaced by a double unit by Margit.*)

BROOKE: We need the bathroom . . . !

TEACHER: Now, Brooke, would you show me about where the bathroom would be. You don't have to put a block there. Would you just show me on the floor here—point to it. Sarah, could I have your little man for a minute? I mean the little man.

SARAH: A doggie.

TEACHER: I thought you had a little man. Could I borrow it for a minute? All right. Thank you. Let's pretend that this is one of the people in our room. Brooke, would you take this person . . . take him through the door in our room. How would they go? Out there and then to where . . . ? Now . . .

BROOKE: And then there's a organ thing . . .

TEACHER: Right down the . . . is that the hallway?

BROOKE: Right here! (*3-45g*)

TEACHER: No wait. Let's just listen to what . . . so the bathroom would be . . . right here.

BROOKE: And the boys' bathroom would be right here.

TEACHER: May I have that (*paper*) . . . All right. Brooke . . . let's make this (*tears paper in two*).

BROOKE: That's the boys' and that's the girls'.

TEACHER: All right. I'll make a line. No, I better not do that. (*The bathrooms are adjacent and she has one piece of paper.*) I'll tear it. You put one for the boys and one for the girls. All right? One for the boys . . . and you put it where it should go.

BROOKE: One for the boys and one for the girls. And put the doggie in the girls—'cause we'll pretend that's a girl. This will be the girls' and this will be the boys'. (*Two sheets in upper right of 3-45h.*)

TEACHER: OK. Thank you. Now we have a bathroom. Do we need any-thing else in the room?

STEVEN: Just the record player.

TEACHER: The record player . . .

PETER: We need the wood projects on top.

SEAN: Yes, the record player.

JENNY H.:   We need another portfolio.

BROOKE: We need another portfolio.

STEVEN: We need another portfolio.

TEACHER: First the record player.

CHILDREN: Over there . . . over there . . .

TEACHER: On this shelf?

CHILDREN: There . . . there . . . there.°

TEACHER: Can you see it? I can barely see it sticking out on the shelf over there. Let's wait on that. Is there any other . . .

BROOKE: But we need another portfolio to change the records. (*The teacher has used a record rack to hold the children's portfolios. Brooke seems to be calling the record rack a "portfolio."*)

TEACHER: And where would that be, Brooke? A place for the records . . . on top of what? Would you put this there? (*One-inch cube visible on "block shelves" in extreme lower left corner of 3-45h.*) We'll pretend that that's it. Brooke says that that's where the records should go. The records are on top of the . . . (*block shelves*).

KERRY: I know another thing we need . . . (*walks across room to large box on block shelves next to record rack*) this, too.

TEACHER: That thing, too. All right. Would you come and take a block and put that where it should go. (*Square block on "block shelves" in extreme left corner of 3-45h.*) Now, you know something . . . I al-most forgot. We're going to have a lot of trouble if I have to leave this here on the floor.

STEVEN: Someone might step on it.

TEACHER: Yeah. Right. Maybe, for awhile we can pick this up . . . If we want to remember all the things that we've put in . . . if I have to take the blocks away, how can I make sure that I'll know where we put these blocks? Jenny?

JENNY H.:   Write where they were.

TEACHER: Write where they were? If I take this down, I'll write the names of the thing . . . like . . .

JENNY H.:   Cubbie over there . . .

TEACHER: Cubbies over there . . . like when I take these blocks up, I'll write "cubbies" and maybe I could even make lines? Shall I make lines?

BROOKE: And then we can make another line like that one.

TEACHER: Brooke has what I think you'll all agree is a good idea. She says that before I take it down, I should draw all around here right next to it so that we know where we put all of these things. And then when I finish with that line . . .

BROOKE: Then you put this down like this and go in here like that.

TEACHER: Brooke, you seemed a little more interested in this than when we started. . . . I'll do every one of these the way you told me to do that one. OK, let's see whose ready to go outside. Now, today we're going to have a problem. As you put your chairs away, you're going to have to walk very carefully around the map and would Miss G. and Miss B. get your things . . . (*The next day the map is colored and hung on the "fat post" [3-45i].*)

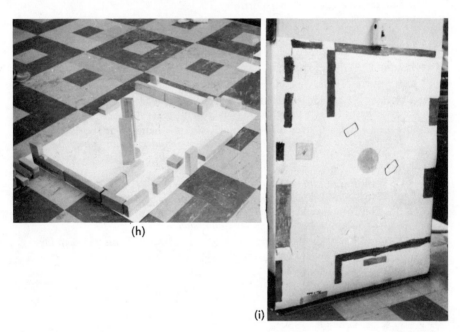

(h)

(i)

A CLOSER LOOK AT MARGIT, KERRY, PETER, HAL, AND BROOKE

Margit.   Margit seems to grasp the spatial relationships in each contribution she makes but does not articulate her thinking. In the initial part of the discussion about the significance of maps she says, "The part that we were talking about was really part of the world." The teacher does not push her to explain what she means. In the discussion about the corner section of the cubbies she says, "It looks longer to me!" The teacher asks, "Which looks longer?" and Margit replies by walking to the corner and pointing, "This!" Because the teacher then places the block on the map it is still not clear what Margit perceives as being "longer." Later she points to where she thinks the block shelves should be placed. At another point she says, "You should put this thing (post) there." When Steven uses a unit block to represent the "fatter" post, Margit says, "But that one's bigger than that one's supposed to be." When the teacher asks, "This post (new one) is bigger than . . ." Margit replies, ". . . than that one. But it's supposed to be because it really isn't bigger than the ceiling." It seems that Margit perceives that the "bigger" post is inappropriately being represented by a shorter block. When the teacher asks, "Margit, is this post (second) higher than this post?" Margit replies, "This one (second post) is fatter than this one (first post) . . . And this (block representing thinner post) is higher." When the teacher questions her thinking, Margit says, "Look! It can't be because we changed. See!" Does her use of the word "changed" refer to the fact that the first post was represented by a double unit block and Steven has "changed" to a single unit to represent the second post? Again it is not clear and the teacher does not help her to clarify what she means. She seems to perceive the relationships but has difficulty articulating her thinking when she perceives more than one dimension.

Kerry.   When Kerry is called on she says, "The mice! The mice." The teacher replies, "But before we put in all those wonderful little things . . ." to which Kerry replies, "The mice are in a cage," suggesting that her perception may be limited to what she is "acting on" this week. (She is in charge of their cleaning and feeding.) Later, she says, "We need the record player," without articulating its location with relation to the other objects already identified on the map. And even later, she walks across the room and points to a large protective radiator cover saying, "I know another thing we need, . . . this, too." When requested, she does accurately place a representative block on the map (3-45h). She seems to focus on bits and pieces of the room and has difficulty articulating their relationship to the whole room or to the map. Does she see the whole?

Peter.   Early in the discussion, when the children are adding the corner section of four cubbies to the teacher's initial row, they discuss the size of block which should be used. When Peter says, "It (unit) wouldn't be long enough. Neither would a square," it is not clear why he feels this way and the teacher doesn't ask him. (A unit block would be proportionately the best and is ultimately chosen.) Later Peter wants to put the oblong table on the other side of the door until he realizes that the door represented on the map is the "red door." He says, ". . . but if that was the place we go out there . . . then it would be on the other side," suggesting that his perception is related to his own body movement through the main entrance to the room. In the discussion about the location of the circle table he is correct and Brooke is wrong. (3-46) He sticks to his perception saying that he can't see the circle table (from where he's sitting). Finally, when Steven suggests adding the second and "fattest" post, Peter says, "There's only one post"—another indication of his single point of viewing. The first post blocks his view of the second post and Peter seems to have his single point of view and, in each instance resists changing his mind despite discussion.

Hal.   In 3-45c Hal has selected three unit blocks and accurately placed them in the corner to represent the two book cases and the toy shelf. (Robert correctly separates the two side shelves slightly.) Later, during

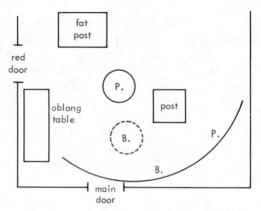

3-46. Floor plan of classroom

the disagreement with Sarah who wants to put the lights on the map, Hal says, "We don't need them." When the teacher asks, "Why not?" Hal explains, ". . . Maps are for the bottoms of things not for the tops of things." He seems to grasp the significance of maps being a two-dimensional representation of the three-dimensional world. Later, when Amanita is arguing with Steven who says that the posts are the same size, Hal says, "They have to be!" The teacher asks, "Why do they have to be?" and Hal replies, " 'Cause the ceiling doesn't get higher on one side." Here again he perceives the significant relationship—the posts have to be the same height because the ceiling is equidistant from the floor throughout the room.

Brooke. In the discussion about the significance of maps, Brooke interjects, "We could make the East River going into the ocean"—a seemingly complex perception. She suggests placing a block to represent the four cubbies at right angles to the blocks the teacher placed as an initial point of reference. "You have to put a little square one right there 'cause then it makes a turn." She changes her mind and says "I mean a rectangle" without any question from the teacher. Although she doesn't explain her thinking, the unit block (a rectangle) she chooses to represent four cubbies is proportionate to the two double units the teacher has placed to represent sixteen cubbies. Brooke later selects a square to represent the sink and accurately places it on the map. She is the one who first verbalizes her recognition of Peter's difficulty in perceiving the location of the "oblong table" in relation to the "red door," rather than the main entrance to the room ("No! We mean the red door."). She is clearly confused about the placement of the circle table but the teacher's question, "Show me what you mean, Brooke" elicits, "If we're going to be on the cubby side and the cubbies are over here and we're facing the post thataway, then the circle table should be over here." Her explanation is not clear to the writer but as other children argue the point she suddenly says, "Me, too!" indicating a change of mind. It appears that she perceived her mistake. Then Brooke suggests, "We need the bathroom," located down the hall from their classroom. She accurately traces the path of the hall, locates the two bathrooms with respect to their relative distance from the room and their position off the hall, and places the two pieces of paper that the teacher has cut. Finally, she is the one who suggests drawing around the edges of the blocks before removing them so that the map can be moved from its location in the middle of the floor. Despite her temporary misperception about the location of the round table, Brooke seems to grasp the essential ideas of this map as a representation of the classroom including the relative size, distance, and direction of objects placed on it.

A TRIP AROUND THE SCHOOL BLOCK

The following dialogue is an interview with a kindergarten teacher. She describes how her children identified the relative location of classrooms from the outside of the school building as well as from the inside.

> INTERVIEWER: I understand you took your children on a walk around the block on which the school is located. Would you tell me in as much detail as you can remember about the children's reactions to this experience?
>
> TEACHER: As I understand it, last year when these children were four, Shirley (*teacher*) took them around the block—it's a pretty standard trip. The purpose of the trip, I think, was to see if they could spot their classroom windows from the outside, so she hung a scarf in the window and they walked all the way around and looked for it (*3-47*).

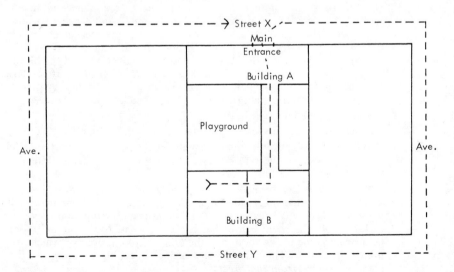

3-47. School block

3- and 4-year-olds' play roof	Rhythms room
4-year-olds' room	

11-year-olds' room	13-year-olds' room	
5-year-olds' lunchroom	music room	12-year-olds' room
upper school lunchroom	art room	shop

3-48.   Rooms in Building B as seen from Street Y

(The four-year-olds' classroom and the two classrooms for the five-year-olds are located in Building B. Since there is no entrance to the school on street Y, walking around the block necessitates walking down the stairs from the second floor in Building B, through the passage and Building A to the main entrance of the school on street X. The classroom these children had last year has windows only on street Y. Their present classroom windows look out over the playground. Their adjacent lunchroom, however, has windows on street Y. Building B is four stories high and has a roof playground for the three- and four-year-olds on top of it.)

TEACHER: Apparently they saw people in their classroom on this trip. I guess they were lucky because the clay teacher was in her room, and the music teacher was in her room and they all looked and waved so they *(children)* could pick out these different rooms from street Y. I hadn't known that when we took our trip around the block this year. All I remembered was having done the same kind of trip with the fives last year when they had absolutely no idea where they were when they went outside. And it took a very long time before one child finally looked and said, "Oh, yes, that's our lunchroom." And I guess because the school takes up buildings on two streets that the idea of going out the door and going so far away *(around the block)* and that's still school, is kind of hard. But this time when we walked around the block, I didn't say anything when we reached here *(Building B on street Y)*. Someone said, "I know what this is. That's our school." And they picked out their lunchroom which hadn't been their lunchroom last year!

INTERVIEWER: That's right!

TEACHER: But they very definitely knew that's what it was.

INTERVIEWER: What's the nature of the window arrangement in this building *(B)* from the outside? Are the rooms arranged in essentially two columns on the four floors?

TEACHER: It's pretty even. Now, I was surprised they knew this was the lunchroom. On the other side *(right side of Building B from street Y)* it's not so surprising because the fours' room is on the top, and they can pick out well the room below that is the thirteens' room but the room below that is the music room and then the art room, both of which are pretty identifiable. The music room has floor-to-ceiling windows and the piano is visible *(from the street)*.

INTERVIEWER: Do the fives go there for music?

TEACHER: Yes, but not as fours they didn't.

INTERVIEWER: This then was the first year that they really knew this room from the inside.

TEACHER: Really knew it, yes. Also they knew that from the yard they could see our room. The first thing they really noticed from the yard was the roof which was their outdoor playground last year. They spotted Shirley (*the fours' teacher*) up there one day and of course she's very tall. Right away "Look there's Shirley!" Mothers of fours would come in the yard to wave to their four-year-old and the fives would stand and look at these mothers. We talked about what they were doing. And one day (*from the yard*) we stood and looked and picked out all the different places, like the rhythms room and what's under the rhythms room and they weren't so sure so we figured it out. And where do you suppose the library is?

INTERVIEWER: How did you figure this out?

TEACHER: Well, we talked about it. For instance, when you go out of our room, straight out on our floor, what is at that end? "Oh, the library." It's on the same floor with us. And when you go to music, is it on the same floor or is it up or down? Do you go up or down to get to rhythms? Some still aren't sure!

INTERVIEWER: In other words, it was really through a discussion on the playground about where you went inside the building to get to these different places which helped them to pick out which room was which.

TEACHER: To pick out the different levels.

INTERVIEWER: Did you carry this beyond your discussion on the playground?

TEACHER: Well, in terms of buildings, the following Monday we came back and everybody started to build.

INTERVIEWER: Did you take the trip on Friday?

TEACHER: No. The trip, I think, was on a Thursday. But anyway, on

3-49.   Rooms in Building B as seen from the playground

rhythms room	roof playground for 3- and 4-year-olds
	3-year-olds' room
9-year-olds' room (store)	11-year-olds' room
library	5-year-olds' room
science	kitchen

Monday when we started building afresh, I think it was the first time I really talked first before building. We had a discussion about what we had seen on the trip, which was really four days ago, and what kinds of buildings we had seen which we had talked about at length all the way around the block. And it was a really very good trip! We talked about what we had seen as a possibility for building—many of them did this—chose to build a building that they had seen. That was the first time that we had a restaurant and a hospital and several specific apartment buildings. And we had seen window washers with a scaffolding and a pulley arrangement which had sparked a lot of interest in pulleys so we had several pulley systems on these tall buildings. It definitely put an impetus into their block play.

This teacher took the children on a trip around the school block and asked them questions while they were walking, when they were in their yard, and in their room, and when they were preparing to go to another room in the school. These five-year-olds had taken this same walk around the block the year before to locate their classroom from the street. Taking the same walk a year later seemed to have helped some children visually locate and identify familiar rooms. This familiarity would seem to derive from the children's having walked up and down stairs to get to the library, the rhythms room, or the shop, as well as looking out of the window from each room—a visual, kinesthetic, and tactile sensing of the dimensions of their school building. The teacher has focused the children's attention on the relative location of these rooms: "When you go out of our room, straight out on our floor, what is at that end? And when you go to music is it on the same floor or is it up or down? Do you go up or down to get to rhythms?"

The scarf in the window, the clay teacher and the music teacher waving from their rooms, and spotting Shirley, their teacher of last year, on the roof playground each served as a familiar point of reference for their developing sense of the dimensionality of their school building. Furthermore, their experiences of looking down on the yard when they were four-year-olds, and now, as five-year-olds, looking up at the roof, seem to provide the children with a kinesthetic and visual "feel" of the spatial relationships of these places.

Visually identifying the rhythms room from the yard, as well as locating the library by discussing how one gets there from a particular point of reference—their classroom—seems to be a way of visually and verbally matching their kinesthetic and visual knowing. By thinking about going up and down stairs, the children are able to clarify their ideas about relative location. Because the children go to the library, the music room, and the rhythms room at least twice a week and have been in the nine-year-olds' room (where the school store is located), they are continually weaving together kinesthetic, visual, auditory, and tactile knowing of the dimensions of their school. The teacher's questions should further serve to bring their sensory knowing to the verbal level. If a child doesn't know when she asks the question, perhaps he will take her question to music, rhythms or to the library. She may even ask it again when he is getting ready to go there independently. Reconstructing buildings (with unit blocks) which a child has experienced kinesthetically and visually should further serve to focus his attention on the dimensions of this space.

WHAT IS A MAP?

In the observation that follows, the teacher is helping the children grasp principles of mapping—representation of the three-dimensional world on a two-dimensional surface. She is also helping them differentiate two-dimensional coordinate relationships of streets and avenues in New York City (east-west, and north-south). Class trips to the Empire State building, the Pan-Am building, and around their school block, plus the teacher's questions, have focused the children's attention on the relative dimensionality of these familiar buildings. Sensing these relative dimensions seems to take primarily a kinesthetic-visual sensing that dimensions are constant despite the variability of points of viewing.

The teacher in the following discussion initially focuses the children's attention on why her printing is blue (streets) and yellow (avenues) in particular places. She then picks up on the children's question of the name of the street that has "no letter." "We didn't write a name here. What about the name of this block?" The discussion then moves on to what the children think is located between the streets which are labeled on the map. The teacher says, ". . . first I walked down eleventh, then fourteenth, twenty-third and thirty-fourth. Is that the way the streets in New York really go?" Finally, in preparation for construction of block buildings on the map, the teacher asks, "Where is school?" Because the discussion jumps from the use of two colors to the continuity of streets beyond their labels, and finally to the location of particular buildings, it is difficult to assess the children's grasp of ideas. Some individual differences are apparent, however. Although Ralph seems unable to grasp the blue-yellow pattern of streets and avenues, he does perceive the continuity of Eleventh Street beyond its label and the bridge that goes "the whole way up Manhattan." Julie, likewise, does not grasp the color pattern but differentiates some letters and numbers and knows the location of her school on the map. Michael differentiates letters and numbers and perceives a bridge running parallel to a street the "whole way up Manhattan."

TEACHER: (*Children are sitting in a semicircle open to a map of the school neighborhood the teacher has painted on the floor. The map is approximately 14 feet by 18 feet. [3-50]*) Why were two colors used for writing on the floor map? (*Yellow for avenues, blue for streets.*)

JULIE: Yellow was for avenues and streets and so were blue.

TEACHER: Why?

RALPH: Yellow was used up first before the streets.

TEACHER: Julie, show me where there is yellow paint. (*Julie walks down Fifth Avenue and across Eleventh Street and then up Sixth Avenue.*) Anyone notice now how yellow was used?

RALPH: Letters.

SEVERAL CHILDREN: Numbers.

TEACHER: Hans, show me where blue writing is. There's something very tricky . . . there's a special difference between where Julie walked and Hans walked. (*Hans has walked across Twenty-third Street, up Sixth Avenue, east on Thirty-fourth Street, up Second Avenue, and west on Forty-second Street.*) Notice the blue and yellow. Both are in numbers and letters (*pointing to an "S" of street*). What does this blue say?

JULIE: Street.

TEACHER: Taya or Geoffrey, can you see this blue? What does it say?

SEVERAL CHILDREN: Street.

TEACHER: It's yellow and says, "avenue." There's another blue word that says, "street." This is tricky here. It says, "St." and means street. You take the first letter and the last letter. Here's another yellow word that says . . .

SEVERAL CHILDREN: Avenue.

TEACHER: Does anyone have a clue now why some are blue and some are yellow?

ARMANDA: 'Cause that's the difference . . .

JULIE: Except look. It has a "3" at the beginning (*34th St.*)

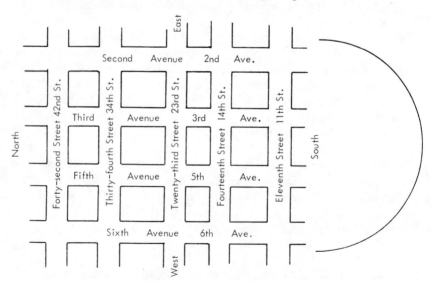

3-50. Floor Map of Community

TEACHER: Armanda says we used yellow and blue so we could tell the difference.

GEOFFREY: 'Cause we ran out of yellow.

MICHAEL: There are different words at the end.

TEACHER: Which part do you see as being different?

MICHAEL: This (*pointing to "Eleventh Street"*) is all letters.

TEACHER: He noticed another big difference.

SASHA: Different parts of the map have no writing.

TEACHER: Different parts of the map have no writing and she thinks they have no name.

JULIE: No letter so no name this block has (*she is pointing to the east end of Eleventh Street*).

TEACHER: Here (*pointing to Eleventh Street*) it says something, and up here (*pointing to "unlabeled" part of Eleventh Street*) is a different block. We didn't write a name here. What about the name of this block?

MICHAEL: I think that's the end of the words.

TEACHER: There are no words here.

RALPH: That's all Eleventh Street.

TEACHER: Even though there is no name, you think it's still Eleventh Street?

RALPH: In between part is also Eleventh Street.

TEACHER: Interesting. Even though there's no writing, this part may be still Eleventh Street. I'm going to walk down this street. Tell me what street I'm walking down.

CHILDREN: Eleventh.

TEACHER: Now to the next street and walk down. Raise your hand. What block am I walking down now?

MICHAEL: Fourteenth.

TEACHER: How did you know? Get up and show us.

MICHAEL: (*Pointing to numerals.*) A "one" and then a "four" after it.

TEACHER: When I was walking down the streets, first I walked down Eleventh, then Fourteenth, Twenty-third and Thirty-fourth. Is that the way the streets in New York really go?

CHUCK: No there are avenues in between.

JULIE: Roads.

MICHAEL: Bridges.

TEACHER: Between Eleventh and Fourteenth Street?

MICHAEL: The bridge goes the same direction as the street.

RALPH: The bridge goes that way.

TEACHER: How far does the bridge go?

RALPH: The whole way up Manhattan.

MICHAEL: The bridge goes into a highway. Then there's grass and there's no bridge.

TEACHER: Are you thinking of the West Side Highway?

JULIE: By the East Side Highway.

ARMANDA: Once I saw a three double-decker bridge.

TEACHER: Between Eleventh and Fourteenth Street?

JULIE: Katie said cars. I said roads and sidewalks.

TEACHER: Where is school?

RALPH: On Eleventh Street.

TEACHER: Can you show us? (*Ralph points to Eleventh Street between Fifth Avenue and Third Avenue.*) What avenue is it near?

JULIE: Third.

TEACHER: So where on Eleventh Street will we build _____ school?

JULIE: Here. (*Points correctly.*)

TEACHER: Who wants to build the Empire State Building? (*The children went as a group to the top earlier in the year. Several children volunteer and four are selected.*) Who wants to build the Pan-Am building? (*Another building they visited. Two children volunteered.*) Who wants to build our school? (*Three children volunteered. Other children wanted to build garages, supermarkets and apartment buildings.*)

A CLOSER LOOK AT RALPH, JULIE, AND MICHAEL

Ralph.   Ralph seems to differentiate the use of yellow and blue paint by the amount available saying, "Yellow was used up first before the streets." The teacher tries to clarify the relationship for the children by having Julie walk on the yellow paint (avenues) and then asking, "Anyone notice now how yellow was used?" Ralph replies, "Letters." Apparently he doesn't grasp the coordinate relationship. In the discussion about the parts of the map that have "no writing," Ralph seems to grasp the continuity when he says, "That's all Eleventh." "In between part is also Eleventh Street." Further on in the discussion when the teacher asks, "How far does the bridge go?" Ralph replies, "The whole way up Manhattan." suggesting that he perceives a bridge (West Side Highway?) which goes "the whole way up Manhattan."

Julie.   Julie, too, is confused by the use of yellow and blue, saying, "Yellow was for avenues and streets and so were blue." Although Julie then walks on the yellow paint of two avenues, she does not respond to the teacher's question, "Anyone notice now how yellow was used?" When the teacher asks, "What does this blue say?" Julie responds, "Street!" She seems to be able to differentiate the word, "Street," but does not grasp the color pattern. Later in the discussion about the parts of the map that have no "writing," she says, "No letter so no name this block has," suggesting that she thinks the street has no name beyond the label.

Michael.   Michael seems to notice the double labeling of each street when he says, "There are different words at the end." When the teacher asks, "Which part do you see as being different?" he replies, "This (Eleventh Street) is all letters." He further differentiates "fourteenth" as consisting of a "one" and then a "four" after it. He seems, too, to perceive the parallel direction of a street and bridge (West Side Highway) when he says, "The bridge goes the same direction as the street." His further clarification, "The bridge goes into a highway. Then there's grass and there's no bridge." suggests that he further perceives the gradual descent of the bridge to ground level in upper Manhattan. This perception would seem to derive from his experience traveling on the West Side highway.

The following day the teacher took the children on a walk down Eleventh Street to First Avenue. She reported that, as a result of this walk, some children understood more clearly that streets were continuous beyond their labels. The children discussed the fact that the school and a whole series of other houses and buildings were also located on Eleventh Street and that the street signs were only on the corners where Eleventh Street crossed Second and First Avenues. It seemed to the teacher that more children were able to perceive the relationship between Eleventh Street on their room map and the experience of walking down Eleventh Street.

RECONSTRUCTING THE SCHOOL NEIGHBORHOOD
AFTER A SUBWAY RIDE

3-51. Reconstruction of the school neighborhood using unit blocks

The teacher took the class on a one-stop subway ride from the underground station at 116th Street (four blocks below their school) to the elevated station at 125th Street. She then constructed a map of the school neighborhood on the floor of her classroom with masking tape. She also held a discussion and raised questions to help the children locate the following on her floor map: (1) the subway line between the uptown and downtown sides of Broadway; (2) their school on 116th Street; (3) the apartment building on 117th Street where many of the children live; and (4) other buildings that had meaning for particular children. The children identified the point at which the subway came out of the ground by looking out of their classroom window and then locating the spot on the floor map.

This model that the children constructed to represent the subway line and selected buildings in their school neighborhood would seem to be evidence of their kinesthetic, visual, and tactile knowing of the dimensional relationships among the buildings included in the construction. The trip on the subway seems to have contributed to their grasp of this three-dimensional spatial experience.

The entrance to the tunnel part of the subway is suggested by the wall in the foreground (3-51); the gradual incline, by the use of ramp blocks; and the elevated station, by a raised bridge. The model of their school in the foreground and buildings on either side of the subway line suggests that the children can visualize the spatial relationships for the neighborhood as a whole as well as for the separate buildings. Their model shows, for example, that the subway comes out of the ground approximately across the street from their classroom windows, their school is approximately the same height as the bridge, and the apartment house in the upper right hand corner is considerably taller. The use of large hollow ramp blocks supported by unit blocks to make a continuous surface for the subway line suggests their grasp of size and shape relationships—height, width, and depth of each block—as well as the relationships among the blocks used. Note the use of the small triangular blocks, each of which is two unit blocks high, as a ramp from the floor level to the first hollow ramp block which is supported at that point by a double unit of the same height (3-52).

The trip on the subway, as well as daily living in the neighborhood, has seemingly provided the children with enough visual, kinesthetic, and tactile knowing to build a model, or map, of their spatial experience. This type of reconstruction seems to require a focusing of attention on the con-

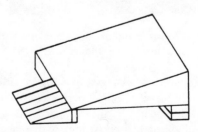

3-52. Children's ramp arrangement representing the subway line

stancy of the spatial dimensions in and around the subway line and neighboring buildings despite the variable points of viewing the children have as they travel among them.

WHAT DOES IT TAKE TO KNOW THE
DIMENSIONS OF SPACE?

Dimension may be defined as extension in a single line of direction as length, breadth, and thickness or depth; or as one of the three coordinates of position—the physical characteristic of length, breadth, or thickness. Dimensions would then include extension in more than one direction—two or more coordinates determining a position in space. Extension in two dimension defines surface area; extension in three dimensions defines volume. Knowing direction seems to take movement on a line through time from a stable point of reference (see "Children Move to Define Directions in Space," pp.83–95). Knowing two or more dimensions (direction relative to a point of reference) would then seem to take (1) movement in two or more directions from a stable point of reference, and (2) sensing the constancy of dimension despite the variability in points of viewing from moving around.

In what ways might a child reveal his ability to know the dimensions of space? To what degree does the teacher in each observation cited above pick up the clues that each child provides? To what degree does she help each child move ahead in his "spontaneous sensing" or "conscious conceptualization" of the dimensions of space?

summary

What children revealed. The dynamic nature of spatial "concepts-in-formation" derived from body movement is revealed in various styles of "knowing" among children. Each child selects particular aspects from each experience the teacher provides on which he focuses his attention. And each child organizes what he selects from each experience in his unique way. Further, individuality is revealed in each child's ability to "spontaneously sense" and "consciously discover" spatial ideas.

1. *Selecting points of reference:* Some children only use self as their point of reference; others may use self in conjunction with points of reference external to self; still others use only points of reference external to self. A child may change his point of reference during a single experience or he may use self in one experience and a point external to self in another. Points of reference vary among children who select the same experience.

2. *Finding a center of balance in space:* Diversity is apparent in children's total body interaction with materials provided, such as trees

for climbing, seesaws, or H-bars, as well as their action on particular materials such as blocks, wood, or boxes for sculpture. Some children seem to spontaneously sense a center of balance while others struggle or give up.

3. *Discovering the time of space:* Styles of body movement and thinking reflect unique rhythms, and organizations of body parts or ideas through time. For some children there is an easy flow of body movement and ideas; other children seem to struggle to organize a rhythm of movement. Observation of children trying to catch a ball will reveal that some have a smooth easy body movement rhythm which coordinates easily with the speed of an approaching ball. Others seem to move arhythmically, body parts fighting each other in movement and/or fighting body perception of the speed and location of the approaching ball. Some children are able to create their own rhythmic flow but are unable to accept an externally imposed rhythm. Success at jumping rope is dependent on ability to sense that external rhythmic pattern and adapt one's body movement to it.

4. *Discovering distance and length:* Some children intuitively seem to estimate distance or length accurately on the first try. Others struggle as if unable to find points of reference for estimating distance or length.

5. *Differentiating shapes:* Children respond in diverse ways to the opportunities that a teacher provides. Teachers in the examples cited in this text provide a tire for climbing around, help children differentiate geometric shape and focus children's attention on the shapes of familiar objects. The children reveal unique abilities and styles of perceiving: some children focus their attention on parts of particular shapes; others focus on the whole object; still others focus on the relationships among the parts of the whole object. Uniqueness is further revealed in the ability to "view from more than one angle" and in styles of organizing what is perceived. Some children, for instance, perceive only "corners" while others focus only on the "whole square or rectangle." Some children perceive only similarities (such as the number of sides or number of "corners" of the geometric shapes) while others perceive only differences, (such as the length of the sides of two geometric shapes) and still others are able to perceive differences as well as similarities.

6. *Discovering direction in space:* Here uniqueness is revealed in the selected points of reference as the children move in space and then in their sense of direction. Some children seem to spontaneously sense direction, while others depend on clues from the teacher or other children.

7. *Discovering the dimensions of space:* The observations reveal unique selections and arrangements of materials. Some children work primarily in one dimension while others use two or three dimensions. In addition, discussions about spatial dimensions reveal uniqueness in (a) the objects or relationships on which each child focuses his attention, (b) children's flexibility in points of viewing, (c) children's ability to verbalize what they perceive, and (d) children's ability to perceive more than one significant relationship.

What Teachers Revealed. Not only did the classroom observations selected for this text reveal styles of learning in children but also diversity
in teachers' "knowing." Teachers' ability to define what it takes to orient
oneself in space was apparent in the nature of the opportunities which
they provided. Their understanding of the role of body movement in the
development of spatial thinking became apparent in their ability to:

1. structure their spatial thinking and provide opportunities that help
   children examine the parts of an object while keeping the whole in
   focus.
2. structure opportunities so that each child can reveal his unique point
   of reference, his unique perceptions, and the structure of his thinking.
3. recognize spatial ideas in the experiences they provide; for example,
   the possible points of reference, the significance of body balance, or
   the role of timing in selected experiences.
4. recognize the significance of and provide opportunities for children
   to view objects from many angles, discover balance in space; and
   recognize the role of time in the structuring of spatial knowing.
5. help children find relevance in classroom simulations (constructions,
   discussions) of spatial ideas derived from the real world.

4

designing curriculum

Conceptualization is in part a product of the interplay among body movement (action), imaging, and speech (language). It is a continual process of juxtaposing the new with the old, the present with the past, as similarities and differences are extracted from experience. Each child structures his own concepts as he discovers patterns in his world. Only from multiple opportunities that permit the interplay of action, image, and speech to select the common elements from the diversity of experience do the dimensions of concepts develop. More specifically, ideas expressed in the words "balance" and "rectangle" are described below as a function of the action-image-speech complex.

The human being "feels" dynamic balance as he learns to crawl, walk, run, hop, skip, jump, climb, pull a wagon, or carry a hollow block. He further feels balance in placing blocks to build a block building, in painting a picture with a "balance" of colors and shapes, in pouring juice, lifting a chair, or weighing objects on a balance scale. From this body action, images are accumulated as the child remembers how to balance and further develops his balancing skill. Then, as he begins using the word "balance" to describe his balancing actions, he is further developing an idea of stability produced by even distribution of weight on each side of the vertical axis. Conscious awareness emerges as "idea" of balance is discovered in a diversity of experiences.

The process of conceptualizing "rectangle" occurs through the same action-image-speech interplay. The body can fill (approach "being") a rectangular shape, walk around a rectangular pool, work on a rectangular table, build with rectangular blocks, fold a rectangular napkin, put a hand in a rectangular pocket, carry a rectangular plank, paint on a rectangular piece of paper, hold a rectangular book and climb through a rectangular space.

Conceptualizing either "balance" or "rectangle" derives from a diversity of experiences with each "idea." An idea grows from one's action, through imaging to speech: the learner comes to "feel," then remember, and finally conceptualize his experience as he discovers the pattern in "idea." The child discovers the "pattern" only if *he* extracts the differences and juxtaposes them with the similarities. The "pattern" of rectangle is a closed two-dimensional figure having four right angles and four straight sides whose opposite sides are of equal length.

Each of these figures is different, but each is a rectangle. Such information processing takes place in time as the individual feels body movement, images these movement experiences, and builds vocabulary.

It then becomes the teacher's role to provide a diversity of experiences for children to feel balance or distinguish a rectangle through the muscles of their bodies in a variety of situations that permit individual functioning and encourages skill development. When the child begins to attach words to his movement and images, concepts are "in-formation." However, the curriculum must necessarily be designed to accommodate each child's particular development. To assess this development, a curriculum designer should ask: To what degree does each child perceive, image, or organize (a) points of reference in space; (b) balance in space; (c) the "time of space"; (d) directionality in space?

It becomes the teacher's role to dynamically describe the depth and range of each child's cognitive functioning as he reveals his developing sense of spatial ideas, and to plan and provide particular opportunities to help each child move ahead in his thinking about space. This becomes a complex task. As teachers improve their ability to assess and respond to children's needs at their individually unique levels, and help them move ahead in their thinking, they will be helping children to cope more satisfactorily with the world they live in. The classroom observations analyzed in Chapter 3 are aimed to help the teacher assess children's behavior and their development of concepts of space and spatial relationships.

This chapter begins with some spatial vocabulary (see 4-1) which is organized to help teachers structure their thinking about space and spatial relationships as a basis for curriculum design. It then goes on to provide more specific suggestions for ways teachers might facilitate children's development of concepts of space and spatial relationships. Hopefully, teachers will use these ideas as suggestions rather than prescriptions.

Some Spatial Vocabulary

Size

big-little	bigger-littler	biggest-littlest
large-small	larger-smaller	largest-smallest
tall-short	taller-shorter	tallest-shortest
fat-thin	fatter-thinner	fattest-thinest

middle sized

medium

huge, enormous, gigantic, wee, tiny

How big is big? How tiny is tiny? Why are some words paired?

- -

Shape

Curved: round, circular, oval, cone, egg-shaped, ball, cylinder, sphere

Angular: triangle, rectangle, diamond, parallelogram, pentagon, hexagon, box, cube, prism, pyramid, parallelpiped, polyhedron, tetrahedron, trapezoid

Wide-narrow, thin-fat, short-long, flat

- -

Direction

left-right	in back of-in front of
up-down	behind-in front
forward-back	above-below
in-out	north-south
over-under	east-west

upright, sideways, horizontal, vertical

Which way is left? Which way is in? Which way is north? Why are some words paired?

- -

Location

left-right	over-under
up-down	behind-in front
front-back	under-on top
top-bottom	inside-outside
latitude-longitude	near-far
indoors-outdoors	in-out

beside, next to, intersection of ___ and ___

Where is the back? Where is over? How far is far? Why are some words paired?

4-1. Some spatial vocabulary

Distance/	near–far	nearer–farther	nearest–farthest
Length	short–tall	shorter–taller	shortest–tallest
	short–long	shorter–longer	shortest–longest
	shallow–deep	shallower–deeper	shallowest–deepest

Measurement of:

height, length, width, depth,
inch, foot, yard, meter, mile, fathom, light year
perimeter, circumference, radius, diameter,
  hypoteneuse

****How far is far? Why are some words paired?

Area

Two-dimensional measurement, surface
"square," square inch, square foot, square yard,
  acre, square mile
___ by ___, height x width, length x width

Volume

Three-dimensional measurement
cubic inch, cubic foot, cubic yard
teaspoon, tablespoon, cup, pint, quart, gallon
___ by ___ by ___, height x width x depth

pail full, truck load, pinch

Time

Sequence: order of succession, discrete events

Eating time → sleeping time → play time →
Outdoor time → juice time → discussion time →
  music time → going home time →
Before, now, after, later, soon, sometime
Morning → afternoon → evening → night →
Sunday → Monday → Tuesday →
January → February → March →
Fall → Winter → Spring → Summer → Fall →
1969 → 1970 → 1971 →
1950's → 1960's → 1970's →
18th century → 19th century → 20th century →

Duration: movement from (beginning) → through
  (time) → to (end of event) How long?

Time to eat, time to sleep, time to play
Morning, afternoon, evening
Second, minute, hour
Day: Sunday, holiday, birthday
Week
Month: January, February, March
Season: Fall, Spring
Year: 1970, 1975
Decade
Century

4-1. Some spatial vocabulary (*cont.*)   **135**

Each community, home, school, teacher, and child is unique. Curricula designed to accommodate such uniqueness provide a firm and valid foundation for each child's growth and development.

discovering space through gross body movement

Figures 4-2a-f are graphic representations of some arrangements of large motor equipment, natural outdoor terrain, and surface patterns organized to highlight the following inherent spatial ideas.

POINTS OF REFERENCE
DYNAMIC BODY BALANCE
TIME OF SPACE

Direction
Size
Shape
Distance/Length
Area
Volume

As children move around, through, over, and under and as they climb, carry, push, roll, jump, and run they are "feeling" spatial ideas through body movement. The extent of each child's independent exploration of movement will proportionately contribute to his development of spatial ideas. Teachers need to help children help themselves. The following are suggested ways in which teachers can encourage children's independent exploration of movement:

1. Ask questions that encourage children to think through and solve their own movement (or construction or manipulation) problems. Wait and let the child struggle a bit!
2. Be familiar with the spatial ideas inherent in each child's activity. Ask yourself: What are his points of reference? To what degree can he achieve a dynamic body balance? What is the nature of the rhythm (time) in his body movement?
3. Provide extended periods of time for children's experimentation and discovery.
4. Provide sufficient space for children's movement exploration, including space for building, space for climbing, or space for running.
5. Use accurate vocabulary when speaking with children about their body movement in space.
6. Arrange equipment to be easily accessible to the children and stimulate awareness of spatial ideas; i.e. Blocks kept on low, shallow shelves and arranged so that their different shapes can be easily perceived from a distance enable children to use them independently and differentiate their sizes and shapes.

7. Provide equipment that encourages children's independence, such as wagons for transporting hollow blocks, sawhorses that children can move and arrange, planks that children can move without adult help.

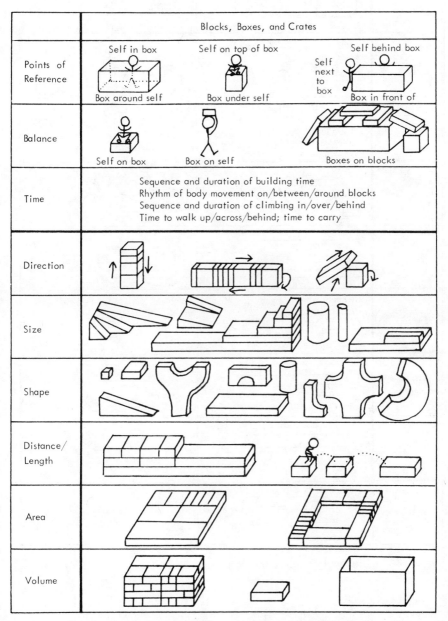

	Blocks, Boxes, and Crates		
Points of Reference	Self in box Box around self	Self on top of box Box under self	Self behind box Self next to box Box in front of
Balance	Self on box	Box on self	Boxes on blocks
Time	Sequence and duration of building time Rhythm of body movement on/between/around blocks Sequence and duration of climbing in/over/behind Time to walk up/across/behind; time to carry		
Direction			
Size			
Shape			
Distance/ Length			
Area			
Volume			

4-2. Discovering space through gross body movement

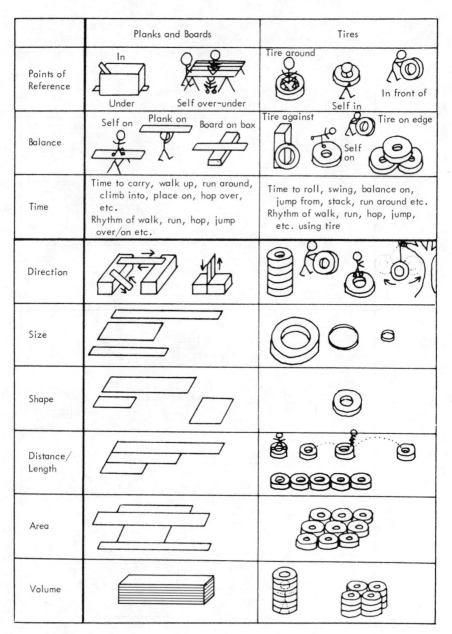

	Planks and Boards		Tires	
Points of Reference	In / Under	Self over–under	Tire around / Self in	In front of
Balance	Self on	Plank on / Board on box	Tire against / Self on	Tire on edge
Time	Time to carry, walk up, run around, climb into, place on, hop over, etc. Rhythm of walk, run, hop, jump over/on etc.		Time to roll, swing, balance on, jump from, stack, run around etc. Rhythm of walk, run, hop, jump, etc. using tire	
Direction				
Size				
Shape				
Distance/ Length				
Area				
Volume				

4-2. **Discovering space through gross body movement** (*cont.*)

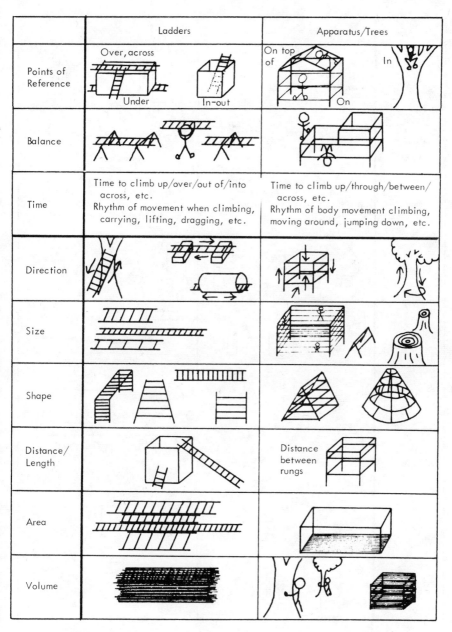

	Ladders	Apparatus/Trees
Points of Reference	Over, across / Under / In-out	On top of / In / On
Balance		
Time	Time to climb up/over/out of/into across, etc. Rhythm of movement when climbing, carrying, lifting, dragging, etc.	Time to climb up/through/between/ across, etc. Rhythm of body movement climbing, moving around, jumping down, etc.
Direction		
Size		
Shape		
Distance/ Length		Distance between rungs
Area		
Volume		

4-2.   Discovering space through gross body movement (*cont.*)

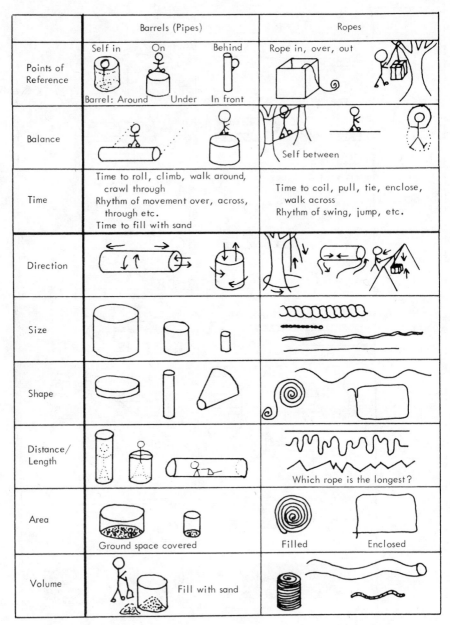

	Barrels (Pipes)	Ropes
Points of Reference	Self in — On — Behind; Barrel: Around — Under — In front	Rope in, over, out
Balance		Self between
Time	Time to roll, climb, walk around, crawl through; Rhythm of movement over, across, through etc.; Time to fill with sand	Time to coil, pull, tie, enclose, walk across; Rhythm of swing, jump, etc.
Direction		
Size		
Shape		
Distance/Length		Which rope is the longest?
Area	Ground space covered	Filled — Enclosed
Volume	Fill with sand	

4-2. Discovering space through gross body movement (cont.)

	Hoops	Balls
Points of Reference	Self in Under On Beside Hoop: Around Over Under	Through Over In On Between Under Around
Balance	On One hand Rolling	One hand Rolling Bouncing
Time	Time to roll, climb through, walk around, balance, stack, etc. Rhythm of movement around, through, etc.	Time to lift, carry, fill, bounce, throw etc. Rhythm of bounce, throw, etc.
Direction	Through Over In-out Up-down Around	Up-down Through
Size		
Shape	Round Circle	Round Sphere
Distance/Length		Far Near
Area		
Volume		

4-2. Discovering space through gross body movement (*cont.*)

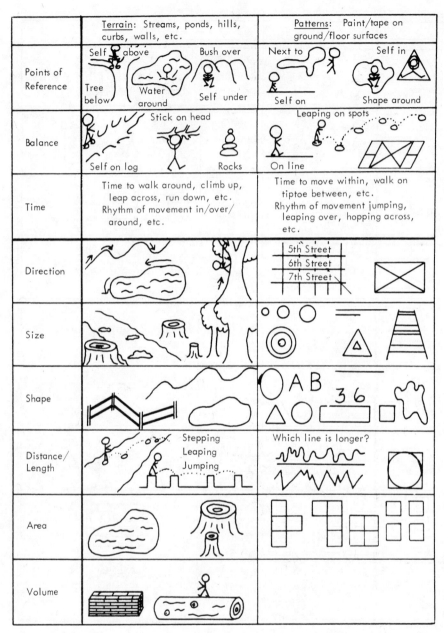

	Terrain: Streams, ponds, hills, curbs, walls, etc.	Patterns: Paint/tape on ground/floor surfaces
Points of Reference	Self above / Tree below / Water around / Bush over / Self under	Next to / Self on / Self in / Shape around
Balance	Stick on head / Self on log / Rocks	Leaping on spots / On line
Time	Time to walk around, climb up, leap across, run down, etc. Rhythm of movement in/over/ around, etc.	Time to move within, walk on tiptoe between, etc. Rhythm of movement jumping, leaping over, hopping across, etc.
Direction		5th Street / 6th Street / 7th Street
Size		
Shape		A B 3 6
Distance/ Length	Stepping Leaping Jumping	Which line is longer?
Area		
Volume		

4-2. Discovering space through gross body movement (*cont.*)

As children develop skill and confidence in their free exploration and manipulation of large and small apparatus, the teacher can structure specific tasks to help them enrich their movement vocabulary and spatial "knowing." Readiness for specific tasks is indicated when a child freely climbs, swings, jumps from, and crawls over available apparatus. The following questions are provided to help the teacher evaluate a child's body awareness in movement.

To what degree does a child—

1. vary his body actions such as balancing, swinging, jumping, running?
2. coordinate the parts of his body in movement? To what degree does each body part complement the total body in movement? To what degree is a child inventive in his use of body parts?
3. vary his body shape in movement? To what degree can he travel in a long pinlike shape? A wide, flat shape? A curled, ball shape? Symmetrically? Asymmetrically?
4. move forward and backwards, up and down, left and right in his movement exploration?
5. vary the floor pattern of his movement? To what degree can he travel in a curved, zigzag, and straight pathway?
6. sense whether his body movement is sudden or sustained, accelerating or decelerating?
7. balance the tension in his body movement? To what degree can he bring firmness or strength and lightness or fine touch to a task? Climbing a rope takes firmness and strength. Keeping a balloon airborne takes fine touch.
8. arrest his body movement when necessary? To what degree can he also achieve a free, ongoingness when the situation allows it?

The teacher's selection of specific tasks also depends upon each child's ability to perceive, image, and structure his body movement in space. Using small groupings of apparatus or apparatus mazes (4-2a–e, 4-3) with mats, or two-dimensional floor patterns (see 4-2f, "Patterns" and 4-4), an entire group of children can be given a single movement task. It is useful to have children fully explore each task in an empty room before trying it out within the additional limitations and complexities which apparatus imposes.[1] For instance, children can be given the task, "Try out different ways of traveling through the room in stretched-out body shapes. Your arms and legs should be extending as far as possible from your body." Then, "Try out different ways of traveling through the room in curled-up body shapes. Pull your arms and legs close to the rest of your body."

[1] Building a body image and "sense of self" depends in part upon being free to try out one's own body movement ideas. A child is freer *and* safer if he is unemcumbered by restrictive clothing. Whenever possible, it is suggested that children do movement exploration in bare feet and underwear, leotards, or shorts.

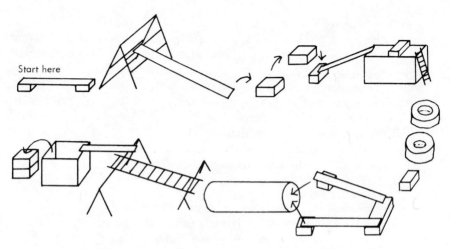

4-3. An arrangement of moveable equipment

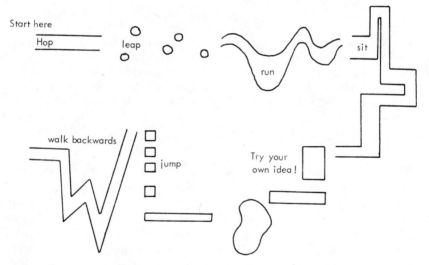

4-4. A surface design for movement exploration

Then, "Now, you decide. Sometimes you will travel in a stretched-out body shape and sometimes you will travel in a curled-up body shape." Finally, apparatus can be arranged throughout the room and these same tasks can be explored on jungle gyms, planks, or while traveling under a hoop supported horizontally by two chairs or over a table or large box.

Some additional traveling tasks are suggested below and should be developed in the same way using open space first and then adding the challenge of apparatus.

"Try out different ways of traveling:

1. in high body shapes; low body shapes.
2. in wide body shapes; narrow body shapes.
3. forward; backwards; sideways.
4. by placing your weight on your bottom only, knees and elbows, back or tummy, hands and feet, or the side of your body.
5. by transferring your body weight from one part to another. (This should lead to experimentation with rocking and rolling.)
6. symmetrically; asymmetrically.
7. using twisting movements.
8. using sliding, turning, jumping, hopping, curling body movement. (Select one or two.)
9. quickly; slowly."

As children become more skillful, the teacher can introduce increasing complexity to the task. She can have the children travel in a curled-up shape or a stretched-out shape and gradually increase or decrease the speed of their body movement. The more the teacher recognizes the spatial ideas inherent in the tasks she designs, the more she will be able to help each child consciously discover the point of reference, dynamic balance, time (sequence and duration), direction, size, shape, distance and length, area and volume in his own body movement. Each child's body movement response to the movement task, and his verbal explanation of how he thought he met the task the teacher set will provide clues to his grasp of spatial ideas. Figure 4-5 (page 146) is provided to help the teacher plan a balanced program of movement experiences using large apparatus, floor patterns, and open space. The bibliography on pages 191–94 suggests additional readings in movement education to provide further understanding. Books about educational gymnastics published in England are particularly useful.

the creative arts: media for space-time exploration

Inherent in each of the creative arts is a multiplicity of space-time ideas. The artist, the dancer, the actor, the musician, and the photographer are masters of space-time relationships, achieved in part through the development of highly differentiated body movement skills. Creativity might be defined as a unique fusion of space and time, the creator having blended them to form a new set of relationships.

The young creator arrives in school with a highly-developed but spontaneous sense of space-time which he reveals in his response to the opportunities the teacher provides. Familiar to every classroom teacher is the "cautious observer," "the explosive explorer," "the deliberate designer," and "the questioning scientist." Each child approaches the cur-

USE OF THE BODY	USE OF SPACE	USE OF MOTION FACTORS*
1) Actions	1) Far-near	1) Time
Balancing Crawling Stepping Running Gripping Swinging Jumping Rocking Rolling Sliding Stretching Curling Turning Twisting Climbing	2) Large-small 3) High-low 4) Directions Up-down Left- right Forward-back	Sustained-sudden Acceleration- Deceleration 2) Weight Firm-strong-solid Fine-light-delicate 3) Space
2) Body parts	5) Floor pathways Straight Angular Curved Twisted	Direct-economical Flexible-indulging 4) Flow

Head
Shoulders, arms
  elbows, hands
Spine
Hips
Legs, knees, feet
	6) Air pathways
	
	Straight
	Angular
	Curved
	Twisted
		Free, ongoing
		Bound, controlled,
		  restrained

3) Body shapes		

Pin-like:
  long and thin
Wall-like:
  flat, stretched
  and wide
Ball-like:
  twisted, rounded,
  curved
 	
Symmetrical-
  asymmetrical
		* Taken from English
		Educational Gymnastic
		Literature and Laban's
		principles of human
		movement.

4-5. Discovering space through body movement tasks

riculum through his own body movement in space-time. His reaction to, and interaction with, the curriculum dynamically restructures his body movements.

Body movement, including action on objects, affords opportunity for children to "feel" spatial ideas and broaden their base of "spontaneous knowing." Creative activities that encourage a maximum amount of decision making through body movement and opportunities to manipulate objects would seem to contribute to this "spontaneous knowing." The teacher's role in facilitating the development of spontaneous as well as scientific concepts about space-time includes—

1. providing opportunities for real and direct sensory experiences with the natural world, people, and materials. It is real and direct involvement with the world that inspires and stimulates thinking, feelings, and actions. The child does not have to be taught to perceive—he is touching, tasting, smelling, seeing, and hearing in every waking hour of his day. However, he needs an environment rich in opportunities for new sensing and responding.

2. thinking through the spatial ideas in the particular tasks she selects.
   a. points of reference
   b. balance (self, objects, self in relation to objects)
   c. time
   d. direction
   e. size
   f. shape
   g. distance/length
   h. area
   i. volume

3. assessing and guiding each child's awareness of these ideas as he works, as well as planning subsequent activities that will help him move ahead in his knowing.

4. focusing the child's attention on space-time relationships through carefully designed questions to him during the activity. (See "Formulating Significant Questions," pages 177–78.)

5. structuring each activity to permit maximum opportunity for decision-making for each child. As decision-making ability increases, the uniqueness of individual thinking emerges. The teacher might ask herself: To what extent can the child select a point of reference, discover balance, order his time, determine shape, try out direction, "feel" distance or length, discover area or volume? To what extent is he permitted to act on—to select, arrange, rearrange, feel, attach, cut, tear, try out—the materials used in each activity? And finally, to what extent is each child's work uniquely his?

6. selecting the materials with which children will work—the quantity, the quality of materials, their relevance to evidenced needs, their appropriateness to the skills of the child, etc.

art

Earlier it was said that body movement serves man's perception and perception directs his body movement. Long before a child handles a crayon, clay, collage materials, or blocks, he has moved through and perceived his world in many ways. His perception of the world and particular objects in the world directs the movement of his crayon, molds his clay, arranges his collage materials and builds his blocks. Conversely, his movements in drawing the crayoned line, molding the clay, arranging the collage materials, and building with the blocks further activates his perception. He senses in order to move, and movement feeds his perception. As he comes to discover the relationship between his movement and the materials he is using, patterns emerge. He discovers how particular movements consistently create particular forms. He can control and predict. He has an image, an idea, a thought. As the child's images and thoughts direct his body movement, so do they direct his creative art. The artist images and thinks about relationships as he structures his materials. Discovering new relationships and building new structures derives from new perceptions—movement that activates sensory modalities in new ways, stimulates new thoughts and, ultimately, new artistic discoveries. The quality of opportunities for feeling, tasting, smelling, hearing, and seeing the world influences the quality of creative art. We now have come full circle: body movement is a fundamental of creative art.

The very young child, or the child who has had limited experience with creative art, needs a variety of opportunities to simply explore the possibilities of materials. Activities which are appropriate to his limited experience with materials and immature control of his body movement

1. allow freedom to his large muscles
2. limit the quantity of materials and processes
3. permit maximum opportunity to discover relationships
4. place emphasis on *sensing* rather than on the product itself.

A child's own body movement, left-right, up-down, and forward-back, builds his spatial knowing. Since a child's early images are three-dimensional and his early thinking focuses on the three-dimensional world, teachers should pay particular attention to planning opportunities for young children to work with three-dimensional art materials.

Whether the child's spatial orientation is based on "spontaneous" or conscious conceptualization, the teacher's role in helping him discover spatial ideas in and through creative art activities includes:

1. providing opportunities for real and direct sensory experiences with the three-dimensional world of nature, people, and materials.
2. thinking about the spatial ideas in the tasks she selects.
3. focusing the child's attention on the space-time ideas inherent in the activities she selects.
4. structuring each activity to provide maximum opportunity for decision-making.
5. testing and selecting the materials she will provide for the children.

Figures 4-6 and 4-7 are provided to assist the teacher in these complex tasks. Figure 4-6 (pp. 150–54) poses some questions to focus teachers' attention on specific spatial ideas inherent in three- and two-dimensional art activities, while 4-7 (p. 155) organizes some "found materials" according to their essential dimensions. Finally, an annotated bibliography on creative art (pp. 189–90) is offered for further study.

dance

From the natural and spontaneous body movements that facilitated his survival, man discovered that he could also communicate ideas through his body movement. The origin of dance can be traced to man's need to express ideas. Imaging "sensed" experiences, man disciplined his body to imitate the movements of animals, praise the gods for a good crop, co-ordinate the movements of his labor, express feelings about sex, birth, maturity, and death. Just as sensed experiences shaped early man's dance, the young child's perceptions of his world shape his dance. Since the way each child is stimulated by his environment affects the quality of the thought which disciplines his body movement, curriculum planning needs to be concerned with providing qualitative opportunities for feeling, tasting, smelling, seeing, and hearing the world. As disciplined body movement, the movements of dance structure space in much the same way that space structures movement. Parts of the body are moving in relation to other body parts as well as in relation to the space itself, or objects within that space.

In dancing, the child deals with his most immediate point of reference —his own body moving in his own space-time. The young child dances naturally in his daily running, hopping, and skipping. However, as he develops a conscious awareness of the space-time relationships in his dancing, he can create new dances. Such conscious awareness develops as his attention is focused on the space-time ideas in his body action.

Body action is gestural, locomotor, or both. Gestures are actions of the extremeties of the body and do not involve transference or support of weight. They can occur towards, away from or around the body. Locomotor movement involves the transference of body weight from one supporting part to another such as in a roll, jump, walk or skip.

Either gestural movement or locomotor movement can be enriched by bending, stretching, or twisting different parts of the body. The body can move symmetrically or asymmetrically; body parts can move simultaneously or successively; one body part can lead the rest of the body; one body part can build its own dance; or two body parts can "play." The child's kinesthetic awareness will emerge only as he discovers a variety of body movement skills that feel good to him. Initially, movement tasks should call into play the child's whole body. The child can jump, "travel"

Three-Dimensional Art	Two-Dimensional Art

Point(s) of Reference

To what degree have opportunities been provided for the child to "act on" creative art materials from different point(s) of reference?

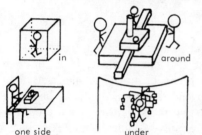

in   around   one side   under

horizontal all sides?   vertical one way

What particular evidence do you have that the child "spontaneously senses"/"is consciously aware of" his selected point(s) of reference in his creative art? To what degree is (are) his point(s) of reference revealed in his product? Is he viewing from the front? the inside? the top? where?

- -

Balance

(3D: L-R; F-B; T-B)   (2D: L-R; T-B)

To what degree have opportunities been provided for the child to "spontaneously sense"/"consciously discover" balance in/through his creative art? Balance of: line, color, texture, size, shape, etc.

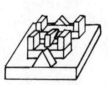

What particular evidence do you have that the child "spontaneously senses"/"is consciously aware of" balance in/through his creative art?

4-6.   Discovering the space of art (cont.)

Three-Dimensional Art	Two-Dimensional Art

Time

To what degree have opportunities been provided for the child to "spontaneously sense"/" consciously discover" the time of space in/ through creative art? Think about "time to experience" (view, perceive) the world (objects) he will represent; time to structure ideas-think; time to "act on" materials; space-time representation - representation of movement, representation of simultaneous time-space.

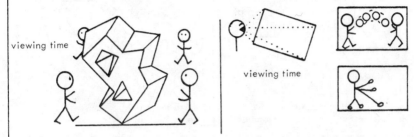

What particular evidence do you have that the child "spontaneously senses"/" is consciously aware of" the time of space in/through his creative art?

- -

Size

To what degree have opportunities been provided for the child to "spontaneously sense"/"consciously discover" (relative) size in/through his creative art? Think about relative size of tools (brushes etc.), surfaces on which to work, objects with which to work etc.

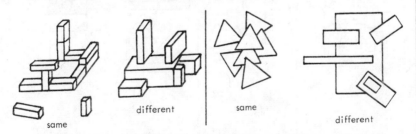

What particular evidence do you have that the child "spontaneously senses"/"is consciously aware of" (relative) size in/through his creative art?

4-6. **Discovering the space of art**

Three-Dimensional Art	Two-Dimensional Art

Shape

To what degree have opportunities been provided for the child to "spontaneously sense"/"consciously discover" shape in/through his creative art? Think about the shape of working surfaces (easel paper etc.) as well as objects with which to work.

different

same

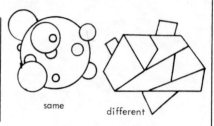
same   different

What particular evidence do you have that the child "spontaneously senses"/" is consciously aware of" shape in/through his creative art?

- -

Direction

To what degree have opportunities been provided for the child to "spontaneously sense"/"consciously discover" direction in/through his creative art? Think about the position of the working surface (horizontal, vertical, diagonal) as well as objects with which children can work (string, wire, long paper).

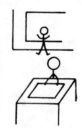

What particular evidence do you have that the child "spontaneously senses"/" is consciously aware of" direction in/through his creative art? Note: point of reference is essential here.

4-6.   Discovering the space of art (cont.)

Three-Dimensional Art	Two-Dimensional Art

Distance/Length

To what degree have opportunities been provided for the child to "spontaneously sense"/"consciously discover" distance/length in/through his creative art? Think about the position of the working surface (horizontal, vertical, diagonal), the objects which have been provided and the surfaces on which to work. (Length of paper, distance between objects, etc.)

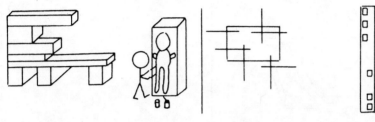

What particular evidence do you have that the child "spontaneously senses"/"is consciously aware of" <u>distance/length</u> in/through his creative art?

- -

Area

To what degree have opportunities been provided for the child to "spontaneously sense"/"consciously discover" area in/through his creative art? Think about size-shape (surface) of materials provided, as well as objects with which to work.

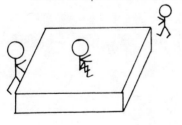 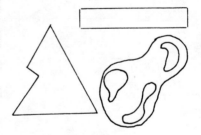

What particular evidence do you have that the child "spontaneously senses"/"is consciously aware of" <u>area</u> in/through his creative art?

4-6. Discovering the space of art (cont.)

Three-Dimensional Art	Two-Dimensional Art
Volume To what degree have opportunities been provided for the child to "spontaneously sense"/"consciously discover" volume in/through his creative art? Think about the range of objects which have been provided. Two dimensional materials become three-dimensional when folded, twisted, interlocked, bent, stacked, tied, crumpled, etc. What particular evidence do you have that the child "spontaneously senses"/" is consciously aware of" volume in/through his creative art?	

4-6. Discovering the space of art (cont.)

Linear Essentially one-dimensional	Flat Surfaces Essentially two-dimensional	Bulk Materials Essentially three-dimensional

Stiff
 	
  Tooth picks
  Sticks
  Dowels
  Popsickle sticks
  Bamboo
  Applicator sticks
	Wood
	Cardboard
	Ceramic tiles
	Asphalt tiles
	Metal sheets
	Leather
		Seeds
		Macaroni
		Dried beans/peas
		Rice
		Corn
		Bottle caps
		Buttons
		Pebbles
		Nuts/acorns
		Shavings
		Sand/salt/sawdust

Controlled
 	
  Pipe cleaners
  Wire
  Rubber tubing
  Straws
  Grasses
  Hose
	Paper (wall-, news-,
	  sand-, corrugated,
	  waffle, metallic,
	  paper towel, roof-
	  ing, gift wrapping,
	  contact, etc.)
		Rug scraps
		Bark

Free
 	
  Yarn
  String
  Tape
  Ribbon
  Trimming
  Binding
  Rope
  Lace
  Rubber bands
	Fabric (burlap,
	  tweed, velour,
	  satin, silk,
	  netting, etc.)
	
	Nylon stockings
	Cellophane
	Tissue paper
	Plastic
		Steel wool
		Cotton
		Excelsior
		Shredded paper
		Gravel
		
		Blocks
		Wood scraps
		Yarn cones
		Spools/reels
		Styrofoam
		Sponges
		Plastic containers
		Cork
		Pine cones
		Boxes (jewelry,
		  toothpaste, pill,
		  soap, furniture,
		  liquor, film, etc.)

To what degree can these materials be used either two- or three-dimensionally Think about bending, twisting, tying, wrapping around, and gluing, nailing, weaving, etc.	To what degree can these materials be used either one- or three-dimensionally Think about cutting in strips, twisting, folding, bending, interlocking, crumpling, packing in, etc.	To what degree can these materials be used either one- or two-dimensionally? Think about spreading, mosaics, slicing, arranging in lines, etc.

in a long thin shape, curl and stretch, or rock and roll with his whole body. Using his whole body, he can float through space, punch the space, or surround a space. Fulfilling movement tasks helps each child focus his attention on his own body movement. The teacher can suggest such tasks as the following:

- Find ways to twist your body or parts of your body. Include your arms, legs, and back.
- Try twisting your whole body to help you move from a lying position into a standing position and back down to a lying position.
- Now make a twisting motif, using your whole body.

Points of reference. In dance, these include body postures as well as floor locations from which movement begins. Children can begin a task, or create a whole dance, in a kneeling, sitting, lying, or tied-in-a-knot position. They can be asked to begin their dance in the middle of the room, under a chair, in a corner, low down (in order to go high), or beside a partner. A dance can begin in a rounded shape, with one body part touching the wall, stretched out, or touching a partner. Such tasks help each child focus his attention on his own point of reference. When a group of children has completed a movement task, the teacher might ask, "Where (or how) did you begin? How do you know that you are in the same place (or position)?"

Time. Time of space in dance includes the tempos and rhythms in body movement. Children will spontaneously dance to their own tempos and rhythms. The teacher can help them to focus their attention on tempo or rhythm by suggesting to them: "Find ways to travel 'over and under,' moving as slowly as you can. Now try the same thing traveling as quickly as you can. Now in your own time create a dance that travels 'over and under' quickly and slowly—a quick-slow-over-under dance. Or EXPLODE into space and then float slowly into a position ready to explode again." A rhythm such as *explode,* EXPLODE, E X P L O D E, *floa . . . . . . t . . . explode,* EXPLODE, E X P L O D E, might be used. Children's appreciation of the contrasts between quick-slow or "explode-float" can be enhanced if the teacher allows plenty of time for exploring each movement separately before combining them in a movement motif. Developing a kinesthetic awareness of the time of one's body movement in space is enhanced through the exploration of body movement rhythms without any musical accompaniment. "Try it in your own rhythm (or time)," a teacher may suggest to her class. Additional rhythm-and-tempo experiences can be provided using poetry, songs, chants, percussion instruments, nonsense words, body sounds (clapping, slapping, stamping, humming, singing, finger or tongue clicking, whistling, blowing, etc.). Such accompaniment can be provided by the teacher alone, one or two children together, or the whole group of children. Each child can use his own sound, or the teacher may suggest a particular kind of sound (such as slapping) for all to explore. The teacher may orchestrate a series of accompaniment sounds such as:

Mmmmmmmmmmm tit, tat, tat, tat, . . . tit, tat, tat, tat.
Rusha, rusha, rusha, rusha, blopp!

```
             over         r  o
   and       and  a        u ; between . . OUT . . . through.
Under                     d  n
```

Sizzle, pop, sizzle, pop, s l i d e . Sizzle, pop, sizzle,
    pop, w r i n g . (*Repeat*)

As children develop rhythmic skill, the teacher can design tasks such as: freeze when you hear ♪ ♩ ♪ ♩ ♪ ♩ and move on the silent part. Or move after the sound: ♩ move ♩ move ♩ move—syncopation.

Balance.   Balance in dance is an integral part of both body movement and body stillness. Balance is also needed in the relationships among dancers in movement and between dancers and the objects that define the space in which they dance. Initially, each child's attention needs to be focused on his own body-sensing of balance or imbalance in dance. In general, as more body surface touches the floor, and body movement is more symmetrical, balance becomes easier. The teacher can help children focus their attention on balance by giving them tasks that contrast easy-balance and hard-to-balance positions and movements. For example, the teacher might suggest:

From a low body shape keep growing higher and higher . . . and higher
—freeze! Try to stay as still as you can. Now begin to grow back into a
low body shape—freeze! What did you notice about your balance when
you were high and when you were low?

Or for another example, she may say, ·

Find a beginning body shape in which one side of your body is a mirror
of the other side. Now make a body-mirror motif—one side must always
mirror the other side in movement. Sometimes travel, sometimes stay on
the spot, sometimes move just part of your body, and sometimes move
your whole body. Now make a movement motif in which the sides of your
body never mirror each other. One body part can go forward while the
other goes back or to the side, one side can go up while the other side goes
down, one side can touch the floor while the other reaches into space. What
did you notice about balance in these two motifs?

Additional questions to help children focus their attention on balance in their dance might be: "When is asymmetrical movement balanced? When is symmetrical movement unbalanced? What causes you to lose your balance? What are some ways to keep yourself from losing balance? How do balanced or unbalanced movements feel? In what ways did you achieve balance? How do you know you are in balance? What kinds of balance does your dance have? How do you know?

Direction.   Direction in dance is defined by identifying a point of reference and moving in relation to it. The body, or parts of the body, can move up, to the left, on a diagonal, or around a particular point of reference. Children's attention can be focused on direction in their dance movement if the teacher sets tasks that help them define their point of reference. "Create a movement motif in which you travel forward and back ending in exactly the same spot and body shape from which you began," she may say; or "Develop an 'up-down' motif using twisting movements"; or "Create a motif in which there is always a part of you moving up while the rest of your body is moving down"; or "Travel around your partner while he moves in a slow zigzag pattern." Additional questions that will help children focus their attention on direction in their dance might be: "In what direction did (or will) you move? Point to it. Why is your 'up' the same as (or different from) Bonnie's 'up'?"

Relationship.   As the child dances he is continually creating relationships among the parts of his body. Relationships can also be developed with a partner or a group of other children; with props, such as hoops or scarves; with sounds, lights, or textures; with feelings of weight, power, happiness, to name just a few. The child's attention can be focused on the relationships in his dance by the teacher's setting tasks such as:

- "Create a movement motif in which your feet are always above your head."
- "Move in the same way (or opposite way) your scarf moves."
- "Move when there is no music," or "Move when your partner stops moving."
- "Create a motif based on the shape (or motion, sound, texture) of this eggbeater."
- "When the sounds are heavy your movement should be _____; when the sound is soft, your movement should be _____."
- "When the flashlight goes out, try to shape your movement the way the light on the floor and wall was shaped."
- "Create an 'opposite' dance with your partner, i.e., while you are rising, he is sinking, and then when you begin to sink, he begins to rise. Or, while you are creating angular movements with your body, your partner is creating curved movements as he travels around you and into the spaces your body parts create. Or, experiment with the ideas of near and far using the same body part or parts as your partner. You might begin with one elbow touching your partner's elbow."

Size and shape.   Body movement in space has size and shape. The whole body or parts of the body can move in large or small spaces, tall or short spaces, curved or angular shapes. The teacher can help children to focus on one factor at a time by setting tasks to explore circular movement or zigzag shapes with the whole body or parts of the body. To introduce a more complex exploration of size, the teacher might say,

- Squeeze yourself into a tiny shape. Now slowly grow into the biggest body shape you can make. Now travel into a different space in that biggest body shape and quickly squeeze back into a tiny shape *(Repeat.)*

To help children focus their attention on shape, the teacher might set the following task:

- Let your whole body grow around a big ball—legs, feet, toes, arms, hands, and fingers surround that big ball. Now gradually squeeze that ball into a smaller and smaller ball. Now move around the outside of that ball.

Sufficient time and emphasis needs to be devoted to each part of such tasks so that children will be able to really feel they now have the "biggest body shape" or they are "around that big ball."

Distance and length.   Distance and length in dance may apply to loco-motor or axial movement. To experiment with feeling distance or length, the teacher may say:

- Walk taking the longest steps you can. Try long steps to the side, . . . and back. Really stretch your legs into a long step. Try running long steps. Now, in your own rhythm, make a long-step dance.
- Let one elbow (knee, wrist, foot) travel far away from the other elbow (knee, wrist, foot). Now, leaving the first elbow (knee, wrist, foot) where it is, take the other elbow (knee, wrist, foot) to meet it. This time let your elbow (knee, wrist, foot) travel far away in a different direction.
- Let your hand travel in long zigzag pathways. Stretch it as far from your body as it will reach. Now stretch it far away from your body in a different direction. Now let it travel in short zigzag pathways. Make those short zigzags far from your body in different directions.

Area.   After the teacher outlines one long or wide area on the floor, she may say to the children:

- Using your whole body, fill the space inside your area. Now cover it in a different way. Try growing from your first way to your second way and back to your first way in your own time. Now travel to another area and slowly fill all its space using your whole body.

Volume.   Volume in dance is concerned with an exploration of all three dimensions of the body, and movement in all three dimensions of a dance space. Children can be helped to "feel" the width, depth, and length of a space as they grow into box shapes, ball shapes, cylinder shapes, cone shapes, and so on. The following is an example of a more complex task to help focus children's attention on the three dimensions of space:

• Find ways to travel forward and back, side to side, and up and down. To focus children's attention on more inventive ways of fulfilling this task, the teacher might use one of the following: Try it moving along straight pathways, moving part of the body in the opposite direction of the traveling, using sudden and direct movements or going in the opposite direction of a partner.

Pushing the air around one's body—away, up and down, forward and back, and side to side—can also help to build an understanding of volume in dance movement.

Figure 4-8 illustrates relationships among ideas related to the space of dance. The questions focus attention on types of body movement, points of reference, time, and balance as each of these factors fits into the child's whole orientation in space. It is hoped that each teacher will help children discover spatial ideas in dance according to their needs. Very young children, and children with limited dance experience, will probably work best with single ideas, such as total body movements, exploring new and varied points of reference for movement, or experimenting with variations in tempo. Children with more experience can focus on more than one idea, such as ways of balancing when changing direction, ways of skipping within different shaped areas. To plan a dance curriculum, the teacher must

1. assess children's particular needs and levels of functioning in dance.
    a. What is each child's range of body movement skill?
    b. To what degree can he select points of reference for his dancing?
    c. What is his ability to vary and control the time of his movement?
    d. What is his ability to balance in his dancing?
2. explore spatial ideas with children as they dance.
3. plan ways to increase children's discovery of ever more complex spatial ideas.

An annotated bibliography of additional readings in dance and movement education is found on pages 190–94.

dramatics

Early man's desire to share and further understand his world was reflected in dramatic dances that recreated hunts, heroic exploits, wars, birth, and death. These dance-dramas served to interpret phenomena man could not otherwise understand. Ritual, magic, and religion emerged from these formalized dance-dramas. Likewise, mimicry and pantomime, well-developed arts in most cultures, developed as special forms of drama and dance.

As early man reenacted his experiences, using dance and drama, so the young child dramatizes his experiences. Dramatic play for the young child not only reflects his world but also serves as a tool for his growth.

Locomotor / Body Movement	Location	Tempo	Self	Reciprocals	Interaction	Size	Distance/Length	
Locomotor Walk　Gallop Run　Skip Jump　Waltz Leap　Polka Hop　Mazurka Slide　Rock/Roll Gestural Bend　Shake Stretch　Bounce Twist　Strike Lean　Swing Curl Contract-Release Gather-Scatter*	Location Behind-in front Below-above Up-down In-out Left-Right etc. Posture Stand Kneel Sit Lie Crouch	Tempo Fast-slow Acceleration-deceleration Duration Rhythm Accent Meter Syncopation Sequence Patterns Beats Rests	Self Around gravitational center Balance-imbalance Objects Props Location is space Size Shape Distance Area Volume	Reciprocals In-out Up-down Forward-back Left-right Over-under Directional Style Zig-zag Curving	Interaction Individual Partner Group Props Balls　Scarves Sticks　Cartons Ropes　Balloons Hoops　Elastic Tubular jersey	Size Big-little Large-small Tall-short Fat-thin Huge-tiny Gigantic-wee Shape-(curved) Round-(Sphere) Circle Oval Twisted Pear	Distance/Length Linear 1-dimension Height/width/depth Long-short Near-far Area Surface 2-dimensions Height-width Length-width	
Use of Body Parts Isolation Opposition Symmetry/Asymmetry Synchronization Movement Qualities* Float　Thrust/punch Flick　Press Glide　Whip/slash Dab　Wring	Rounded Elongated Angular Twisted	Accompaniment One's own body movement rhythm Body sounds Nonsense words Action words Chants Percussion Songs Poetry	Self in relation to objects Self - walls Self - other people Self - props	Directional Relationships Around Diagonal	Sensations Visual Auditory Kinesthetic Tactual Gustatory Olfactory	Shape-(angular) Triangle Square Jagged Sharp	Volume 3-dimensions Height + width + depth	
BODY MOVEMENT	**POINTS OF REFERENCE**	**TIME**	**BALANCE**	**DIRECTION**	**RELATIONSHIP**	**SIZE/SHAPE**	**DISTANCE/AREA/VOLUME**	**TOWARD ORIENTATION IN SPACE**
*Taken from Laban principles of movement. (See movement education bibliography, pp. 190-95.) How might you help children discover their space of dance using more than one of these ideas? i.e. "Try leaning back when you run."	From a standing position where is up?	How fast is fast? Clap your hands as you take each step. What is the difference between Johnny's walk and Sue's?	What is balance? Create a controlled but "tippy" dance. Create a dance in which you balance against the wall and/or other people sometimes.	Where is up? Where is back? Where is left? How will you help children discover it? i.e. standing on your ...nes find a way to go up.	Begin standing back to back with your partner... Mirror/lead/answer your partners movements with...	How big is big? How round is round? Try making sharp movements with your arms.	How near is near? How deep is deep? Move around the edge of this room as you....	How do you find out where you are when you are lost?

4-8. Discovering the space of dance

What he "plays," he comes to understand. This early play-making is invaluable to his social and emotional development, for it calls the whole self into action. It increases the child's understanding of space-time for, in order to mirror his world in the first place, the child must imagine a space and time for himself. Moreover, in ordering his ideas for play, he must use the ideas of sequence, duration, and direction.

As his play develops, the child becomes ready to play and replay his thinking. He may work with a group to act out a familiar story. His play-making is then an improvised sequence of events taking place in a particular space. Some five- and six-year-olds will want to use props and costumes to replay their story for others. Although spontaneity is a key to success and satisfaction for both teacher and children, there are space-time factors that teachers can help children to discover.

"Coming to know" through dramatics depends on the quality of the sensory experiences which are used to build dramatic themes. Developing children's sensitivity to the attitudes and qualities of movement in people and animals is essential. Trips through the city streets, to shops, into factories, through fields and barns and dairies can provide sensory experiences to enrich dramatic ideas. Recording these experiences in words, paint, music, or movement helps to clarify images and further enhance this knowing.

Point of reference. Spatial ideas are inherent in any dramatic theme. In dramatics a point of reference is concerned with where a dramatic idea begins, both in space and in time. The teacher can help children to focus their attention on their point of reference by asking, "Where is the street cleaner before he goes to work? What time is it? Where in his house is he? Show me what you think he is doing." Or, "Where are the crabs? When do they dig into the sand? Make your whole body into a crab and show us where your crab begins."

Balance. In dramatics as in dance, balance has to do with one's own body posture in developing dramatic characterizations as well as balance in the use of dramatic working space. The teacher can help children focus their attention on balance by setting tasks such as, "Try out some movements of your woods creature. Does he climb, hop, suddenly jump, stand on one leg, move on one knee and one hand?" To develop children's awareness of balance in the working space, the teacher can direct children to, "Look for the empty spaces and move into them. Try to find a 'tree' that is all alone for your tree animal to live in." People or animals can balance on or against small supports, pretend to be on a rocking ship, or walk a circus tightrope.

Time. The time in dramatics includes both sequence and duration. The teacher can help children focus their attention on the sequence of their story by saying, "Let's retell the whole story together. What happens first? Then what happens? How does it end?" Or, "What does the shoemaker do first? Then what does he do?" She can help children focus their attention on duration by asking, "In our story, how long does the sun shine?" "How long does it take the firemen to put the fire out?" Time is also inherent in dramatics when percussion instruments are used to emphasize character traits or the quality of particular events. Rhythmical patterns played on percussion instruments can enhance the movement quality of a thunder storm, a scampering mouse, an angry monster, or a twinkling star. Or, using a sequence of two or three different rhythms (played by the teacher or several children) each child can be encouraged to develop his own dramatic movement story. As children's skill develops, percussion sequences can be lengthened and more complex rhythmic patterns can be used.

Direction.   Direction in dramatics occurs when a child acts out ideas such as retreating in fear, climbing a tree to find food, sinking into the sea, pushing through a crowd, or making way through the forest underbrush. The teacher can encourage children to express such directional movement in various ways, depending, of course, on the character being portrayed and the nature of the environment. As a child moves through the woods, for instance, he should remember there are low branches to crawl under, big logs to climb over, rocks to go around, and deep ditches to cross.

Size.   Size in dramatics includes awareness of the size of a person, animal, or object portrayed, and its corresponding range of motions. It is also inherent in the size of objects carried, or walked around, or pushed. Finally, the size of the space used for these dramatic activities must be considered. The teacher can help children focus their attention on size in dramatic experiences by suggestions such as: "Let's see how big your ocean creature is. Is it a huge monster with huge fins or legs which takes huge steps in the water? Or is it a tiny creature with tiny fins or legs which can only take tiny steps?"

Shape.   In drama this includes awareness of the shape of whatever is portrayed. Children should be encouraged to sense the form of their sea or forest creatures, the shape of cobwebs or caves where these creatures might live, the shape of objects held, pushed, carried, or walked into, and so on. Teachers can help children focus their attention on shape by suggesting: "Let me see the shape of your insect. Where are its legs? Are they close together, far apart, in a long line, bent or straight? Is its back rounded or flat? How does it move in that shape?" Or, "As you travel through the passageway, show us by the way you move where it is wide and low, where it is narrow, where it is round, where it dips down, and where it bends."

Distance or length.   Awareness of distance or length in drama occurs when a child demonstrates the length of steps his character takes, the length of a path through a garden or alley, the height of a ladder, the length of thread used to sew a pair of shoes, and so on. The teacher can help children focus their attention on length by designing tasks that contrast short and long movements. She may suggest: "Try a kangaroo hop. Now try a grasshopper hop." Having the children act out moving along a wall, tightrope, or around the edge of an object can also help to focus attention on length.

Area or volume.   A sensing of area in drama can be derived from the children's awarenes of the floor space in an imaginary building, sections of an imaginary garden, or parts of an imaginary garage. To focus attention on volume, the teacher can suggest such dramatic tasks as: "Show us the shape and size of your 'house' by the way you move in it. How wide is it? How deep is it?" or "Show us the volume of your package by the way you hold it and what you take out of it."

For further reading in creative dramatics with young children, see the annotated bibliography on pages 195–96.

music

As primitive man found that he could control his laughter, cries of pain, and other sounds of emotional expression, he also found he could create sounds by striking stones, hollow logs, or sticks, blowing through hollow reeds, and causing other objects to vibrate. Such musical achievement reflects thinking through movement. For early man, this resulted in singing and dancing ceremonies associated with hunts, war, birth, sickness, or death. As rhythm derived from body movement so inner rhythms also induced body motion. Rhythm is a defining quality of music and dance. Body movement was early man's first instrument of music-making. The vibration of his vocal cords and the controlled sound patterns of his body movement such as clapping, stamping were the foundation of music.

Like primitive man, children also discover that they can control their body movements that create sound. Every child develops his own sense of rhythm as he learns to move. Movement efficiency depends on rhythm. (See Chapter 2, pp. 26–31.) A young child intuitively uses his voice and his body in rhythmic patterns as he plays. Gaining more control over his body and voice, he can discover and create new music patterns. Such control derives from his focused attention on his own music making. As an organization of sounds in time, music making reflects body control as well as thinking. It is through body movement that the young child can organize his musical thinking. Rhythm, melody, and dynamics in music are "sensed" through body movement. Clapping, hopping, skipping, or galloping reflect a sense of rhythm; when these activities are accompanied by music, the child can further clarify his musical ideas about rhythm, tempo, and dynamics. As the child develops control of his movement, he can express such musical concepts as melody. The movement of his body in space can express the shape, length, and direction of melody as well as the changing intensities of the beat. Spatial ideas can be explored through experiences with rhythm, melody, and tempo as music embodies points of reference, balance, time (rhythm, meter, tempo), direction, distance/length, and volume. For further ideas for providing young children with experiences in music, see pages 196–97 for an annotated bibliography.

photography

Photography provides many opportunities for discovering and developing space-time concepts and relationships. A photograph freezes both space and time. It can freeze location, change the sense of time of a movement, and create the illusion of movement. It can illustrate multiple angles of viewing simultaneously; it can distort size, shape, distance, or balance. It can change perceived spatial relationships among objects. Although a photograph is two-dimensional, it can increase a child's awareness of three-dimensional knowing. How?

An object may be photographed from many angles. The school playground, for instance, might be photographed from the roof of an adjacent building, the director's office, the top of the jungle gym, inside a block building on the playground, a limb of a nearby tree, or a point down the street. Simultaneous viewing of this series of two-dimensional photographs can expand children's three-dimensional knowing. A teacher might ask, "What do you see in this photograph? What is different or the same about these two photographs?"

Photography can also be used to focus children's attention on the rotation and revolution of the earth around the sun. Outdoor photographs of shadows taken from the same spot at different times can provide visual aids for discussions about the rotation and revolution of the earth around the sun and how man has come to define time. Photographs of shadows of different objects taken at the same time can provide visual aids for discussions about (1) the similarities and differences in two- and three-dimensional shape, and (2) relative as well as measured length and area. Children might use photography to illustrate ideas of up-down, over-under, around, through, shape, size and negative space. Photographs of moving objects such as swings, balls and body movements can be used for discussions about the shape of that object's movement, the distance it moved or the area needed for movement.

Photography can be used to provide opportunities for children to discover—

1. movement in space—the space of movement
2. points of reference for viewing space
3. balance-imbalance in space
4. the time of space
5. directions in space
6. distance in space
7. area
8. volume

space trips for young children

Body movement in space builds the foundation for later conceptualization of space. Perception of space comes from direct muscle involvement— kinesthesis. This kinesthesis is the foundation for the child's construction of images and subsequent understanding of the relationships among the objects in his world. "Knowing" the space in a classroom, for instance, requires many experiences of moving around among the tables, chairs, bookcases, block shelves, workbench, easels, and so on. "Knowing" the school building requires many experiences of climbing the stairs, walking through the hall, riding the elevator, walking through doors, and finding the office. What experiences are required for knowing the immediate neighborhood?

Such muscle-knowing is crucial but not sufficient. The known parts must be fit together. What is the spatial relationship between the easel and the block shelves, the easel and the tables, and the tables and the sink? Where is the elevator in relation to the classroom? Where is the classroom in relation to the three-year-olds' room? Where is it in relation to the front entrance? The whole can only be known through a particular organization of the parts—each part has one, and only one, place. To perceive the whole involves a simultaneous juxtaposing of what parts of the whole are to the front, back, left, right, top, and bottom. A complex imaging task at best!

Space walks need to highlight distinct space differences as "differences stick out in untutored perception." Walking from narrow spaces into open spaces, from high places to low places, and from empty spaces to cluttered spaces emphasizes difference in space.

The teacher might plan a trip to focus children's attention on the shapes of the spaces through which they will pass. Such a trip might take children up a narrow stairway to the roof, under the water tank on the roof, down on the elevator to the basement, through the storage room, out the service entrance, across the courtyard, between the school building and the adjacent building, back through the front door, and along the corridor to their room. Children's attention can also be focused on direction during such a space walk. In this case, the teacher might say to the children:

As we're taking our space walk today we are going to look for up spaces, through spaces, under spaces, between spaces, behind spaces, over spaces, across spaces and around spaces. While we're walking we'll just look, listen, and feel the spaces. When we come back we'll talk about them.

What did you notice about the space in the stairwell (or under the water tank, in the storage room, on the roof, in the elevator, in the courtyard, between the two buildings, in the front hall, along the corridor)? What happened to you when we went through that space? Now, if we wanted to tell someone about it without words, what could we do? (Blocks, paper, box sculpture.) How was each space (name pairs) connected to every other space? How will we show that each part was connected to every other part?

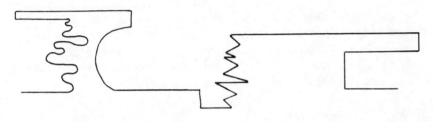

4-9. Diagram of a space walk

globes, mapping, and maps

Self is the first and most meaningful point of reference for perceiving space. Hence, the child's self should be the teacher's point of reference in her curriculum planning. The second most meaningful points of reference for the child are familiar objects and places through, in, over, and around which he has moved. Using three-dimensional models for mapping projects helps children grasp the idea of reduced scale in mapping. From three-dimensional models, children's use of such concrete materials as blocks or cardboard boxes, helps them further make the transition toward two-dimensional representation of objects in the real world characteristic of maps.

globes

A classroom globe allows the children to experience the abstraction of the entire three-dimensional world on the surface of a sphere. A globe demonstrates particular spatial ideas:

1. The earth is a sphere. Travel takes place around it.
2. There is more water than land on our earth. How much more?

3. Distances can be judged relative to the whole earth.
4. The relative location of the north and south poles and the equator can be seen.
5. The axis of the earth which is a straight line passing through the north and south poles, and a point on the surface of the globe are necessary points of reference for defining north-south and east-west.
6. The role of gravity as it relates to the earth as a sphere can be demonstrated by placing an object against the globe and pulling it away along an imaginary radius.

from three-dimensional representation
to abstraction

Moving from three-dimensional representation to two-dimensional representation requires abstraction—the ability to image the third dimension when only two dimensions are represented. As an individual moves through and perceives the three-dimensional world from many angles, he gradually builds images from his body movement experiences. Hence, mapping experiences should derive from body movement experiences in and around the objects and areas being mapped.

mapping

A map is a graphic representation of the three-dimensional world on a two-dimensional surface. To make a map one must be able to:

1. abstract two dimensions from the three-dimensional world of objects in a given space, and graphically represent this abstraction.
2. identify points of reference on a two-dimensional surface. What does it take to know where you are in a room? Since walls and objects define the space in a room, knowing one's location would take defining one's position relative to two adjacent walls—a vertical and horizontal

    coordinate. A vertical and horizontal coordinate defines points of reference—constancies.

    Yet each child's points of reference may be different—variability. He must move from his selected points of reference. The direction of his movement on his map must be relative to the direction of his movement in the three-dimensional world.
3. perceive sizes relative to the real world and the two-dimensional representation of it. The object that takes up the greatest amount of surface space in the portion of the world represented, must take up the greatest amount of space on the map.

Figure 4-10 illustrates this discussion. Children's ability, however, must guide the teacher in her curriculum planning. She must assess their level of skill and then help them define their points of reference. Answers to the following questions may provide clues in this complex evaluation:

1. What specific evidence do I have of each child's ability to abstract two dimensions from the three-dimensional world?
2. What specific evidence do I have of each child's ability to differentiate points of reference on a two-dimensional surface that represents a three-dimensional space?
3. What specific evidence do I have of each child's ability to perceive size relationships between the real world and a model of it?

commercial maps

Commercial maps afford opportunities for children to discuss segments of their spatial world. Maps of places immediately familiar to the child would be the logical point of reference for the teacher's curriculum planning. Maps of the classroom, the school building and grounds, the immediate neighborhood sequentially define foci for study. Maps of the community, city or town, and county would come later. Commercial maps of different projections such as Homolosine, Lambert, Robinson, or Mercator, can facilitate children's grasp of specific spatial ideas. Maps are used most effectively in conjunction with trips through the areas represented on the map.

measurement of space

Before children are ready to formally measure quantity, they need many experiences that provide "feel" of length, area, and volume through body muscles, and opportunity to actively work with units of measure. Walking the length of a plank, reaching around a hollow block, covering a table with newspaper, filling a crate with blocks, pouring sand, mud, flour, or water from one container to another are foundation activities for formal measurement of length, area, and volume. Children's readiness to begin more formal measuring experiences is indicated as they begin to estimate and compare relative size of objects, either through actions or verbalization. They use comparative statements as they begin to measure: "I'm bigger than Susan;" "My board is longer than yours;" "Hey, your block is bigger;" "We need more newspaper 'cause our table is bigger." (Note how a point of reference is always indicated.) These are clues that children are ready for further measuring experiences. The teacher then should provide units of measure of multiple sizes and shapes if children have not already had them, with encouragement to find out how long

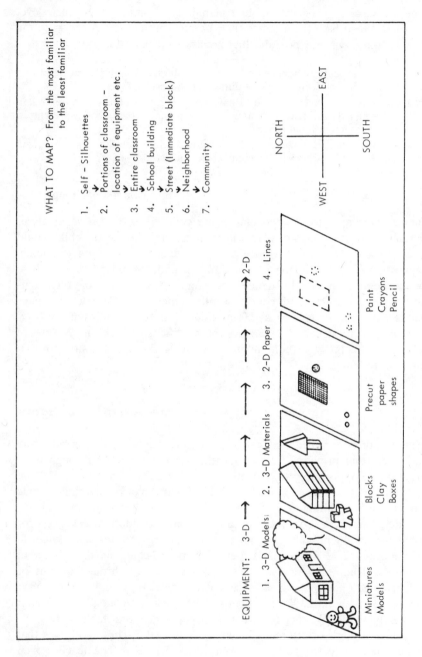

WHAT TO MAP? From the most familiar to the least familiar

1. Self – Silhouettes
2. Portions of classroom – location of equipment etc.
3. Entire classroom
4. School building
5. Street (Immediate block)
6. Neighborhood
7. Community

NORTH
EAST
WEST
SOUTH

EQUIPMENT: 3-D

1. 3-D Models
2. 3-D Materials
3. 2-D Paper
4. Lines

Miniatures
Models

Blocks
Clay
Boxes

Precut
paper
shapes

Paint
Crayons
Pencil

4-10. Mapping: from three dimensions to abstraction

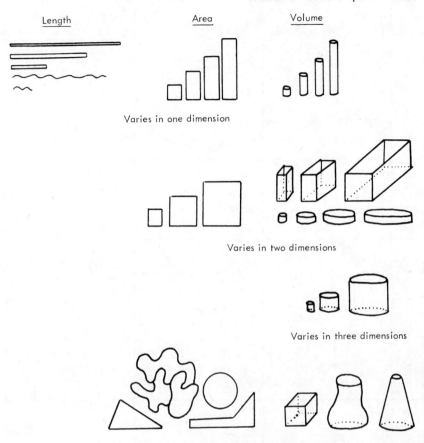

4-11. Some units for measuring length, area, and volume

something is, or "How many blocks did it take to cover the floor of your house?" or "How much sand is in ———?" "Which one is longer (or covers a larger space, or holds more)? How do you know?" Discovery that it takes more small units or fewer large units to fill a given space is crucial to later grasp of number ideas. Figure 4-11 suggests some possible units of measure for such learning.

Since self is the first and most meaningful point of reference, using the body as an initial unit for measuring length, area, or volume is recommended. Repeated use of a single unit of measure is the next step toward abstraction. Subsequently, estimation using this single unit of measure provides practice in comparing relative size and is a powerful tool for self-correction. Finally, a standard unit, such as a yardstick or measuring cup, can be introduced. Figure 4-12 suggests objects that can be used for

	BODY OR PART OF BODY	SINGLE UNIT OF MEASURE	ESTIMATION	STANDARD UNITS OF MEASURE
Distance/Length Self Classroom length and width Plant growth Shadow Length	Hands, feet Body length of a tall child Finger width Length of a short and a long (child's) foot.	A length of rope A length of string A stick A block (unit)	"About . ."	Ruler Yardstick
Area Table top/self Hop scotch court Shadow area Floor space for an animal cage	Hand span "Lying-down bodies" Feet Feet or hand span	A unit block A sheet of paper A piece of wood A piece of fabric Squares on graph paper	"About . ."	Ruler Yardstick Graph paper
Volume Fish tank Pail full Block	Handfuls (water)	A can A bottle A plastic container	"About . ."	Teaspoon Tablespoon Cup Pint Quart Gallon

4-12. Measuring distance, area, and volume

	Body or Part of Body	Single Unit of Measure	Estimation	A Standard Unit of Measure
Classroom length and width	Our room is 8 1/2 Sue's long and 5 Sue's wide.	Our room is 7 of these sticks long and 3 1/2 sticks wide.	Jim thinks our room is 8 of him long and 5 of him wide. Bonnie thinks our room is 10 of her long and 6 of her wide.	Our room is 30 feet long and 12 feet wide.
Area of table top	It takes 15 of Ann's hands to cover the table	It takes 4 1/2 quad blocks to cover the table.	Sally thinks it will take 20 of her hands to cover the table. Bill thinks 8 of his hands will cover the table.	Our table is 2 1/2 feet long and 1 1/2 feet wide. It is 3 3/4 square feet.
Quantity of water in our fish tank	There are fifteen handfuls of water in our fish tank.	Our fish tank contains 12 soup cans of water.	John thinks there are 20 cups of water in our fish tank. Julie thinks 40 handfuls of water would fill the fish tank.	Our fish tank holds 8 quarts of water.

4-13. Recording measurement of distance, area and volume

measurement of distance or length, area, and volume, beginning with parts of oneself and moving toward standard units of measurement. Children need to become thoroughly familiar with each object as a unit of measure before moving to a more refined unit of measure. The teacher must assess her childrens' ability and their grasp of measurement in order to select her point of reference for planning measuring experiences.

Recording discoveries is the next step toward abstraction. Again, children should be helped to think of a way. Figure 4-13 is provided as an example of how selected objects of measurement from Figure 4-12 might be recorded.

It becomes the teacher's role to 1) know sequences of development in children's ability to measure distance, area, and volume, 2) assess children's readiness to move ahead, and 3) plan sequential activity. Very young or immature children may need to spend the entire year measuring quantity through gross motor activity. (See "Gross Body Movement" on pp. 136–45.) Other children may advance more quickly to use a single unit of measure and a standard unit. Rulers, yardsticks, teaspoons, tablespoons, cups, and quarts can eventually be provided. Answers to the following questions should help to clarify both teacher's and children's thinking regarding a crucial idea in measurement: How long is long? How far is far? How big is big? How full is full?

measurement of time

Movement in space is a measure of time. Early man defined time as he observed recurrent phenomena in his world—sunrise and sunset, the overflow of the Nile, the movement of stars, the waxing and waning of the moon, the ebb and flow of tides, and changing seasons.

Knowing time takes a sensing of the amount of movement which occurs in given quantities of space. "Time is embedded in a series of events—in a continuum in which space and time are not differentiated." [1] The young child is initially concerned with the time dictated by his physiological needs—hunger, fatigue, elimination. Later he develops a sense of the time of space as he reaches out to catch a ball, runs when asked to hurry, fills a pail with sand, crawls through a long pipe, hops along a wall. Sensing when to reach, leap, or hop is a time-space coordination. Very young children need a variety of experiences with space-time if they are to develop efficiency in their sense of timing. As they come to feel their activity as an ongoing movement, they are building a foundation for later grasp of duration.

[1] K. Lovell, *The Growth of Basic Mathematical and Scientific Concepts in Children* (London: University of London Press, 1961), p. 78.

Movement in space defines time. Just as early man developed a routine to fit the time patterns in his world so children discover and respond to regularity and patterns in their "time of space." Early man adapted his activities to the patterns of change in his environment. He had a time for waking, sleeping, working, resting, planting, and harvesting. His sense of time emerged from the weaving of his physiological needs with the patterns created by the rotation and revolution of the earth.

In like manner, children develop their sense of time by weaving the demands of the social world with their physiological needs. Since children's grasp of sequence precedes their grasp of duration, it becomes the teacher's role to help them discover, first, the sequence and ongoingness of time through their own body movements and the patterns of change in their world created by the rotation and revolution of the earth; secondly to help them discover the limits of an activity (its beginning and end) and labels for measuring duration. Discovering pattern is based in finding regularities in perception and since regularity is most easily found in the time of the present, a teacher's focus should necessarily begin here. To help the child discover the time of space, the teacher should

1. provide a predictable but flexible schedule of daily activities, as well as allowing time to practice particular space-time skills—ball throwing, jumping, climbing, running, etc.
2. focus the child's attention on the predictability of each movement or activity. As the child comes to know the time of his body movement, the teacher can help him discover some basic sequences of daily life, such as the change from day to night, day to day, month to month, or season to season.
3. help each child develop a time vocabulary. Although words can be meaningless unless they are associated with kinesthetic knowing, words facilitate a grasp of increasingly complex relationships and associations.
4. help each child learn to use clocks and calendars when he gives evidence of his spontaneous knowing and ability to image the time of space. (*Caution:* Telling time is dial reading; reciting the day of the week, month, or year can be meaningless memorization of words.)

Figure 4-14 is provided to help the teacher focus her attention on 1) man's organization of time-space, and 2) the role of body movement in children's discovery of time-space ideas.

measurement of weight

Weight is a measure of gravitational pull. Conceptualization of weight is based on kinesthetic knowing—feeling gravitational pull. The young child initially senses his own weight through his various movements, such as

	SEQUENCE (order of succession, discrete events)	DURATION movement from (beginning) → through (time) → to (end of event)
Minute(s)	Sequence of activities: Getting up → dressing → eating → going to school	Through the time it takes: to eat breakfast and/or go to school; for all the sand to fall into the bottom of the timer; the second hand to move around clock.
Hour(s)	Sequence in daily activity: i.e., outdoor time → juice time → music time → indoor time → lunchtime → 1:00 → 2:00 → 3:00 →	Through the time it takes from the beginning, through to the end of (an) hour(s), i.e. High tide + low tide; lunch time + rest time; amount of movement in sun shadow or minute hand of clock.
Day(s)	Sequence of weekly activity: i.e. Music day → "Miss J. comes" day → day when mother drives car pool → days when daddy stays home; Mon. → Tues. → Wed. →	Through the time it takes from AM to AM; light + dark; day + night; time for shadow to move or hour hand to move on clock.
Week(s)	Sequence of activity which takes place in (a) week(s). Week when mother helps at school or Mrs. Z. walks you to school. 1st week → 2nd → 3rd week →	Through the time it takes from Sunday to Sunday; change in position of moon or stars.
Month(s)	Sequence of holidays + birthdays. i.e. My birthday, Easter, daddy's birthday; January → February → March →	Through the time in a month; four weeks; time for stars to move a given distance.
Season(s)	Sequence of outdoor activity: swim, football → basketball → baseball; swim → skate → bicycle ride; winter →	Through the time when particular clothes are worn/activities are engaged in; spring tides/winter tides/harvest time
Year(s)	Sequence of grades (years) in school; 1969 → 1970 → 1971 →	Through the time between single holidays; all one does while he is ___ years old.

4-14. Body movement, the foundation of time-space "knowing"

rolling, balancing on small body parts, or hanging. Using one's muscles to lift and carry builds a "spontaneous knowing" of the weight of objects. The child gradually discovers similarities and differences among familiar objects of differing densities. He discovers that size and shape are not necessarily relevant factors of weight. The young child's early knowing of weight is comparative—objects are heavier, lighter, or weigh the same as other objects. As the young child makes such observations he is showing readiness for more specific measurement of weight. A balance scale can provide opportunity to discover the comparative weights of two or more objects. Through the use of standard weights (1-, 2-, 5-, and 10-pounds) children can discover how much sand, flour, beans, blocks, or cotton it takes to equal x pounds. Initially a single pound weight can be used, but as the children become more skillful, fractional as well as large weight units can be introduced. As children indicate readiness, the teacher's role is to:

1. provide opportunities for children to hang from tree limbs and bars.
2. provide varied opportunities for children to push, pull, lift, and carry objects of varying sizes and weights. (Blocks, sand, water, leaves, pebbles, rocks, lumber, sawdust, etc.)
3. focus children's attention on comparative weights of objects by asking significant questions while the child is feeling the weight.
4. provide a balance scale with time to discover weight of objects of varying densities.
5. provide standard units of measure for discovery of standard weight.
6. help children discover ways of recording comparative weight and standard weight by using graphs, illustrations, etc.

formulating significant questions: a powerful teaching and learning tool

The nature of teachers' questions affects the nature of children's thinking and their responses. Her organization of relevant ideas is reflected in her questions and in turn contributes to the quality of children's verbal or action responses.

Questions that focus children's attention on relevant ideas but are open enough to encourage individual viewing of an idea seem to elicit the most revealing responses from learners.

Encouraging individual responses to an idea helps children find personal relevance, build a meaningful thought structure, and discover patterns and relationships among ideas. That the teacher refrains from evaluation further promotes difference of opinion and thinking through of an idea. Difference of opinion seems to be a powerful tool in stimulating thought. If teachers are really going to educate children they must begin by focusing children's attention on the structure of ideas and help each child find personal relevance. Answers to questions which have circulated through the arteries and veins of thought are more readily absorbed in the body of knowing than are those which are spread on the skin and never reach the circulatory system. It becomes the teacher's role to:

1. clarify for herself the structure of her thinking.
2. formulate questions and provide opportunities to help each child to reveal the unique structure of his thought.
3. provide significant opportunities for each child to fill the gaps in and rearrange the pieces of his experience.

In short, raise questions that will help children construct knowledge. A relevant unanswered question is a fertile seed with powerful potential; however, it requires a rich environment of selected nutrients if the organism of knowing is to grow .Some growth-stimulating questions are:

- Can you say more about that?
- What do you mean? (Can you show us what you mean?)
- Why do you think _____?
- What would happen if _____?
- Who has another (different) idea?
- _____, what do you think about this?
- What is another way to do it?
- How do you think we could find out?
- What do you think we should try now?
- What ideas do you have about _____?

These are general questions. Their significance lies in how they will be used. Each question refers to a specific context; but each is open to encourage each child to answer according to the nature and structure of his thinking.

general
bibliography

anatomy

MORTON, DUDLEY J. and FULLER, DUDLEY DEAN. *Human Locomotion and Form.*
Baltimore: Williams and Wilkins, 1952

anthropology

LEE, DOROTHY. *Freedom and Culture.* Englewood Cliffs, N.J.: Prentice-Hall,
1959.

art, art education, visual arts

ARNHEIM, RUDOLF. *Art and Visual Perception.* Berkeley: University of Cali-
fornia Press, 1967.
HARRIS, DALE B. *Children's Drawings as Measures of Intellectual Maturity.* New
York: Harcourt Brace Jovanovich, 1963.
KEPES, GYORGY, ed. *Education of Vision.* New York: Braziller, 1965.
————, ed. *The Nature and Art of Motion.* New York: Braziller, 1965.
————. *The New Landscape in Art and Science.* Chicago: Paul Theobald
and Co., 1956.

————, ed. *Sign, Image, Symbol.* New York: Braziller, 1966.

————, ed. *Structure in Art and Science.* New York: Braziller, 1965.

LOWENFELD, VIKTOR. *Creative and Mental Growth.* New York: Macmillan, 1957.

MACHOVER, KAREN. *Personality Projection in the Human Figure.* Springfield, Ill.: Charles C. Thomas, 1949.

MONTGOMERY, CHANDLER. *Art for Teachers of Children.* Columbus, Ohio: Charles E. Merrill, 1968.

SCHAEFER-SIMMERN, HENRY. *The Unfolding of Artistic Activity.* Berkeley: University of California Press, 1950.

SHAHN, BEN. *The Shape of Content.* Cambridge: Harvard University Press, 1957.

child development

STEVENSON, HAROLD W., ed. *Early Behavior: Comparative and Developmental Approaches.* New York: John Wiley, 1967.

communications

MARTIN, JOHN J. *The Dance.* New York: Tudor, 1947.

MC LUHAN, MARSHALL. *The Medium is the Massage.* New York: Bantam Books, 1967.

————. *Understanding Media: The Extensions of Man.* New York: McGraw-Hill, 1965.

dance

H'DOUBLER, MARGARET N. *Dance, A Creative Art Experience.* Madison: University of Wisconsin Press, 1959.

economics

BOULDING, KENNETH E. *The Image.* Ann Arbor: University of Michigan Press, 1956.

education

GERHARDT, LYDIA A. "The Role of Body Movement in the Child's Conceptualization of Space: A Multidisciplinary View." Ed.D. dissertation, New York University, 1970.

MINOR, FRANCES. "Toward an Art-Science of Questioning: A Critical Inquiry into a Strategic Teaching Function." Ed.D. dissertation, Teachers College, Columbia University, 1967.

PHENIX, PHILIP H. *Realms of Meaning.* New York: McGraw-Hill, 1964.

WHEELWRIGHT, PHILIP. *Metaphor and Reality.* Bloomington: Indiana University Press, 1962.

genetic epistomology

PIAGET, JEAN. *The Origins of Intelligence in Children,* trans. Margaret Cook. New York: Norton, 1952.

————. *The Construction of Reality in the Child* trans. Margaret Cook. New York: Basic Books, 1954.

————. *The Language and Thought of the Child,* trans. Marjorie Worden. New York: Humanities Press, 1959.

————. *Play, Dreams and Imitation in Childhood,* trans. C. Gattegno and F. M. Hodgson. New York: Norton, 1962.

————, and INHELDER, BARBEL. *The Child's Conception of Space,* trans. F. J. Langdon and J. L. Lunzer. London: Routledge and Kegan Paul, 1956.

mathematical education and mathematical philosophy

CHURCHILL, EILEEN M. *Counting and Measuring.* Toronto: University of Toronto Press, 1961.

SPENCER, PETER LINCOLN and BRYDEGAARD, MARGUERITE. *Building Mathematical Concepts in the Elementary School.* New York: Holt, Rinehart & Winston, 1952.

WHITEHEAD, ALFRED NORTH. *Symbolism, Its Meaning and Effect.* New York: Macmillan, 1927.

philosophy

CASSIRER, ERNST *Substance and Function and Einstein's Theory of Relativity,* trans. William Swabey and Marie Swabey. New York: Dover, 1923.

FRASER, J. T., ed. *The Voices of Time.* New York: Braziller, 1966.

HANSON, NORWOOD R. *Patterns of Discovery.* Cambridge: Cambridge University Press, 1958.

KOSLOW, ARNOLD, ed. *The Changeless Order.* New York: Braziller, 1967.

LANGER, SUSANNE K. *Mind: An Essay on Human Feeling.* Baltimore: Johns Hopkins Press, 1967.

————. *Philosophy in a New Key.* Cambridge, Mass.: Harvard University Press, 1942.

LEVITAS, GLORIA G. *Culture and Consciousness.* New York: Braziller, 1967.

physical education

BROER, MARION R. *Efficiency of Human Movement*. Philadelphia: Saunders, 1966.

BROWN, ROSCOE C., JR. and CRATTY, BRYANT J., eds. *New Perspectives of Man in Action*. Englewood Cliffs, N.J.: Prentice-Hall, 1969.

CRATTY, BRYANT J. *Movement Behavior and Motor Learning*. Philadelphia: Lea and Febiger, 1967.

———. *Movement, Perception and Thought*. Palo Alto, Calif.: Peek, 1969.

———. *Perceptual-Motor Behavior and Educational Processes*. Springfield, Ill.: Charles C. Thomas, 1969.

GODFREY, BARBARA B. and KEPHART, NEWELL C. *Movement Patterns and Motor Education*. New York: Appleton-Century-Crofts, 1969.

METHENY, ELEANOR. *Movement and Meaning*. New York: McGraw-Hill, 1968.

MOSSTON, MUSKA. *Developmental Movement*. Columbus, Ohio: Charles E. Merrill, 1965.

———. *Teaching Physical Education*. Columbus, Ohio: Charles E. Merrill, 1966.

physiology and neurophysiology

LURIA, ALEKSANDR ROMANOVICH. *Higher Cortical Functions in Man*. New York: Basic Books, 1966.

———, and YUDOVICH, F. I. *Speech and the Development of Mental Processes in the Child*. London: Staples Press, 1959.

SHERRINGTON, C. *Man on His Nature*. New York: Cambridge University Press, 1951.

psychiatry

SCHILDER, PAUL. *The Image and Appearance of the Human Body*. New York: International Universities Press, 1950.

THOMAS, ALEXANDER; CHESS, STELLA; BIRCH, HERBERT G.; HERTZIG, MARGARET E.; and KORN, SAM. *Behavioral Individuality in Early Childhood*. New York: New York University Press, 1963.

psychology

BARSCH, RAY H. *Achieving Perceptual-Motor Efficiency, A Space-Oriented Approach to Learning*. Seattle, Wash.: Special Child Publications, 1967.

BARTLETT, SIR FREDERIC C. *Remembering, A Study in Experimental and Social Psychology*. Cambridge: Cambridge University Press, 1932.

———. *Thinking, An Experimental and Social Study*. New York: Basic Books, 1958.

BARTLEY, S. HOWARD. *Principles of Perception.* New York: Harper & Row, 1958.

BRUNER, JEROME S. *On Knowing.* Cambridge: Harvard University Press, 1962.

CARR, HARVEY A. *An Introduction to Space Perception.* New York: Longmans, Green, 1935.

CHURCH, JOSEPH. *Language and the Discovery of Reality.* New York: Random House, 1961.

VON FIANDT, KAI. *The World of Perception.* Homewood, Ill.: Dorsey, 1966.

FREEDMAN, SANFORD J., ed. *The Neuropsychology of Spatially Oriented Behavior,* Homewood, Ill.: Dorsey, 1968.

FURTH, HANS G. *Thinking Without Language.* New York: Free Press, 1966.

———. *Piaget and Knowledge.* Englewood Cliffs, N.J.: Prentice-Hall, 1969.

HALL, EDWARD T. *The Silent Language.* New York: Fawcett World Library, 1959.

HEBB, D. O. *The Organization of Behavior.* New York: John Wiley, 1949.

HELLMUTH, JEROME, ed. *Learning Disorders, vol. 1.* Seattle, Wash.: Special Child Publications, 1965.

———. *Learning Disorders, vol. 2.* Seattle, Wash.: Special Child Publications, 1965.

HUNT, J. MCV. *Intelligence and Experience.* New York: Ronald Press, 1961.

ITTELSON, W. H. and CANTRIL, H. *Perception, a Transactional Approach.* New York: Random House, 1954.

KEPHART, NEWELL C. *The Slow Learner in the Classroom.* Columbus, Ohio: Charles E. Merrill, 1960.

———. *Success Through Play.* New York: Harper & Row, 1960.

KOHLBERG, LAWRENCE. "Early Education: A Cognitive-Developmental View," *Child Development* 39 (December 1968): 1013–62.

LOVELL, KENNETH. *The Growth of Basic Mathematical and Scientific Concepts in Children.* London: University of London Press, 1962.

SCHACHTEL, ERNEST G. *Metamorphosis.* New York: Basic Books, 1959.

VERNON, M. D. *A Further Study of Visual Perception.* New York: Cambridge University Press, 1952.

VINACHE, W. EDGAR. *The Psychology of Thinking.* New York: McGraw-Hill, 1952.

VYGOTSKY, LEV SEMONOVICH. *Thought and Language.* Cambridge, Mass.: M.I.T. Press, 1962.

WERNER, HEINZ. *Comparative Psychology of Mental Development.* Rev. ed. New York: International Universities Press, 1964.

WERTHEIMER, MAX. *Productive Thinking.* New York: Harper & Row, 1959.

WHITE, C. T., and CHEATHAM, P. G. "Temporal Numerosity: II. A Comparison of the Major Senses," *Journal of Experimental Psychology* 58 (December 1959): 441–44.

WITKEN, HERMAN A. *Psychological Differentiation.* New York: John Wiley, 1962.

dictionary

GOVE, PHILIP BABCOCK, ed. *Webster's Third New International Dictionary of the English Language Unabridged.* Springfield, Mass.: Merriam, 1968.

annotated

bibliography

**books for young children containing
concepts of space and spatial relationships**

ATWOOD, ANN. *The Little Circle*. New York: Charles Scribner's Sons, 1967.
Full-color photography shows a circle is more than a blackboard zero.
BAIER, HOWARD. *Now This, Now That*. New York: Holiday House, 1957.
Encourages reader to look at things from different distances and different
angles as it develops such comparative vocabulary as, big-little, up-down,
taller, straight, under, on, near-far.
BECKY. *Tall Enough Tommy*. New York: Children's Press, 1948.
Tommy thought his height was just right. Tim was too tall; Susan was too
short. But one day a new turning bar appeared at the playground that was
too tall for him and the only way he could use it was when Tim gave him
a boost.
BEIM, JERROLD. *The Smallest Boy in the Class*. New York: Wm. Morrow, 1949.
The antics of the smallest boy in the class, used to develop the ideas of
comparison as big, biggest, small, smallest, tall, tallest, and tiny.
BENDICK, JEANNE. *Shapes*. New York: Franklin Watts, 1968.
Shape, line, plane figures, three-dimensional figures, symmetry.
———. *Space and Time*. New York: Franklin Watts, 1968.
Scientific description of the complex relationship between concepts of time
and concepts of space.

BERKELEY, ETHEL S. *Ups and Downs,* illus. Kathleen Elgin. New York: William R. Scott, 1951.
This book asks questions and gives information about up-down, top-bottom, high-low, over-under, etc.

BLACK, IRMA S. *Busy Water,* illus. Jane Castle. New York: Holiday House, 1958.
Water flows down, gathers momentum and increases its size as it is combined with other springs, rain, brooks, rivers, and the ocean. Changes in size and shape of water.

BLAIR, MARY. *The Up and Down Book.* New York: Golden Press, 1964.
This very simple picture book illustrates "up" and "down" as a child views his world. "The clouds are up. The grass is down." "My head is up. My feet are down." A more complicated relationship is introduced when, "I stand up on the swing. I hang down from the swing."

BORTON, HELEN. *Do You See What I See?* New York: Abelard Schuman, 1959.
This story is about lines, shapes, and colors. There are tall-short, curvey and slanted lines. There are some lines that are placed side by side. Slanted lines are like the slanted lines in a see saw. They are curved like a swan, or arranged like balls. Lines make up squares, rectangles, and triangles.

BRANLEY, FRANKLIN M. *Big Tracks, Little Tracks.* Illus. Leonard Kessler. New York: Crowell Collier and MacMillan, 1960.
Cleverly illustrated book about the tracks made by people, their household pets, and other animals. Relates size of the tracks to the size of their makers.

———. *North, South, East and West,* illus. Robert Galster. New York: Thomas Y. Crowell, 1966.
Easy text which develops the language of position.

BUDNEY, BLOSSOM. *A Kiss is Round,* illus. Vladimir Brobri. New York: Lothrop, Lee, and Shepard, 1956.
Things in the real world which are round—written in rhyme.

BURTON, VIRGINIA LEE. *Mike Mulligan and his Steam Shovel.* New York: Houghton Mifflin, 1939.
A hole gets bigger the more you take away from it!

CARROLL, RUTH. *Where's the Kitty?* New York: Henry Z. Walck, 1962.
Ideas of "under," "in," "behind," etc.

CHARLIP, REMY. *Where is Everybody?* New York: William R. Scott, 1957.
Spatial relationships in the outside world—prepositions used in abundance as each new piece is added to the story.

DE REGNIERS, BEATRICE. *How Joe the Bear and Sam the Mouse Got Together.* New York: Parent's Magazine Press, 1965.
A large bear and a small mouse with similar interests could not live, play ball, ride a bike, or play music together because of their difference in size; but they could eat ice cream together, so that's just what they did.

EMBERLY, ED. *The Wing on a Flea—A Book About Shapes.* New York: Little, Brown, 1961.
A beautifully illustrated story about things in the world which are triangular, circular, and rectangular.

FLACK, MARJORIE. *Tim Tadpole and the Great Bullfrog.* New York: Doubleday, 1954.
Through time Tim Tadpole grows into a great big bullfrog.

FREEMAN, DON. *Fly High, Fly Low.* New York: Viking Press, 1958.
Pigeons fly high and low, up and down, away from and toward.
FRITZ, JEAN. *Growing Up,* illus. Elizabeth Webbe. Chicago: Rand McNally. 1956.
Builds concepts of relative size as the child grows up. He is always bigger than something and smaller than something.
GAG, WANDA. *Snippy and Snappy.* New York: Coward-McCann, 1935.
Ideas of relative size—how does a chair look to a little mouse?
HADER, BERTA, and HADER, ELMER. *Lost in the Zoo.* New York: MacMillan, 1957.
How do you remember how you came into the zoo?
HAWKINSON, JOHN, and HAWKINSON, LUCY. *Little Boy Who Lives Up High.* Chicago: Albert Whitman, 1967.
Ricky lives in a high rise apartment house. He can look down on his world and see small trees and cars. But when he goes down in the elevator things change; now Ricky is small and the trees are tall.
HEIDE, FLORENCE, and VAN CLIEF, SYLVIA. *How Big Am I?* Chicago: Follett, 1968.
A little boy compares his size to animate and inanimate objects.
HOGAN, INEZ. *Twin Lambs.* New York: E. P. Dutton, 1951.
This story about twin lambs who wander away from their flock develops ideas of same size, same shape, together, and distance.
HORWICH, DR. FRANCES R. *My Goldfish.* Chicago: Rand McNally, 1958.
Round small bowl, large rectangular aquarium, and thin goldfish can swim through a castle. Larger, fat goldfish cannot!
———. *Growing Things.* Chicago: Rand McNally, 1956.
All sorts of possibilities for measurements. Measure plant, compare it to child's measurements, etc.
JEAN, PRISCILLA. *Pattie Round and Wally Square.* New York: Ivan Oblensky, 1965.
A sad square who longs to be round like a circle, Wally Square is showed by Pattie Round a new world of squares.
JOHNSON, RYERSON. *Let's Walk Up the Wall,* illus. Eva Cellini. New York: Holiday House, 1967.
KAHN, JOAN. *Seesaw,* illus. Crosby Bonsall. New York: Harper and Row, 1964.
Two children seesawing tell what they see when they are "up" and "down": flies, treetops, climbing rose, mole's hole, dewdrop, garden hose, etc.
KALUSKY, REBECCA. *Is It Blue as a Butterfly?* illus. Aliki. Englewood Cliffs, N.J.: Prentice-Hall, 1965.
A child tries to guess what her father has brought her. "Is it the size of a whistle?" "Sometimes!" "Is it big as a cuckoo clock?" "Sometimes." What is it? (Balloon!)
KAUFMAN, JOE. *Big and Little.* New York: Golden Press, 1966.
Pictures and simple text comparing large and small objects.
KESSLER, ETHEL, and KESSLER, LEONARD. *Are You Square?* New York: Doubleday, 1966.
Using questions, the authors focus the reader's attention on shape.
KESSLER, LEONARD. *I Made a Line.* New York: Grosset and Dunlap, 1962.
Position vocabulary used as a boy thinks about his drawings of lines.

KLEIN, LEONORE. *How Old Is Old?*, illus. Leonard Kessler. New York: Harvey House, 1967.

What is old? What is young? Four is old for a mouse. A three-year-old is a grown up horse. Giant tortoises live longer than any other animals.

———. *What Is an Inch?*, illus. Leonard Kessler. New York: Harvey House, 1966.

Book of how we measure an inch. We can't use our bodies for measuring because everybody is different. Ruler is universal measurement. An inch can be measured up, down, sideways, or diagonally. Asks reader to measure for himself. Discusses twelve inches equals a foot, cubic foot, square inch, square foot, yard and square yard, millimeter, centimeter, and kilometer.

KRASILOVSKY, PHYLLIS. *The Very Little Boy*, illus. Ninon. New York: Doubleday, 1962.

Language of comparison used in this story of a very little boy as he grows into a bigger boy.

———. *The Very Little Girl*, illus. Ninon. New York: Doubleday, 1953.

A very little girl who thinks that everything is bigger than she is finally grows bigger.

KRAUSS, RUTH. *The Big World and the Little House*, illus. March Simont. New York: Harper & Row, 1964.

Relative size of objects in the world.

KUSKIN, KARLA. *Square is a House*. New York: Harper & Row, 1960.

Relative size of objects in the world.

LENSKI, LOIS. *Big Little Davy*. New York: Oxford University Press, 1956.

When Davy was a baby he liked to do some things, but as he got bigger he liked to do different things, such as help his mother and daddy. Finally, he is so big that he goes to school.

LIONNI, LEO. *On My Beach There are Many Pebbles*. New York: Ivan Obolensky, 1961.

Sizes and shapes of pebbles are differentiated.

MACDONALD, GOLDEN. *Big Dog, Little Dog*, illus. Leonard Weisgard. New York: Doubleday, Doran, 1943.

The story of a large dog and a small dog with an explanation that because of their size differences, each notices different objects while walking down the street.

MARINO, DOROTHY. *Edward and the Boxes*. New York: J. B. Lippincott, 1958.

Edward finds appropriate-sized boxes for his pets—relative size!

MILGROM, HARRY. *Adventures with a Ball*, illus. the Strimbans. New York: Dutton, 1965.

Characteristics of a sphere.

RAMIREZ, CAROLYN. *Small as a Raisin, Big as the World*. Irvington-on-Hudson, N. Y.: Harvey, 1961.

Compares sizes of objects familiar to a young child.

RAND, ANN. *The Little River*. New York: Harcourt Brace Jovanovich, 1959.

Changes in size and shape of water as it gently flows from mountain to sea.

SKAAR, GRACE. *The Very Little Dog*. New York: William Scott, 1949.

Growth of a little dog—in time!

SCHICK, ELEANOR. *5A and 7B*. New York: Macmillan, 1967.

Living at the same address does not assure that you know everyone else who lives there!

SCHLEIN, MIRIAM. *Heavy is a Hippopotamus.* New York: Young Scott Books, 1954.
Size and weight are not relative!
———. *Shapes,* illus. Sam Berman. New York: Young Scott Books, 1952.
Roundness, squareness, and straightness.
SCHNEIDER, HERMAN, and SCHNEIDER, NINA. *How Big is Big?,* illus. A. F. Arnold. New York: William Scott, 1946.
Beautifully conceived story about relative size and the need for a point of reference in qualitative discussions of size. A classroom "must."
SCHWARTZ, JULIUS. *Uphill and Downhill.* New York: McGraw-Hill, 1965.
Author is a science teacher who introduces concepts of up, down, gravity, how a snowball gets bigger as it rolls down the hill, why trees are smaller at the top of the hill, how hills are used for lifting and rolling (inclined plane).
SHAPP, CHARLES, and SHAPP, MARTHA. *Let's Find Out What's Big and What's Small,* illus. Vana Earle. Eau Claire, Wisc.: Hale, 1959.
Size of different objects in the child's world.
SMITH, ROBERT PAUL. *Nothingatall, Nothingatall, Nothingatall,* illus. Alan E. Cober. New York: Harper & Row, 1965.
This is essentially a song about the world that a child makes up before he goes to sleep. He begins with the earth (point of reference) and gradually "thinks down" to a coal mine, a gold mine, a river and then "nothingatall." Then he reverses the order and "thinks back up" but continues to air, clouds, space. And on top of space is "nothingatall."
STOVER, JOANN. *Why? Because.* New York: David McKay, 1961.
Uses some language of geometry as it gives some amusing reasons. For example, "A ball is round because if it were square, it couldn't roll."
SULLIVAN, JOAN. *Round is a Pancake.* New York: Holt, Rinehart and Winston, 1963.
Round objects pictured and named in rhyme.
TAMBURINE, JEAN. *Almost Big Enough.* New York: Abingdon Press, 1963.
It takes a long time but finally one grows "big enough."
TRESSELT, ALVIN. *Follow the Road,* illus. Roger Duvoisin. New York: Lothrop, Lee and Shepard, 1956.
The road travels through hillsides and meets people, and animals. Then it goes to cities via turnpikes.
———. *How Far is Far?* New York: Parents Magazine Press, 1964.
Deals with "as far as," "as deep as," "as high as," and "as big as," using a child, a water bug, a rabbit, tree roots, and a baby as points of reference.
WARD, LYND. *The Biggest Bear.* Boston: Houghton Mifflin Co., 1952.
A pet bear grows and grows and grows until he becomes a gigantic problem. Each illustration shows him getting bigger and bigger in relation to Johnny.
WEBBER, IRMA. *It Looks Like This.* New York: William R. Scott, 1959.
This story tells of four mice who live in a barn. They each live in different parts of the barn and argue about what a cow, a pig, and a donkey look like from their point of view. In the middle of the argument a big cat comes in and they see him from all sides, thus realizing each one had been right. To know an object you must view it from all sides!

————. *Up Above and Down Below.* New York: William R. Scott, 1943.
A first science book about plants, animals, earth and sunlight. Plants grow above and below the ground. Animals can live above or below the ground.
WING, JENRY RITCHET. *What is Big?* New York: Holt, Rinehart and Winston, 1963.
Compares the size of a child with that of larger and smaller animals.
WITTE, EVE and WITTE, PAT. *Look! Look!* New York: Golden Press, 1961.
Backward-forward, up-down, taller-shorter, fast-slow, big-little.
WITTRAM, H. R. *Going Up, Going Down.* New York: Holt, Rinehart and Winston, 1963.
The elevator shaft in a children's toy shop becomes a number line, the basis for questions about sequence and direction of numbers.
ZION, GENE. *All Falling Down,* illus. Margaret Bloy. New York: Harper & Row, 1951.
Everything falls down: snow, leaves, nuts, sand castles, shadows, and some stars.

books about art

ARNHEIM, RUDOLF. *Art and Visual Perception; A Psychology of the Creative Eye.* Berkeley: University of California Press, 1967.
A comprehensive view of the relationship between perception and art including chapters on shape, form, space, movement, etc. A thinking text for teachers.
BIBER, BARBARA. *Children's Drawings from Lines to Pictures.* New York: Bank Street College of Education Publications, 1962.
Small booklet which describes the development of drawings of children from age two to five.
BLAND, JANE COOPER. *Art of the Young Child.* New York: Doubleday, 1957.
Theory and practice in art with two- to five-year-olds. Some practical suggestions for collage, clay, mobiles, stabiles, etc., are included.
Bureau of Elementary Curriculum Development. *Art for Elementary Schools.* Albany, N. Y.: The State Education Department, 1967.
Practical suggestions, recipes. Ideas about work with crayons, chalk, papier mâché, paper, textiles, painting, etc.
COLE, NATALIE ROBINSON. *Children's Arts from Deep Down Inside.* New York: John Day Co., 1966.
Teachers discover art with children: block printing, clay, line, and color. Sensitive.
GALDSTON, OLIVE. *Play with Puppets.* New York: Play Schools Association, 1965.
Practical suggestions: first puppets, bag puppets, quickie puppets, sock puppets, papier mâché puppets, finger puppets, rod puppets, string marionettes.
GREENBERG, PEARL. *Children's Experiences in Art: Drawing and Painting.* New York: Reinhold, 1966.
In-depth study of children's two-dimensional art.

HARTLEY, RUTH E.; FRANK, LAWRENCE K.; and GOLDENSON, ROBERT M. *Understanding Children's Play.* New York: Columbia University Press, 1952.
Excellent discussion of blocks, clay, graphic materials, finger painting, etc. from a social-emotional point of view. Practical suggestions and notes on interpretation.

JOHNSON, HARRIET M. *The Art of Block Building.* New York: Bank Street Publications, 1945.
Developmental discussion of children's block building from age two to five.

KELLOG, RHODA. *Analyzing Children's Art.* Palo Alto, Calif.: National Press Books, 1969.
Primarily an attempt to classify young children's scribbles according to their placement on the paper: use of space.

LINDSTROM, MIRIAM. *Children's Art.* Berkeley: University of California Press, 1960.
A study of normal development in children's modes of visualization, through stages of development between ages two and fifteen.

LINDERMAN, EARL W., and HERBERHOLZ, DONALD W. *Developing Artistic and Perceptual Awareness.* Dubuque, Iowa: William C. Brown, 1964.
Focused on developing artistic and perceptual awareness. Some practical suggestions.

LOWENFELD, VIKTOR. *Your Child and His Art.* New York: Macmillan, 1956.
Answers to parents' (and teachers') questions about children's artwork—particularly painting.

————, and BRITTAIN, W. L. *Creative and Mental Growth.* New York: Macmillan, 1964.
Developmental view of creative art. Helps to focus teachers' attention on evaluation of children's art.

MATTIL, EDWARD L. *Meaning in Crafts.* Englewood Cliffs, N.J.: Prentice-Hall, 1959.
Theory and practical application in a multiplicity of art activities—modeling and sculpturing, printing, puppets, drawing and painting, seasonal activities, papier mâché, weaving, stitchery and applique.

MONTGOMERY, CHANDLER. *Art for Teachers of Children: Foundations of Aesthetic Experience.* Columbus, Ohio: Charles E. Merrill, 1968.
Excellent discussion of "what goes on" in the thinking-feeling processes of artwork. Includes practical suggestions for artwork such as: rubbings, printing, found materials, collage, puppets, clay, three-dimensional art.

books about movement education (dance and gymnastics)

ANDREWS, GLADYS. *Creative Rhythmic Movement for Children.* Englewood Cliffs, N.J.: Prentice-Hall, 1954.
Theory and practice of "creative rhythmic movement" in the elementary school. Contains suggested piano music, an excellent section describing ways to make home made instruments, and bibliography.

BAILEY, EUNICE. *Discovering Music with Young Children.* New York: Philosophical Library, 1958.
Teacher and children discovering music and dance together: examples and practical suggestions for the teacher of the three- to seven-year old.

BARRETT, KATE ROSS. *Exploration, A Method for Teaching Movement.* Madison, Wisc.: College Printing and Typing, 1965.
Excellent practical suggestions in particular kinds of movement exploration: locomotion, axial movement, etc.

BILBROUGH, A., and JONES, P. *Physical Education in the Primary School.* London: University of London Press, 1963.
Practical suggestions for developing movement education programs with elementary school children. Exploration and creativity are emphasized.

CAMERON, W. MC D. *Education in Movement, School Gymnastics.* Oxford, England: Alden and Mowbray Ltd., 1963.
Practical suggestions for developing movement education programs, including floor work and exploration of large apparatus.

GODFREY, BARBARA G., and KEPHART, NEWELL C. *Movement Patterns and Motor Education.* New York: Appleton-Century-Crofts, 1969.
Theory and practice in movement education. Authors analyze locomotor patterns, balance patterns, and handling objects (hitting, pushing, pulling, etc.). Useful for analysis of movement patterns.

GRAY, VERA, and PERCIVAL, RACHEL. *Music, Movement, and Mime for Children.* London: Oxford University Press, 1962.
A practical guide for teaching music and movement in the nursery school and primary grades. Based in Laban theory, it gives specific suggestions for developing movement-music ideas using percussion instruments, songs, stories and recorded music. Appendices of records, musical terms and "follow-up" lessons are included.

HACKETT, LAYNE C., and JENSEN, ROBERT G. *A Guide to Movement Exploration.* Palo Alto, Calif.: Peek Publications, 1966.
Practical suggestions for movement problems. Analyzes walking, running, jumping, hopping, sliding, skipping, general locomotion, with formulated questions to encourage children's problem solving.

HARTLEY, RUTH E.; FRANK, LAWRENCE K.; and GOLDENSON, ROBERT M. *Understanding Children's Play.* New York: Columbia University Press, 1952.
Specific observations and analysis of children's behavior during music-dance experiences are included in one chapter.

Inner London Education Authority. *Movement Education for Infants.* London: The County Hall, 1967.
Practical suggestions of activities and experiences for five- to seven-year-old children. Excellent.

JAMES, J. MYRLE. *Education and Physical Education.* London: G. Bell and Sons, 1967.
This little paperback book attempts to describe how "physical" can be a medium through which "education" can come about. Mrs. James is concerned with individual differences among children: attitudes, ego-involvement, social development, the development of intellectual concepts and processes of thought. Although she does not discuss these ideas in great depth, she opens the door for the reader.

JORDQN, DIANA. *Childhood and Movement*. Oxford: Basil Blackwell and Mott, 1966.

Based on Laban theory, this booklet gives practical guidance to teachers interested in understanding, organizing, and developing gymnastics programs in primary and secondary schools. Although limited in depth and scope it is clear, specific, and full of ideas for both the beginning and experienced teacher.

KIRCHNER, GLENN; CUNNINGHAM, JEAN; and WARRELL, EILEEN. *Introduction to Movement Education: An Individualized Approach to Teaching Physical Education*. Dubuque, Iowa: William C. Brown, 1970.

This is a sound practical guide for developing a movement education program in the elementary school. It includes lesson plans, ideas for curriculum building, excellent bibliographies, a list of available films, a list of "human" resources, and suggested sources for purchasing equipment. Numerous photographs help to bring the text alive.

LABAN, RUDOLPH. *Modern Educational Dance*. 2d edition revised by Lisa Ullman. London: MacDonald and Evans, 1963.

This little book is the bible of Laban theory. It describes Laban's sixteen basic movement themes including notational symbols for the elements of "effort" and "space." This is a must for understanding Laban's theory of movement.

LIDSTONE, JOHN and WEINER, JACK. *Creative Movement for Children: A Dance Program for the Classroom*. New York: Van Nostrand, 1969.

Written for the classroom teacher this text illustrates, in numerous series of photographs, the development of specific movement themes: locomotion, "sliding clay," "jumping wire," "turning piano," and images of space and time. It ends with "the dance class" where "the whole secret is feeling."

LONDON COUNTY COUNCIL. *Education Gymnastics, A Guide for Teachers*. London: The County Hall, 1963.

Specific ideas for building a gymnastic lesson beginning with a limbering-up activity, developing a theme, and carrying the theme into apparatus work. A separate chapter is devoted to such movement themes as whole body work, supporting the body weight on the arms, leg work, apparatus work, learning to receive and transfer weight, lifting and lowering weight, curling and stretching, twisting, shape, symmetry and asymmetry, rhythm and phrasing, circling, swinging and the use of momentum, successive and simultaneous movement, parts of the body leading the movement, and losing and recovering balance. Laban factors of time, space, weight, and flow are briefly explained.

LOWNDES, BETTY. *Movement and Drama in the Primary School*. London: B. T. Batsford, 1970.

More practice than theory about the role movement and drama can play in the education of the child age 5–11. Contains excellent practical ideas for building sensory awareness through touch, taste, smell, visual observation and sound. Separate chapters on body awareness, locomotion, creative movement, mime and verbal drama improvisations. Based in Laban theory.

MAULDON, E., and LAYSON, J. *Teaching Gymnastics*. London: MacDonald and Evans, 1965.

A popular teaching resource in England, this practical text is designed for both the classroom teacher and the specialist. It gives useful points on how to develop a movement lesson and describes in some detail the development of specific gymnastic themes for both the primary school and secondary school teacher.

METTLER, BARBARA. *Materials of Dance as a Creative Art Activity.* Tucson, Ariz.: Mettler Studios, 1960 (published by the author).
Excellent suggestions through organization of ideas which teachers might explore with children. Needs interpretation for individual groups and age levels.

Ministry of Education. *Physical Education in the Primary School; Part I: Moving and Growing.* London: Her Majesty's Stationery Office, 1952.
Theory articulated with lovely photographs that differentiate the uniqueness of individual physical development and body movement style.

————. *Physical Education in the Primary School; Part II: Planning the Programme.* London: Her Majesty's Stationery Office, 1953.
The practice of theory (explained in Part I) through photographs, drawings, and explanations.

MORISON, RUTH. *A Movement Approach to Educational Gymnastics.* London: J. M. Dent, 1969.
Although written for secondary students and teachers in training, this book has many useful ideas for working on particular movement tasks which young children could easily be helped to discover. It includes extended sections on locomotion (transference of weight, traveling, flight), and actions emphasizing balance (weight bearings, actions of "arriving," and on-and-off balance actions).

MOSSTON, MUSKA. *Developmental Movement.* Columbus, Ohio: Charles E. Merrill, 1965.
Excellent practical suggestions for increasing such skills as balance, agility, strength, and flexibility through the use of simple equipment—ropes, sticks, lines on the floor, etc. Illustrated with thought-provoking stick drawings.

————. *Teaching Physical Education from Command to Discovery.* Columbus, Ohio: Charles E. Merrill, 1966.
Concerned primarily with styles of teaching this text is written to help the teacher of physical education discover approaches that encourage children to develop physical skills through problem-solving.

MUNDEN, IVY. *Physical Education for Infants.* London: University of London Press, 1953.
This is a practical guide for classroom teachers interested in developing movement education curriculum in the nursery school, kindergarten, and grades 1 and 2. Separate chapters are devoted to each age level and enhanced with photographs that illustrate group activity on a broad range of apparatus.

NORTH, MARION. *Composing Movement Sequences.* London: Werner Studios, 1961 (published by the author).
This simple handbook gives specific suggestions to the teacher of movement without being prescriptive. Some chapters are: "Introduction of a Session," "The Main Part of the Session," and "Variations on Movement Themes."

Practical ideas for movement experiences based on swinging, stretching, traveling, turning, jumping, etc. are provided.

―――. *A Simple Guide to Movement Teaching.* London: Werner Studios, 1959 (published by the author).

A beautifully explicit booklet giving specific suggestions to the teacher of movement. Separate chapters are devoted to the use of space, body accents and stresses, recovery, body balance, the use of percussion, images from nature, group movement projects and objective movement training. Line drawings of children in action serve to illustrate the underlying ideas.

RANDALL, MARJORIE. *Basic Movement; A New Approach to Gymnastics.* London: G. Bell and Sons, 1961.

As its title suggests, this small text describes the new "individual differences" approach to the teaching of gymnastics. Gymnastics curriculum is built on Laban's theory of space, time, weight, and flow in movement. Although primarily theoretical, it is filled with practical suggestions for implementing the theory.

REDFERN, BETTY. *Introducing Laban Art of Movement.* London: MacDonald and Evans, 1965.

A brief summary of Laban's theory of movement as it derives from and applies to industry, theatre, therapy, and education.

ROBINSON, CHRISTOPHER M.; HARRISON, JULIE; and GRIDLEY, JOSEPH. *Physical Activity in the Education of Slow-Learning Children.* London: Edward Arnold, 1970.

This book is filled with practical suggestions for planning movement experiences for "slow-learning" children. Based in Laban theory, suggestions are made for different age groups in educational gymnastics, skills and games, and educational dance, in roughly equal amounts.

RUSSELL, JOAN. *Modern Dance in Education.* London: MacDonald and Evans, 1958.

This little book is written for the beginning teacher of dance at all educational levels from nursery school through teacher training. Miss Russell discusses the theory underlying the "art of movement" as described by Rudolph Laban and briefly interprets this theory into application at various levels. Although brief, it is clear, straight forward, and offers a broad range of ideas for the beginning teacher of dance.

―――. *Creative Dance in the Primary School.* London: MacDonald and Evans, 1965.

Written for students and teachers who wish to introduce dance in the primary school, this book gives practical suggestions and examples of work suitable for various age groups from five through eleven years. Based in Laban theory of movement, it is both theoretical and practical. The planned series of photographs is sensitive, inspiring, and real.

SHEEHY, EMMA D. *Children Discover Music and Dance.* New York: Teachers College Press, 1968.

A recently reissued early childhood text based in sound theory of child development. Although concerned more with music than dance, it contains excellent chapters on percussion instruments, dance, guiding movement and accompaniment, and phonograph records.

WOODLAND, E. J. M., ed. *Poems for Movement; A Teacher's Anthology*. London: Evans Brothers, 1966.
Written for teachers of children between five and eight, this is a collection of "poems for movement." For the hesitant teacher there are specific suggestions for accompanying movements using Laban's ideas of space, time, weight, and flow. Separate sections are devoted to seasons, flowers and trees, animals, "things to do," "busy days," people, and "play, fantasy, and magic."

books about dramatics

ALINGTON, A. F. *Drama and Education*. Oxford, Eng.: Basil Blackwell, 1961.
A condensed description of movement, mime, improvisation, speech, "play making," and dramatic literature in education. About 30 pages dealing with the child from 5–7. A sound philosophy of creative and interpretive dramatics is presented.
BRUCE, V. *Dance and Dance Drama in Education*. New York: Pergamon Press, 1965.
In this small paperback, Bruce has built a rationale for dance and drama in education. Her theory, philosophy, and few practical suggestions are based in Laban principles of movement.
DURLAND, FRANCES CALDWELL. *Creative Dramatics for Children*. Yellow Springs, Ohio: Antioch Press, 1952.
Practical suggestions for leadership as well as content. Focused on elementary school level.
GOODRIDGE, JANET. *Drama in the Primary School*. London: Heinemann Educational Books, 1969.
Although devoted to the primary school, this small paperback contains excellent ideas for building dramatic ideas using a framework of Laban theory.
HARTLEY, RUTH E.; FRANK, LAWRENCE K.; and GOLDENSON, ROBERT M. *Understanding Children's Play*. New York: Columbia University Press, 1952.
Excellent chapters on dramatic play of the preschool child, describing it as "Mirror of the Child" and "Instrument for Growth."
KASE, ROBERT C. *Stories for Creative Acting*. New York: Samuel French, 1961.
Includes a special section devoted to 4 to 7-year olds.
LEASE, RUTH, and SIKS, GERALDINE BRAIN. *Creative Dramatics*. New York: Harper & Row, 1952.
Specific suggestions for working with young children. Theory and guidance techniques.
LOWNDES, BETTY. *Movement and Drama in the Primary School*. London: B. T. Batsford, 1970.
More practice than theory about the role movement and drama can play in the education of the child age 5–11. Contains excellent practical ideas for building sensory awareness through touch, taste, smell, visual observation and sound experiences. Separate chapters on body awareness, locomotion, creative movement, mime and verbal drama improvisations.
MC CASLIN, NELLIE. *Creative Dramatics in the Classroom*. New York: David McKay, 1968.

A simple but thorough analysis of creative dramatics, including numerous practical suggestions for the beginning as well as the more experienced teacher.

MORGAN, ELIZABETH. *A Practical Guide to Drama in the Primary School.* (Published by the author), 1968.
Written especially for the classroom teacher, this small text deals with the practical problems of teaching drama in education. It includes introductory exercises designed to give children an awareness of their hands, feet, and heads, with specific suggestions for teaching method. A separate chapter is devoted to the role of the "movement lesson" in drama.

RASMUSSEN, MARGARET, ed. *Creative Dramatics.* Washington, D. C.: Association for Childhood Education International, 1961.
Focused on the elementary school. Description of some particular community projects. Also some practical suggestions and ideas. Pamphlet form.

SIKS, GERALDINE BRAIN. *Creative Dramatics, An Art for Children.* New York: Harper & Row, 1958.

SPOLIN, VIOLA. *Improvision for the Theatre.* Evanston, Ill.: Northwestern University Press, 1963.
Loads of theatre "exercises" includuing a section on "where." Excellent ideas that would need adaptation for young children.

WARD, WINIFRED. *Playmaking with Children.* New York: Appleton-Century-Crofts, 1947.
Theory and practice with particular suggestions for working with the 5- to 7-year-old.

————. *Stories to Dramatize.* Archorage, Ky.: Children's Theatre Press, 1952.
Selected stories for specific age groups, i.e., 5- to 7-year-olds.

books about music

ARONOFF, FRANCES WEBBER. *Music and Young Children.* New York: Holt, Rinehart & Winston, 1969.
Theory and practice in music through movement. Focuses on teaching musical concepts through body movement.

BAILEY, EUNICE. *Discovering Music with Young Children.* New York: Philosophical Library, 1958.
Anecdotal descriptions of teachers discovering music with English children ages two to seven. Creative. Takes clues from children.

HARTLEY, RUTH E.; FRANK, LAWRENCE K.; and GOLDENSON, ROBERT M. *Understanding Children's Play.* New York: Columbia University Press, 1952.
One chapter devoted to music and movement. Anecdotal material and analysis as well as suggestions to teachers.

MAYNARD, OLGA. *Children and Dance and Music.* New York: Charles Scribner's Sons, 1968.
Mainly theory but some practical suggestions for working in music and dance with children.

SHEEHY, EMMA D. *Children Discover Music and Dance.* New York: Teachers College Press, 1968.

A readable and comprehensive description of musical activities in early childhood education. Theory and practical suggestions.

song collections for young children

ABESON, MARION, and BAILEY, CHARITY. *Playtime with Music.* New York: Liveright, 1967.

COLEMAN, SATIS, and THORN, ALICE G. *Singing Time.* New York: Day, 1929.

LANDECK, BEATRICE. *Songs to Grow On.* New York: Edward B. Marks Music Corp., 1950.

———. *More Songs to Grow On.* New York: Edward B. Marks Music Corp., 1954.

LLOYD, NORMAN. *The New Golden Song Book.* New York: Golden Press, 1962.

McCALL, ADELINE. *This Is Music for Kindergarten and Nursery School.* New York: Allyn and Bacon, 1966.

MacCARTENEY, LAURA PENDLETON. *Songs for the Nursery School.* Cincinnati, Ohio: Willis Music Co., 1937.

SEEGER, RUTH CRAWFORD. *American Folk Songs for Children.* New York: Doubleday, 1948.

books about mathematics

CHURCHILL, EILEEN M. *Counting and Measuring: An Approach to Number Education in the Infant School.* Toronto: University of Toronto Press, 1961. An excellent discussion of theory with some practical ideas re: young children's development of space, measurement and number ideas.

FROBISHER, BERYL, and GLOYN, SUSAN. *Infants Learn Mathematics,* illus. Robin Kempster. London: Ward Lock Educational Co., 1970. A practical little book by two teachers who have experimented with the Nuffield Mathematics Project and tried to amalgamate their ideas under a single cover. Separate sections deal with language, sorting, classifying, sets, one to one correspondence, ordinal number, cardinal number, patterns of number, shape, movement, time, money, weight, capacity, length and height.

GALE, DONALD H. *The Teaching of Numbers.* London: Hulton Educational Publications, 1965. Using Piaget's developmental ideas, this little book contains practical suggestions for providing experiences for children in: seriating and sorting, weight, classification, area, length, thickness, group patterns, size, quantity, position, space and time.

LOVELL, KENNETH. *The Growth of Basic Mathematical and Scientific Concepts in Children.* London: University of London Press, 1962. Separate chapters devoted primarily to theoretical foundations for children's grasp of concepts of number, substance, weight, time, space, length, area and volume.

MARSH, LEONARD G. *Children Explore Mathematics.* London: A. and C. Black, 1968.

Based in the idea that mathematical ideas emerge from the child's "own activity with the materials," this book contains two useful sections about mathematics and the young child: How many? and How much? In addition it has an outline of categorical mathematical ideas.

Mathematical Association. *Primary Mathematics, a Further Report.* London: G. Bell and Sons, 1970.

This is a survey of recent developments in primary mathematics in England. It discusses such timely issues as: the importance of understanding, awareness of differences and likenesses, changes in approach, and how to introduce children to the new ideas.

Mathematics in Primary Schools. London: Her Majesty's Stationery Office, 1969.

Excellent discussion of theoretical understandings underlying mathematical learning with illustrations and examples.

Nuffield Mathematics Project Publications. New York: John Wiley, 1968.

I Do and I Understand	*Computation and Structure (2)*
Pictorial Representation	*Shape and Size (3)*
Beginnings	*Computation and Structure (3)*
Mathematics Begins	*Mathematics: the First 3 Years*
Checking Up 1	*Your Child and Mathematics*
Graphs Leading to Algebra	*Environmental Geometry*
Shape and Size (2)	

Excellent series of booklets describing theory and practice of the Nuffield Foundation mathematics education study. It contains numerous practical suggestions and illustrations of children's work as part of each mathematical idea which is developed.

SPENCER, PETER LINCOLN, and BRYDEGAARD, MARGUERITE. *Building Mathematical Competence in the Elementary School.* New York: Holt, Rinehart and Winston, 1966.

Good organization of key mathematical ideas with chapters devoted to quantity, sets, number and numeration, whole numbers, mathematical language, etc. Sample experiences are provided. The book is focused on the elementary school.

Index

DATE DUE

JAN 3 0 '75			
MAR 1 4 '75			
MAR 2 4 '77			
OCT 1 3 '77			
APR 2 0 '78			
MAY 6 '78			
FEB 8 '79			
FEB 2 3 1979			
MAR 1 6 1979			
MAR 1 3 1980			
APR 9 1981			
MAR 1 1, 1982			
NOV 1 1 1982			
NOV 2 9 1989			
GAYLORD			PRINTED IN U.S.A.